Visul Anthropology
In India
And Its Development

Visual Anthropolopgy
In India
And Its Development

K.N. SAHAY

GYAN PUBLISHING HOUSE
New Delhi - 110002

Published by

GYAN

Gyan Publishing House
5, Ansari Road
Daryaganj, New Delhi-110002
Phone: 011-47034999, 9811692060
E-mail: books@gyanbooks.com

Distribution Network
gyanbooks.com
India, USA, Canada, UK, Australia, France

ISBN: 978-81-212-0434-7 (HB)
First Published, 2014

Printed at: Gyan Press, Delhi.

Visual Anthropology in India and Its Development
Author: K.N. Sahay

To
Satyajit Ray
An
Unending Thirst
for
Realistic Film in Indian Society
and Experiment

CONTENTS

INTRODUCTION

Since I was a Post-graduate student of anthropology and later a researcher, I was deeply interested in photography connected with fieldwork. My interest continued growing in anthropology and subsequently I got a Faculty in the Department, Ranchi University. At that time Margaret Mead was one of the few exponents and developed the idea of photography - still and movie, among children in Bali sometime in Nineteen forties onward. Later on, of course coming from media, Satyajit Ray created New-wave films in India, coming through Italy and America. Being a genre of Indian films, he conceived and directed the first film *Pather Panchali* in 1955 and subsequently a series of others exclusively different from commercial films. In seventies, Mrinal Sen, Shyam Benegal and few others followed the Indian New-wave films. Of course, such films were technically not anthropological as Margaret Mead and her colleagues had made. However, the New-wave films created profuse 'ethnographic data' closely bearing with anthropological or ethnographic films which we could not ignore. As such, I tried to explore it in Indian anthropology and it emerged a new dimension of visual anthropology. Earlier, Jean Rouch and Marielle Delorme of France and later on, Asen Balikci of Canada interacting with me, did influence

It was in that background, earlier Professor L.P. Vidyarthi, my senior colleague and Chairman of this Department was elected as a President of the I.U.A.E.S. (1973-78) and I.C.A.E.S. (1978) and India was considered as a host country ensuing 1978 International Congress. The President involved a series of close and active colleagues with organizational aspect of the Congress, and created several Commissions on I.U.A.E.S. The International Commission on Visual Anthropology was one of them. Looking my personal interest in photography and visual anthropology, the President nominated me as the Co-Chairman (IUAES, 1973-78), while Dr. Masao Oka was the Chairman from Japan.

In this background, the Visual Anthropology in India did humble beginning when I had convened the first meeting of this International Commission at Ranchi in February, 1977. Miss Yasuko Ichioka, Junichi Ushiyama besides Dr. Masao Oka all coming from Tokyo, Mrs. Marielle Delorme from Paris, and the Guest President (IUAES), celebrated the meting. Later on, activities did very fast and consequently culminated the 1978 Symposium on Visual Anthropology at Delhi.

II

Being from the host country as said, I had tremendous responsibility. However, I was given a free hand to organize the Delhi Symposium. Earlier, I was invited to visit Tokyo and Paris to study the position of Visual Anthropology. At Tokyo I was also given brief orientation on film-making and made two small films connected with training. There also I saw a few dozens of ethnographic films coming from different countries. I had heavy correspondence almost throughout the world and in the country itself, I made extensive journey contacting relevant persons while organizing the Symposium.

In the Symposium a number of anthropologists from ten different countries were participated. They presented several papers, screened a number of ethnographic films and did threadbare discussions for five days. It was really the First International Symposium on Visual Anthropology in the country. It was successful and indeed, marks the major landmark.

While organizing this Symposium, initially I conceived seminal ideas. Subsequently I published and edited a small but not the least, important bi-annual *Visual Anthropology Bulletin* (1979-82). It was certainly the first relevant Journal on the subject at least in Asia. I also published nine basic articles on Visual Anthropology bearing with India and produced an ethnographic film on fascinating dances in Ranchi (silent).

Later on, the Second International Seminar on Visual Anthropology, of course on a different context, was organized at Jodhpur in 1987. Incidentally, I was still closely involved and helped the INTACH (The Indian National Trust for Art and Cultural Heritage, New Delhi) and the A.S.I. (The Anthropological Survey of India, Calcutta) to organize this event.

III

In all, the manuscript has six important chapters in first part - mostly trend setters, three chapters containing subsidiary features in second part, and five relevant Appendices. The brief relevant points connected with different nine chapters are given as below:

The opening chapter has earliest effort of anthropological film making in India. It includes documentation of ethnographic films, the international body in India, Symposium at Delhi and Seminar at Jodhpur. The filming of the rich cultural heritage of the country; stock-taking; realistic fiction films; national, regional, and global networks; educational, archival, and research activities are explored. Besides, the author looks to future tasks to be undertaken by Visual Anthropologists in India.

The second chapter deals with the brief history of Ethnographic films in India. It studied the films since 1896 with Silent era and the Talkie era in early thirties. Such early films were related to some glimpses of the life and culture of Indian people. After Independence, rapid development of different types of documentaries of Film Division of the Government of India, of State Governments, Burmah-Shell, and Ethnographic films on Anthropological Survey of India, Tribal Research Institutes, several Universities and Centres, mostly coming from Western countries, and individual anthropologists, were produced. A number of New-wave films as well as some old realistic feature films were also produced and were relevant.

The third chapter considers the background and concept of Indian Fiction films—specially New-wave, old realistic feature films, films on Television, typology, selection and analysis of films. Films as cultural documents and a source of awareness, powerful agency of change, dual nature of film's impact on society; positive and negative, bridging people and their culture with films, have also been mentioned.

The fourth chapter has a bearing with the last one i.e., the article, 'Visual Anthropology and Indian Fiction Films'. Earlier it was circulated to five different Indian and American scholars for comments. In this chapter these comments have been received and the author did the reply.

The fifth chapter discusses an approach to cultural documentation and revitalization with special reference to India. It mentions cultural documentation in Visual Anthropology apart from ethnographic films bearing on specially new-wave films, other realistic fiction films, some Tele-films and T.V. features. The documentation of certain traditional cultural values and through films could be of immense help in cultural revitalization under acculturative situations.

The sixth chapter makes an analysis of two Indian fiction films — *Manthan,* a feature film of Shyam Benegal and *Admi aur Aurat* - a Tele-film of Tapan Sinha. They constitute a model perspective in Visual Anthropology developed earlier in chapter three.

The seventh chapter discusses the First International Symposium on Visual Anthropology at New Delhi. The Symposium was celebrated for five days and twenty-eight ethnographic films were screened and discussed.

The eighth chapter includes details of nearly two hundred 'Films of Ethnographic Interest on India' collected from different sources in this country and outside mostly having technical details and brief summary.

The concluding Tenth chapter presents a model syllabus for Visual Anthropology which may be useful for Indian Universities or similar Centres.

The whole content makes a complete theme on what is going on in Visual Anthropology in India, its development and the task ahead. It makes the first attempt to bring together widely diffused relevant data and it can claim to be prestigious publication on Visual Anthropology in this country.

This book has bearing with media, social communication, sociology, ethnography, development, applied aspect, history and the like.

IV

The nine chapters discussed above, were originally published in different research Journals. Now they have been mostly revised and modified to suit this book. They are being referred to and acknowledged as given below:

Chapter One was taken from *Visual Anthropology*, Vol. 4, Pp. 25-41, 1991, Harwood Academic Publishers GmbH, Printed in the United States of America; Chapter Two from *Visual Anthropology Bulletin*, Vol. 4, No. 1, 1982, 48/3K, Bariatu Housing Colony, Ranchi; Chapter Three from *Journal of Social Research*, Vol. 29, No. 2, 1986, Pp. 1-41 (Under Special JSR Treatment), Department of Anthropology, Ranchi University; Chapter Four from *Journal of Social Research*, Vol. 31, No. 1 & 2, 1988, Pp. 119-33 (Special JSR Treatment: Comments and Reply); Chapter Five from *Journal of Social Research*, Vol. 30, No. 1 & 2, 1987, Pp. 111-19; Chapter Six from *Journal of Social Research*, Vol. 31, No. 1 & 2, 1988, Pp. 9-32; Chapter Seven from *Review of Ethnology*, Vol. 5/16-26, Pp. 203-6, 1977, Austria; Chapter Eight is based on *Visual Anthropology Bulletin*, (Vol. 1, No. 1, 1979, Pp. 3-6) and *Current Anthropology* (Vol. 21, No. 2, 1980, Pp. 271-73, U.S.A.); Chapter Nine from *Visual Anthropology Bulletin*, Vol. 1, Nos. 1 & 2, 1979, Vol. 1, No. 1, 1980, and Vol. 3, No. 1 & 2 1981.

Coming to Appendices, there are five. The First One was taken from different Editorials on *Visual Anthropology Bulletin*, (Vol. 1, No. 1, 1979; Vol. 2, No. 1, 1980; Vol. 3, No. 1, 1981; and Vol. 4, No. 1, 1982). The Second and Third Ones taken from *Visual Anthropology Bulletin* (Vol. 2, No. 1, 1980). The Fourth and Fifth ones were the write-ups of my reminiscences sent long back respectively to the Nippon A-V Productions of Tokyo, and *Chitra Bani,* Calcutta for their use.

There are twelve photographs in this book collected from *Satyajit Ray's Art,* Firoze Rangoonwalla, Clarion Books, 1980 (1), Shyam Benegal's *The Churning (Manthan),* Screenplay by Vijay Tendulkar, Seagull Books, Calcutta, 1984 (2 and 3), *Splice,* Samik Bandhopadhyay, June, 1986 (4), and *A Portrayal of People: Essays on Visual Anthropology in India,* Anthropological Survey of India and Indian National Trust for Art and Cultural Heritage, New Delhi, (1987 (5 to 12). These sources are also being acknowledged.

V

While the book is being published, I am reminded of my tender feelings to Professor L.P. Vidyarthi and Professor Masao Oka who are no more. If they were alive, I wish they must have enjoyed the writing.

I am thankful to Dr. Binod C. Agrawal, Secretary, ICAES, 1978 who initially did some help when I was organizing the Symposium.

I am grateful to the members of the Commission on Visual Anthropology (IUAES, 1973-78) for helping me and the delegates who participated in the Delhi Symposium. In particular, I was like to mention that Miss Yasuko Ichioka, Mr. Junichi Ushiyama, Mrs. Merielle Delorme, Dr. Jean Rouch, and Dr. Anna Hohenwart-Gerlachstein had close interactions with me, and I cherish.

Dr. M.C. Chaudhry, Director, Department of Teaching Aids, N.C.E.R.T., Ring Road, New Delhi was very kind and allowed me to use the Auditorium for five days during the Symposium.

Sri Chidananda Das Gupta, Director, INTACH, New Delhi roped me with the plannings and organization of the Visual Anthropology Seminar at Jodhpur. Professor I.P. Singh, Head, Department of Anthropology, Delhi University gave me generous gesture and spiritual help when I was developing Visual Anthropology in India. I express my gratitude.

I have been close with Sri Sushanto K. Chattopadhyay (Retired Cine Photographer, A.S.I., Calcutta) and from time to time I have used his experience connected with Visual Anthropology.

Sri Sanjay Kumar S. Rajeev Kumar, Anjani, and Manoj helped me in different types of secretarial assistance connected with my various writings and the book.

KESHARI N. SAHAY

PART ONE

Chapter I

The Development of Visual Anthropology in India and the Task Ahead*

Visual anthropology is inextricably connected with photography, whether it be still photographs or films on the life and culture of various peoples that are used for teaching, research, feedback, or other applied purposes.

Visual anthropology in India is still in a state of formulation and has yet to emerge as an organised and effective discipline. One has to go back as early as the end of the last century to understand its genesis. It is linked with the beginning of movie films in India when one could hardly think of anything like visual anthropology. Nevertheless, many early film pioneers in the country could very well be said to be the precursors of visual anthropology. Efforts having a bearing on visual anthropology in the beginning were widely diffused and contributions relevant to it have been made by persons and organisations of diverse backgrounds not necessarily connected with anthropology. However, it is only recently that some people have been forcefully pleading the necessity of developing visual anthropology as a useful discipline, keeping in view the world trend in anthropological studies, and its vast scope in India.

Thus, any attempt to construct a history of visual anthropology in the country will require piecing together the diffused efforts of the early decades and discussion of some important events in recent times that have smoothed the way to the creation of visual anthropology in India.

Revised version of the earlier paper published in *Visual Anthropology*, Vol. 4, Pp. 25-41, 1991, Harwood Academic Publishers GmbH, U.S.A.

In India, a number of the early films were made by pioneer photographers and others who did not come from the profession of anthropology, though their short films were generally shot on a wide range of real life situations that occurred naturally and were close to ethnographic films. Unwittingly, they were creating an informal tradition of Indian visual anthropology.

Earliest Efforts

Indian films date back to 1896 when the first fiction film was shown in the Watson's Hotel in Bombay by the agents of the Lumière brothers of France. In the early years, films were mostly documentary and ethnographic in character though obviously they lacked anthropological and methodological sophistication, and related to life and culture and important events in India. A significant development took place when the operators who followed came with their projectors and cameras, often combined into one, and found the scenic grandeur of India a good source to feed their constant need of filmable materials. *Coconut Fair* and *Our Indian Empire*, the latter showing the monuments of Delhi and the famous Imambara Palace of Lucknow, were the first two films of this kind, made in 1897 by unknown cameramen, and were also perhaps the first documentary films about India. In Calcutta, it was Mr. Stevenson who brought the first 'bioscope' show to the city in October 1898 at the Star Theatre [Rangoonwala, 1975:12]. The same year, Mr. Stevenson shot local items known as *A Panorama of Indian Scenes*, including the procession of Parashnath through the streets of Calcutta. At about the same time in Bombay, Mr. Anderson showed some documentaries based on Indian scenes: *Train Arriving at Bombay Station* and *Poona Race '98*. In early 1899, Mr. P.A. Stewart announced some more 'local scenes' in his shows at Trivoli.

The 'first really Indian footage' was canned by Mr. Harischandra S. Bhatvadekar, who shot a film on a wrestling bout at Bombay's Hanging Gardens in 1897 entitled *The Wrestler*. Another short was made by him which showed some monkeys being trained by their master. In 1900 a film titled *Fatima, an Indian Dancer* was shown in Bombay. In the mid-1900s Mr. F.B. Thanawalla's film, *Taboot Procession,* covered the annual pageant of the Muslims as it passed through the busy Kalbadevi roads. In 1903 Hiralal Sen of Calcutta presented a series of his films, *Indian Life and Scenes*. These films included scenes of Indian domestic life as well as events from Indian history and Hindu mythology.

In 1906 the Elphinstone Company produced several shorts: *Grand Parashnath Procession; Bathing Ghat of Howrah; Goat Sacrifice at Kalighat; Dancing of Indian Nautch Girls;* and *Grand Masonic Procession.* At about the same time, the Paris Cinematograph showed films on *Scenes of Native Life in India* which included the *Malabarese, Charming Snakes, Juggling a Girl,* and *Dancing*. The names of the filmmakers, however, remain unknown.

In 1910, the Excelsior Cinematograph of Bombay presented coverage of the annual Muslim Festival of Muharram in Delhi. *Fugitive Dalai Lama* was another special attraction, which is of special historical significance now, showing the Tibetan leader's flight from the Chinese to seek protection in the then British Indian Territory and the big reception given to him. In 1911-12 the coming of George V to India and the Delhi Darbar attracted the attention of many filmmakers who covered the various events connected with the Darbar.

Films relating to some aspects of feudal life in India were also produced: *Marriage of a Maharaja* [1911], *Coronation of Maharaja Holkar at Indore,* filmed by Gaumont and the Excelsior Cinematograph, coverage of a garden party for Sir Shapurji Broacha, all in 1912. In about the same year a film, *Benaras* or *Kashi,* depicting the scenes of religious life in the sacred city of the Hindus, was made by an unknown cameraman and shown at the American-Indian Theatre. Another short depicted the *Ganapati Festival,* exclusively photographed for Cinema de Lux [Rangoonwala 1975; Raha 1974:63-66; Srivastava n.d.].

In the years that followed, the Indian film industry made rapid growth. The talkie cinema came into being on 14 March, 1931, when *Alam Ara*, the first Indian talkie feature produced by Ardeshir M. Irani, was released at the Majestic, Bombay [Kak 1980:5] and themes of films now shifted from shorts and documentaries depicting situations and events from real life to the classics, religious and mythological aspects of Indian culture, historical events, reformation themes, or those made for pure entertainment. Under the impact of Western culture, films based on themes of war and propaganda also inspired governmental and private agencies.

Documentation Becomes Meaningful

A systematic and more meaningful history of ethnographic films or documentaries with an ethnographic bias relating to glimpses of life and culture of Indian people, however, did not start until India gained freedom in 1947 when a national government was formed and an urgent necessity was felt to project the rich cultural heritage of India through the medium of short films. The Films Division, Government of India, under the Ministry of Information and Broadcasting came into existence in 1948.

With an annual target of 157 short films and a weekly national news review, Films Division is the world's largest single short film unit. Out of the 157 films, about 50 are produced for the Defence and Agriculture ministries; the remainder cover miscellaneous subjects. The films for general release are dubbed in 15 languages, and distributed in the country's 11,000 theatres to a weekly audience of some 60 million [Tandava 1983:62].

So far, over four thousand documentary films have been produced. They relate to a broad range of themes. Of all these films, those coming under the categories of 'Biographies', 'Arts', 'Festivals', 'People of India', and 'Experimental Films' are of special interest and relevant to the present context. The Films Division has compiled a voluminous catalogue of its films made between the years 1949 and 1972 and some other catalogues of selected films from time to time.

Besides the Films Division, a number of state governments have also produced several short films through their Departments of Information, Publicity, or Public Relations. Such documentaries of the Governments of Assam, Meghalaya, Arunachal, Manipur, Tripura, West Bengal, Madhya Pradesh, Orissa, and Himachal Pradesh which show dances, festivals, arts and crafts, economic life, historical events, or the nature of cultural change among the tribal and non-tribal peoples of the respective states may specially be mentioned.

By and large, the films of the Government of India and the state governments mentioned above have a running time between ten to thirty minutes. They are too short to depict a complete or systematic picture of even a single aspect of life and thus lack scientific precision. Nevertheless, they give us some glimpses of life and are in some measure important visual documents of culture.

Among private companies Burmah-Shell, India, planned and produced forty half-hour documentary films between 1954 and 1968 for Burmah Shell Oil Company, with Indian production units, for distribution in various regional languages within India. Among those which are of special interest, mention may be made of the series on village life in Travancore, West Bengal, and East Punjab. Other series related to family life in Andhra Pradesh and Karnataka, and the life of weavers, tanners, martial dancers, Oraons, fishermen, and so forth.

A significant development took place in the field of ethnographic films when the Anthropological Survey of India, a Government of India body, took up this task and produced under the supervision of anthropologists, more than fifty ethnographic films since 1954. These films cover a wide range of communities, regions, and aspects of Indian life. Out of the total, thirty-seven films are in colour. The running time varies between eight and fifty-seven minutes, though in a majority of the cases they are more than thirty minutes in duration. These films mainly relate to the life of tribal communities from different parts of India: the Abor, Onge, Nicobarese, Khasi, Riang, Juang, Toda, Gaddi, Asur, Birhor, Olari Gadaba, Bison Horn Maria, Rabari, Monpa, Garo, Lanjia Saore, Cholanaikan, Lahaulees, and Spitialees. They also cover arts and crafts, and festivals and fairs held in different parts of India. Most of these films are without sound though in recent years efforts have been made to produce sound films.

Some of the tribal or cultural research institutes started by the state governments in the early fifties, especially in Madhya Pradesh, Bihar, and West Bengal, have also made some ethnographic films relating to the life of some of the tribal communities in their respective states.

It is of interest that several universities in the United States, Europe, and elsewhere offer courses on South Asia with the help of ethnographic films produced either by foreign anthropologists or agencies who have been working independently in India or in collaboration with Indian counterparts. Here, mention may be made of the Department of South Asian Studies, University of Wisconsin, Madison, State University of New York, and others. The former made a film series called *Contemporary South Asia*. The State University of New York, through an arrangement with James Beveridge Associates, produced a series of biographical films on the *Music of North India*. The fifth edition of *Films for Anthropological Teaching* published by the American Anthropological Association [Heider 1972] includes half-a-dozen interesting films on the Ganges, a mountain community, North Indian village life, Tibetan traders, and other topics.

One of the recent films in this context is *The Ho; The People of the Rice Pot* (70 minutes) by Michael Yorke of London. This is a detailed ethnographic film backed by data sheets for classroom discussion and analysis. Margaret C. Fairlie of Ithaca College, New York, directed and edited two films on *Tribal Groups of Central India; Lifeway, Ceremony, and Dance* in 1971-72 which present a unique educational contribution. These films record the ceremonial rites and dances of four tribal and caste populations against the exotic backgrounds of their contrasting ways of life, economics, and ecological settings.

Interaudiovisual [1980], an official organisation in France, in its list of ethnographic films published in 1980 mentions nearly a dozen ethnographic films on India produced since 1965 by a number of French agencies such as SERDDAV, S. Genevoix, les Films de l'Adagio, INA, CNRS, and others. These films depict the Ganges, Pushkar, a Buddhist village, boatmen, dances, singers, and ballads. The *Encyclopaedia Cinematographica* [Wolf 1977:174-77] published by the Institut für den Wissenschaftlichen film, Göttingen, also lists a number of ethnographic films from India on the Bhil, Baiga, Toda, Kond, Hindus, life in Mithila (North Bihar), Nagas, and others.

Besides these films, some professional film directors, either on their own initiative or sponsored by others, have from time to time produced or directed documentaries or films of ethnographic interest on India. Paul Zils, a German, directed a film, *Our India,* in the mid-fifties which not only showed glimpses of contemporary life but depicted a few scenes from Indian history as well. Roberto Rosellini, the famous Italian director, came to India in the late fifties and made an abortive attempt to produce *India*. Satyajit Ray made a documentary on the life of the Sikkimese. Other names that come to mind in this connection are K.A. Abbas, Sukhdev, Shyam Benegal, Mani Kaul from Bombay, and Barindranath Saha, Sushil Karan, Tarun Mazumdar, Ashish Mukherjee, and Harisadhan Das Gupta from Calcutta. This list is not, of course, exhaustive [Sahay 1983:53].

Thus, in the light of these facts relating to the development of ethnographic films in India it may be said that since the end of the last century when the technique of cinematography was imported to this country by agents of the Lumière brothers of France and used for making short films of a documentary and ethnographic character, several isolated attempts have been made by different persons and organisations coming from different backgrounds or those connected with anthropology to make meaningful documentary and ethnographic films. However, such materials are widely scattered and the efforts which have so far gone into the making of such films lack coordination, system, and a 'convergent point' on the national level that are necessary for the systematic growth of a discipline. Many people interested in the making of such films do not know about others engaged in this field, or how their films could be made available. Many films of the early pioneers seem to have been 'lost' or may be lying in unknown places, in a precarious condition due to lack of proper facilities or knowledge about preservation. There is also lack of proper technical knowledge on the part of many persons who want to make such films. Besides, visual anthropology is a costly proposition and lack of funds is still another big hurdle in the making of films.

India Honoured by an International Body

Against this background, a very significant development took place in the field of visual anthropology in India when the ICAES nominated an Indian—K.N. Sahay from the Department of Anthropology, Ranchi University (the present author)—to act as its co-chairman from 1973 to 1978. A preliminary meeting of the commission[2] was convened at Ranchi in February 1977. Besides its chairman and other members from Japan (Masao Oka, chairman; Junichi Ushiyama, member; Yasuko Ichioka, member) and France (Marielle Delorme, who represented Jean Rouch), the meeting was attended by L.P. Vidyarthi, President, IUAES [1973-78] and ICAES [1978] as a guest participant.

Matters relating to cooperation with other organisations connected with ethnographic films, substantial financial support for the activities of the commission, the necessity of preparing, on an urgent basis, a catalogue of bibliographies of ethnographic films, and production of ethnographic films on themes specially relating to Third World countries like India were discussed. It was also decided to hold a symposium on visual anthropology and an exhibition of ethnographic films during the Xth ICAES at New Delhi. Dr. Sahay was entrusted with the task of exploring funds for this purpose, doing the necessary correspondence, and organising the symposium on behalf of the commission. He approached nearly half-a-dozen international and national bodies for necessary funding but unfortunately nothing could be procured from any source except the Finance Committee of the ICAES, which granted a modest amount. The co-chairman also visited Tokyo and Paris in 1977 at the invitation of Dr. Masao Oka, the chairman of the commission and Nippon Audio-Visual Productions (NAV), Tokyo, Japan, and Dr. Jean Rouch, General Secretary, CIFH, Paris, respectively. (His foreign travels were sponsored by NAV while hospitality in Paris was given by CIFH.)

The commission felt that since nearly two dozen committees and organisations connected with ethnographic films throughout the world had prepared their respective indices of ethnographic films, what was needed was the creation of a bibliography of all such bibliographies or indices of films. Jean Rouch of the Musée de l'Homme was requested to accomplish this task through his organisation, while Junichi Ushiyama of NAV Tokyo, a member of the commission, was requested to prepare an index of ethnographic films on Asia and Oceania. Anna Hohenwart-Gerlachstein of Vienna, another member of the commission and chairman of the Commission on Urgent Anthropology, strongly pleaded for cooperation between the two commissions and consequently published a few notes in her newsletter relevant to those interested in Visual Anthropology. Sahay took up the matter of preservation under proper conditions of the valuable ethnographic films of the Anthropological Survey of India, the necessity of adding a sound track to these films, making copies available to other institutions and researchers, and developing this wing under the guidance of a senior anthropologist of the ASI, with its director and some senior officials of the Department of Culture, Ministry of Education, Government of India.

The First International Symposium at Delhi

Subsequently, a definite advance was made when a five day International Symposium on Visual Anthropology was organised at Delhi, in the auditorium of the NCERT in December 1978, on behalf of the commission.

The symposium was a great success. Originally, it was scheduled for only three days, but was extended for two more.

In addition to the symposium, there was a screening of some three dozen ethnographic films for participants in the Xth ICAES. Marielle Delorme of Paris organised this programme at Vigyan Bhavan, the main venue of the ICAES, on behalf of the commission. The symposium was attended by delegates from ten countries: Japan, Korea, Tunisia, Australia, France, Austria, the Federal Republic of Germany, Canada, the United States, and India. It consisted of seven sessions where a number of papers and ethnographic films were presented and discussed.

This symposium was the first organised activity in India relating to visual anthropology on country-wide and international levels, which will hopefully go a long way in shaping the future of visual anthropology in the country. For India, this event constituted an important landmark in the history of visual anthropology, where, among other things, possibilities were explored to ensure international cooperation to develop it with special reference to Third World countries. An emphasis was laid on establishing a global network of regional and national centres in visual anthropology to coordinate the filming, indexing, educational, archival, and research activities. The symposium created a deeper interest in ethnographic filming among a section of young anthropologists, other scholars, and amateur filmmakers, and inspired them to explore the rich prospect of ethnographic films in India.

It was with this in view that the biannual, *Visual Anthropology Bulletin*, containing news relating to ethnographic films and short articles, was edited and published by K.N. Sahay beginning in June 1979.

On the last day of the symposium, a meeting of the Commission on Visual Anthropology was held in which the following resolutions were adopted:

Whereas the increasingly rapid loss of cultural variety in the world has intensified the need to prepare permanent researchable, illustrative records of vanishing ways of life and culture; and whereas the visual potential of film makes it well suited to presenting and preserving multicultural viewpoints in records of human heritage; and whereas humanistic film studies heighten national and international awareness of the needs of ethnic groups by presenting in accessible and understandable form information vital to their social, cultural, and political life;

For these reasons it is resolved:

1. That the Resolution on Visual Anthropology passed at the IXth International Congress of Anthropological and Ethnological Sciences, Chicago, September 1973, be hereby reaffirmed and emphasized.
2. That film studies be undertaken which go beyond the particular belief system of a single culture to present multicultural viewpoints.
3. That new kinds of humanistically oriented centres be created to take advantage of the multicultural potential of the visual media for furthering human understanding.
4. That the technologically advanced nations be encouraged to lend resources, training, and effort to developing nations, particularly those with broad independent cultural traditions, to develop local talent and expertise in visual anthropology.
5. That, since much of anthropology is in the Western cultural traditions, a new type of humanistic orientation be developed in which the non-verbal potential of film is employed in cross-cultural studies and documentation.
6. That freer international movement of educational, cultural, and scientific film materials be encouraged.
7. That a joint international commission on ethnographic film and urgent anthropology be formed to bring together from time to time the existing Commission on Urgent Anthropology and the Commission on Visual Anthropology.
8. That, in pursuit of the goals delineated above, a global network of regional and national centres, in visual anthropology be established to co-ordinate the filming, indexing, educational, archival, and research activities required.

Second International Seminar at Jodhpur

The first Delhi Symposium on Visual Anthropology, held in 1978, deeply inspired and stirred the imagination of a few people. It led to a second International Seminar of this type—*A Portrayal of People*, organized at Jodhpur from 15 to 19 December 1987. The idea of this seminar was conceived by Jayasinghji Jhala (currently at Harvard University), an enthusiastic young man and filmmaker who was an active participant in the Delhi Symposium and presented two ethnographic films, *Apatani Sacrifice* and *Forgotten Headhunters*. Jhala gave concrete shape to his idea with the help of the Indian National Trust for Art and Cultural Heritage (INTACH), New Delhi, which is associated with Pupul Jayakar and Rajiv Gandhi. Later on, the Anthropological Survey of India joined in a big way and co-sponsored the seminar, which took place with K.S. Singh, the Director General, A.S.I., as its General President and Mr. Jayasinghji Jhala as the Co-ordinator of Programmes. Besides a large number of Indian delegates, nearly twenty foreigners participated, including Asen Balikci, Chairman of the International Commission on Visual Anthropology, and John Marshall. Nearly fifteen papers and several interesting ethnographic films were presented and thoroughly discussed. The seminar resolved to undertake the following tasks: to lend support to institutions and stimulate interest within the ministries of the Government of India; to identify Indian filmmakers and encourage a dialogue between them and anthropologists on issues of common interest; to promote films in India which would include the establishment of an archive and the hosting of an annual ethnographic film festival; to identify individuals and organizations with the skills, time, and shared sense of purpose with whom collaboration can be undertaken to establish workshops and scholarships; and to promote interaction between Indian visual anthropologists and their counterparts elsewhere in the world [Menon 1987:11]. Only time will tell how far these ideas are translatable into reality.

The Task Ahead

India is a society with varied geographical, racial, economic, linguistic, religious, and cultural groups. It has a rich variety of culture ranging from that of pre-farming and folk communities to complex urban and industrial societies. One can find here societies which represent all the stages in the evolutionary process of cultural development. There are tribal groups as primitive as cave-dwellers, hunters, food-gatherers, or shifting agriculturists. On the other hand, some of the groups are so acculturated that they have completely taken to the urban or civilized way of life. A large variety of caste, creed, and religious groups, along with rural and urban styles of life and a wide range of ecological settings which helped to develop different types of culture, present still other dimensions of Indian life and civilization. Indian civilization itself has an orthogenetic growth with a very long history, and unity amidst diversity has been one of its basic characteristics. A host of religious centres situated in different parts of the country, the institution of pilgrimage, and the religious intelligentsia connected with it foster a sense of unity amidst elements of heterogeneity. It all promises a vast scope for visual anthropology.

In view of all this, there are a number of tasks before us which must be accomplished on an urgent basis to develop visual anthropology in this country. The first and the foremost task is a stock-taking exercise to locate the various persons and organisations from India and abroad who have been connected with the making of ethnographic and relevant documentary films in the past and the present; to collect details of such films, evaluate their quality, classify them meaningfully, and index them scientifically to make them useful to the students and researchers of visual anthropology, planner or whosoever is interested.

Some of the organiations, such as the Anthropological Survey of India, various research institutes, public relations departments of state governments, film divisions and the like, have their own catalogues of films. It would be necessary to make an annotated bibliography of all such catalogues. The documentaries made by persons or organisations not connected with anthropology should be scrutinized carefully and only those films which are ethnographic in nature and relevant to anthropology should be selected.

Locating documentaries by pioneers in the silent era may prove to be a difficult task as the whereabouts of some are unknown, many have been completely destroyed, and still others have been stored in improper and bad conditions. One has to know about and retrieve them, and preserve them under proper conditions.

There are several communities living in precarious conditions. As a result of the negative forces of modernity they have been exposed to or the change in the ecological balance and the new forest legislation. Their customs and practices are fast disappearing. Some of the tribes—Onge, Little Andamanese, Shompen, and Jarwa—are even threatened with cultural and physical extinction. In view of this we are faced with the proverbial question of 'now or never' and visual anthropology has to act fast by making a list of priorities for the purpose of filming such communities.

Visual anthropology has still to take shape in our country. So far attempts made in this field are highly diffused. One of the reasons for this is the lack of information among those interested. Some people have the necessary resources and potential to contribute to this field but have no idea of the work done by pioneers or others in this field. Again, there are anthropologists devoid of the knowledge of cinematography, and film-makers interested in the subject but devoid of the knowledge of anthropology. Under the circumstances, dissemination of information relating to ethnographic films, technical or otherwise, or the persons connected with them, developments in the field, and available funds, is greatly needed. All these objectives can be fulfilled by establishing on an urgent basis a National Centre of Audio-Visual Data with a network of five regional sub-centres in different parts of the country.

Such an Audio-Visual Data Centre should visually document the variety of culturally patterned human behaviour which reflects diverse, sometimes unique, expressions of basic human potential on the one hand, and emerging developments in societies that lead to modernisation on the other [ICEF 1978:2].

Audio-visual materials will help us to study non-verbal communities and 'body language'. Such material may also serve as a scientific tool allowing the repeated examination of movement and behaviour, segmented into regular units and slowed down for microanalysis as developed by American scholars like Gregory Bateson, Ray Birdwhistell, Edward Hall, Alan Lomax, Margaret Mead, and others in their film analysis [ICEF 1978:2]. Sorenson wrote:

> ...We need better understanding of how man fits into and copes with the world and its transformations, including those he himself generates. These

newer technologically based ways of life change perhaps even more rapidly than do isolated cultures. Our incomplete understanding of the dynamics of such change, or its socio-biological significance, frequently forces us to make uniformed and arbitrary decisions about its direction. Movement into the future would be less traumatic and more adaptive if we had greater understanding (Sorenson 1975:463].

He talks further of four basic functions of such audio-visual data centres:

Repository and Archiving: which will store and preserve film records of man's varied ways of life; maintain facilities and equipment to locate, view, and abstract specific kinds of visual data from the collections; and provide a means to duplicate sequences needed for research and educational projects;

Acquisitional: which will undertake and support programmes to document vanishing cultures and changing patterns of human behaviour and encourage local production of visual documents; accept gifts of films for desposit; copy undeposited original films before they are edited; and purchase endangered prints of early films;

Research: which will support the scientific study of various ethnographic and 'research films'[3], already archived; promote studies of various filming approaches; and support studies to increase the potential of film as a scientific and humanistic resource;

Educational: which will support and conduct seminars, training fellowships, workshops, etc., in the visual documentation of changing culture and human behaviour; support the production of educational materials from holdings; and support studies of new ways to use visual materials in education [reworded from Chanock and Sorenson 1975: 473-74].

The heterogeneity of visual data in India, the complexity of its culture and civilization, and the richness of its religious and philosophical traditions provide ample scope for research and new experiments in the visual presentation of anthropological material. *Lost Child* and *Trip*, the two films made by Jagat Murari and Pramod Pati respectively, of the Films Division, Government of India, are symbolic presentations of certain philosophical thoughts [Sahay 1980:1]. *Duvidha* (Dilemma), directed by Mani Kaul and based upon a Rajasthani folk tale dealing with spirit possession and exorcism, is another significant film which opens a new vista in cultural studies as it has a distinctive style.

The data centre will also work as a liaison agency between the government and the persons or organisations interested in making relevant films. It will assume a greater importance if it acts as a storehouse and disseminates all kinds of relevant information pertaining to visual anthropology in this country and abroad through published materials of seminars and symposia, or newsletters, bulletins, and journals. Several other dimensions of ethnographic filming can also be explored by the audio-visual data centre. It may be of interest to note that films have a commercial side in an international market. Hence, they may be commercially exploited, which could gradually create requisite funds to enrich the data centre.

Films have a great feedback[4] value and this aspect should be fully utilized. It has been observed that the lack of knowledge about others' culture often breeds misunderstanding while a knowledge of it promotes mutual appreciation and trust among people. It would be useful to telecast a regular series of films about the different peoples of India as this will foster a sense of mutual understanding and integration on a national level. Such films may be of one hour's duration and could be shown once or twice a week or Indian television.

Films dealing with comparative, cross-cultural subjects of universal interest and importance like *rites-de-passage*, economy, religion, dances, crafts, tribal problems, and the like, might be telecast. Such films serve a useful purpose by radiating new ideas and insights among the people and are an important source of 'controlled change' in the desired direction. They would also be useful to planners and administrators and enable them to have a better understanding of the needs of the communities they work for.

The introduction of various 'video booths' in our museums on the pattern of the National Museum of Ethnology at Osaka, Japan, known as *Videotheque* in that museum, would be significant. Visitors could then see international ethnographic films of their choice. The Japanese museum has thirty-seven video booths, a control room with a small computer, automatic video cassette tape players, special robots, and so on [Omori 1978:1]. Such booths in Indian museums, apart from facilitating human understanding and national integration, will also work as an important tool for anthropological research.

The vastness of the field in India is not met by the poor resources, and indeed, there are hardly any funds available for ethnographic filming. It calls for priorities to be fixed in terms of geographical areas least covered, communities still untouched, and those aspects of culture that are changing fast owing to the impact of modern forces. A phased programme for ethnographic filming is obviously implied. A comprehensive filming programme for India has to be carefully evolved to include many representative communities of the country and the various facets of Indian life. Here one has also to keep in mind the need for cross-cultural visual data from different parts of the world. The *Visual Anthropology Bulletin*, published in Ranchi, has taken stock of ethnographic films about India.

This objective can be fulfilled by locating interested visual anthropologists, scholars, filmmakers with anthropological insight, institutions, and government officials interested in ethnographic filmmaking. They would form a national committee with regional offices which would provide an infrastructure of experts and work in close collaboration with the audio-visual data centre. This national committee would pursue the matter with central and state governments, especially the Ministry of Information and Broadcasting, the Films Division, and the Public Relation Departments and create an awareness for the promotion of ethnographic films by requisitioning the services of visual anthropologists. The various Tribal Welfare Research Institutes of state governments and the departments of anthropology in various universities can also contribute significantly to ethnographic filming. Some have audio-visual wings with cameramen, but due to financial constraints and lack of adequate technical know-how or interest, they are sitting idle.

Apart from this, the departments of anthropology in various universities should introduce visual anthropology as a part of their curriculum.[5] This will help to popularise the subject and go a long way in serving the cause of visual anthropology in the country. The bias against the use of film in teaching on the part of older anthropologists is probably due to a lack of technical knowledge, the paraphernalia associated with it, and the heavy financial commitment involved. However, the apathetic attitude has to be removed and a new generation of teachers must come forward. A special provision should be made for fellowships and scholarships in visual anthropology, to be awarded by universities, the national committee, or the audio-visual data centre.

The government has realized the necessity of promoting 'film culture' on the campus and in 1984 the UGC came up with a proposal to establish film societies in the universities [Khanna, 1984:1-9]. Bangalore University is the first to introduce a short course in film appreciation [Bahadur, 1976:106]. Such developments are likely to have a favourable result and may directly or indirectly strengthen the cause of visual anthropology in India.

So far, the Anthropological Survey of India, the largest anthropological institution in the world in terms of its extension and spread, with headquarters in Calcutta, has been the major producer of ethnographic films. Unfortunately, this important wing has been virtually a one-man show, functioning under Sushanto K. Chattopadhyay, its ciné cameraman, stationed at Calcutta (now retired), though there are also a few other cameramen at some other stations. Of course, Sri Chattopadhyay worked in association with anthropologists of the ASI, but he alone has been responsible for shooting, editing, and processing the films. The ASI can strengthen this wing by appointing an anthropologist of the rank of a Deputy Director who has an orientation and personal interest in filmmaking and who can be assisted by other trained anthropologists.

Nippon Audio-Visual Productions of Tokyo has been organizing the Tokyo Festival of 8mm films every year since 1973 in cooperation with the Japanese Television Network and newspapers to encourage more and more Japanese to film the life and traditional culture of their country [Sahay 1979:11]. Junichi Ushiyama, who organises this festival, told the author that he met with tremendous success. Such a festival could be organised by the national committee on an all-India and regional basis to help locate talent and at the same time add to the body of visual data on India. Talented persons can be encouraged to pursue visual anthropology as a profession. In fact, such an effort to organise an all-India festival of short films by Indian Amateur filmmakers has already been started by the Students' Association of the Film and Television Institute of India, Poona [Sahay 1981b:6].

So far native communities have been studied and filmed by outsiders. But under the fast changing circumstances, it would be worthwhile to train native talent to make ethnographic films about their own culture. Methodologically, it would be significant to note the difference of perspective between our conception of the native culture and the insider's conception and projection of it as reflected in ethnographic films. Secondly, Indians should be encouraged to make films on the life of non-native communities coming from the mainstream of society with a view to gauge their understanding of other cultures.

Another area which needs to be explored under visual anthropology is the 'New Wave', 'Art', or 'Realistic' fiction films being produced in India (as elsewhere) for the last few decades. The films of Satyajit Ray, Mrinal Sen, Shyam Benegal, Sathyu, Mani Kaul, Govind Nihlani, Girish Karnad, and a host of others can be mentioned in this connection. Besides the short films focused on real life situations and events which occur naturally and spontaneously, ethnographic films may also include, under a separate sub-category, those films which are not pure fiction but in a considerable measure present a faithful and vivid depiction of the typical lifestyle, problems, and events connected with a particular cross-section of the society. They could be ethnographically and anthropologically useful.[6]

Such films influence society in two ways: materially and non-materially. On the material level films influence fashion, dress and decorations, manners, etiquette, style of living, crime patterns, and material goods. But the impact works more powerfully on the non-material aspects of life—belief and value systems, ideals, morals, attitudes, levels of aspiration, horizons of knowledge, and awareness of various situations. This is significant, for any real change in a society must be preceded by a change in the ideational aspect of life. However, films, besides being an agency of change, also reinforce some of our basic traditional norms and values. They can thus be an effective instrument of cultural revitalization.

Students of the Film and Television Institute of India, Poona, and the Institute of Film Technology at Madras have to make diploma films on completing their courses. Some of these students could be encouraged to make ethnographic or relevant documentary films.

The magnitude of work before us also calls for international cooperation especially in matters relating to technical, organizational, and financial aspects of the endeavour. Here one is reminded of some of the resolutions adopted at the meeting of the Commission on Visual Anthropology held at New Delhi in 1978 which envisaged that:

> new kinds of humanistically oriented centres be created to take advantage of the multicultural potential of the visual media for furthering human understanding; the technologically advanced nations be encouraged to lend resources, training, and effort to developing nations, particularly those with broad independent cultural traditions to develop local talent and expertise in visual anthropology; and the necessity of a global network of regional and national centres in visual anthropology; be established to coordinate the filming, indexing, educational, archival, and research activities required.

Now is the time to see that such resolutions no longer remain confined to paper but sincere efforts are made to implement them in the larger interest of the global community of visual anthropologists. The Commission on Visual Anthropology of the ICAES and those immediately connected with it should pursue the matter to ensure some results.

NOTES

1. This paper is a thoroughly revised and enlarged version of a paper published earlier in *A Portrayal of People: Essays on Visual Anthropology in India*, Anthropological Survey of India, New Delhi and INTACH, New Delhi, 1987.

2. A detailed report of this meeting of the Commission on Visual Anthropology held at Ranchi was published in *Review of Ethnology*, Newsletter No.2, 1977-78, pp.203-06.
3. "The research film method provides identified and annotated visual records useful for continued study and use. These visual records are unedited and not in themselves "films" in the usual sense: there is no attempt in them to present a coherent statement or point of view. Not designed to demonstrate a conclusion or to impose preconceived ideas, they are intended to facilitate review and study of passing, naturally occurring phenomena. They are not constructed to conform to the aesthetic models of our age or to present worked out concepts. Rather they are designed to serve as information potential: they are ordered and annotated—but not edited, rearranged or abstracted. Thus the name *research films* [Chanock and Sorenson 1975:432].
4. Jean Rouch [1975:100] has the following to say about feedback: "This extraordinary technique of 'feedback' (which I translate as "audio-visual counter-gift") has certainly not yet revealed all of its possibilities, but we can see already that, thanks to feedback, the anthropologist is no longer an entomologist observing his subject as if it were an insect (putting it down) but rather as if it were a stimulant for mutual understanding (hence dignity)".
5. Earlier, the author had published "A Model Syllabus for Visual Anthropology" [Sahay 1981a:1-2] as one of two papers about teaching visual anthropology on the post-graduate level to suit Indian universities. It was later expanded into "A Model Curriculum in Visual Anthropology" [1986-87] for the U.G.C.'s Curriculum Development Programme in post-graduate anthropology and sociology at the Department of Anthropology, Ranchi University, Ranchi, and sponsored by the University Grants Commission, New Delhi.
6. K.N. Sahay's paper "Visual Anthropology and Indian Fiction Films", *Journal of Social Research* 29(2), September 1986.

REFERENCES

Bahadur, Satish, 1976, The Context of Indian Film Culture. In *Film Miscellany*, p.106. Pune: Film and Television Institute of India.

Chanock, F.O., and E.R. Sorenson, 1975, Research Films and the Communications Revolution. In *Principles of Visual Anthropology*. Paul Hockings, ed. Pp.431-38. The Hague: Mouton.

Heider, Karl G., 1972, *Films for Anthropological Teaching*, Fifth Edition. Washington, DC: American Anthropological Association.

Interaudiovisual, 1980, *Ethnographic Film French Production*, Pp 1-335. Paris.

ICEF, 1978, International Ethnographic Film Decade. Unpublished manuscript of a proposal submitted by the Executive Committee of ICEF, Wenner-Gren Foundation

Kak, Sidharth, ed., 1980, *Cinema Vision India* I(1):5. Bombay: Adarsh Nagar.

Khanna, Arun, 1984, U.G.C. Report Proposes Growth Strategy for University Film Club. *Screen*, 22 June, Pp. 1-9.

Menon, Ritu, 1987, A Portrayal of People. In *The Indian National Trust for Art and Cultural Heritage* (INTACH), Number 11:11. New Delhi.

Omori, Yasuhiro, 1978, The Development of Ethnographic Film by Videotheque in Museums. Paper presented at the Symposium on Visual Anthropology, Xth ICAES, organised by the Commission on Visual Anthropology of IUAES [1973-78], Delhi, December.

Raha, Kironmoy, 1974, Indian Cinema. In *Chitra Bani: A Book on Film Appreciation*. Gaston Roberge, ed. Pp. 163-66. Calcutta: Chitra Bani.

Rangoonwalla, Firoze, 1975, *Seventy-five Years of Indian Cinema*. New Delhi: Indian Book Company.

Rouch, Jean, 1975, The Camera and Man. In *Principles of Visual Anthropology*. Paul Hockings, ed. Pp. 84-102. The Hague: Mouton.

Sahay, K.N., 1979, A Popular Movement for Folk Film Making in Japan. *Visual Anthropology Bulletin* I(1):11.

—— 1980, Editorial. *Visual Anthropology Bulletin* II(1):1.

—— 1981a, A Model Syllabus for Visual Anthropology. *Visual Anthropology Bulletin* III(2):1-2.

—— 1981b, National Amateur Short Film Festival 1981, India. *Visual Anthropology Bulletin* III(1):6.

—— 1983, Ethnographic Films in India: Prospect, Priorities and Proposals. In *Methodology in Anthropological Filmmaking*. Nico C.R. Bogaart and Henk W.E.R. Ketelaar, eds. Pp. 49-59. Göttingen: Edition Herodot.

—— 1986, Visual Anthropology and Indian Fiction Films. *Journal of Social Research*, 29(2):1-41.

—— 1987, History of Visual Anthropology in India. In *A Portrayal of People: Essays on Visual Anthropology in India*. Pp. 49-74. New Delhi: Anthropological Survey of India and Indian National Trust for Art and Cultural Heritage.

Sorenson, E.R., 1975, Visual Records, Human Knowledge, and the Future. In *Principles of Visual Anthropology*. Paul Hockings, ed. Pp.463-76. The Hague: Mouton.

Srivastava, Bachchan, n.d., *Bharatiya Filmon Ki Kahani* (Hindi). Delhi: Pocket Books.

Stiglmayr. E., 1977-78, A Detailed Report of the Meeting of the Commission on Visual Anthropology at Ranchi. *Review of Ethnology Newsletter*. 2 November, Pp. 203-206.

Tandava, G., 1983, The Documentary: Systematic Images. In *Indian Cinema Superbazar*. Aruna Vasudev and Phillipe Lenglet, eds. P. 62. New Delhi: Vikas Publishing House, Pvt. Ltd.

Wolf, G., ed., 1977, *Encyclopaedia Cinematographica*. Pp. 174-77. Göttingen: Institut für den Wissenschaftlichen Film.

Chapter II

A Brief History of Ethnographic Films in India*

Indian Cinema is a little over eighty years old when there used to be only silent films. It is significant that India provided incentive to many foreign and Indian film-makers to make films on the life and culture of India in all its diversities right from the days of silent films. The history of Indian films goes back to the 7th July, 1896 when the first Movie film was shown in the Watson's Hotel in Bombay by the agents of the Lumiere Brothers of France. Since then, a number of films were shown to Indian public.

A significant development took place when the foreign operators who came with their projectors and cameras (often combined into one), found the scenic grandeur of India a good source to feed their constant need of filmable material. *Coconut Fair* and *Our Indian Empire,* the latter showing the monuments of Delhi and the famous Imambara Palace of Lucknow, were the first two films of this kind made in 1897 by unknown Cameraman which were also perhaps the first documentary films on India. In Calcutta it was Mr. Stevenson who brought the first 'Bioscope show' to the city for the first time in October 1898 at the Star Theatre.[2] In December 1898, the Star Theatre came up with one more of Mr. Stevenson's locally shot items known as *A Panorama of Indian Scenes,* which included many actuality materials including the procession of Pareshnath through the streets of Calcutta. At about the same time in Bombay, Mr. Anderson, who had brought his Scopograph operated on elecuric light, showed some documentaries based on Indian scenes viz., *Train Arriving at Bombay Station* and

---

* Revised version of the earlier paper published in *Visual Anthropology Bulletin*, Vol. IV, No. 1, 1982.

Poona Races '98. In early 1899 Mr. P.A. Stewart announced some more 'local scenes' in his shows at Trivoli.

But the 'first really Indian footage' was canned by one Mr. Harischandra S. Bhatvadekar alias Save Dada who got together two well-known wrestlers and shot a reel on their bout at Bombay's Hanging Gardens in 1897 entitled *The Wrestlers*. He also made another short showing some monkeys being trained by their master. On the New Year's day in 1900, a film was shown in Bombay named *Fatima, an Indian Dancer*. In the middle of 1900, Mr. F.B. Thanawalla made a film *Taboot Procession* which covered the annual pageant of the Muslims as it passed through the busy Kalbadevi roads.

In the early months of 1901, Hiralal Sen of Calcutta shot scenes from the famous dramas and filmed seven such extracts from plays like musical Opera *Alibaba*. In January 1903, Hiralal came up with a new package programme of his own films, called *Indian Life and Scenes*. These films included scenes of Indian domestic life besides events from Indian history and Hindu mythology. In the year 1903 a number of Cameramen shot films on *Delhi Darbar*.

The year 1906 witnessed the production of several shorts by Elphinstone Company viz., *Grand Pareshnath Procession, Bathing Ghat of Howrah, Goat Sacrifice at Kalighat, Dancing of Indian Nautch Girls*, and *Grand Masonic Procession*. At about the same time the Paris Cinematograph showed films on *Scenes of Native Life in India* which included *The Malabarees, Charming Snakes, Juggling a Girl and Dancing*. But the names of the film makers, however, remain unknown. In 1907 the Elphinstone Company made a film on *Amir of Kabul's Procession*.

In 1910, the Excelsior Cinematograph of Bombay made a coverage of the annual Muslim festival of the Mohurrum in Delhi. *Fugitive Dalai Lama* was another special attraction, and of special historical significance now, which showed the Tibetan Head's flight from the Chinese to seek protection in the then British Indian territory and the big reception given to him. In 1911-12, coming of George V to India and the next

Delhi Durbar attracted the attention of many film makers. The Excelsior made a detailed coverage of the different ceremonies of the King's arrival, the procession shot from a specially commissioned Tram Car travelling from Sir J.J. Hospital to Hornby Road and a Garaba dance performed by Parsi girls before the King.

Some other films made in the early part of the second decade of the present century which specially depicted some aspects of life style of some feudal Kings of India, were *Marriage of a Maharaja* shown in 1911 while *Coronation of Maharaja Holkar at Indore* filmed by Gaumont and the Excelsior Cinematograph coverages of *Garden Party to Sir Shopurji Broacha,* all shown in 1912. In about the same year a film, *Benaras or Kashi* which depicted the scenes of religious life in the Sacred City of Hindus was made by an unknown Cameraman and shown at the America-India Theatre. Another short depicted the *Ganapati Festival* exclusively photographed for Cinema de Lux.[3]

In the years which followed, Indian film Industry made a rapid growth. The Talkie cinema came into being since early thirties and the themes of these films mainly related to Indian classics, religious life, mythological aspects of culture, historical events, reformistic themes or those meant for pure entertainment, in many cases, under the impact of Western culture. The two world wars inspired several Governmental or private agencies to make documentary films based on the themes of War and propaganda.

A systematic and meaningful history of Ethnographic films or documentaries with ethnographic bias, relating to some glimpses of the life and culture of Indian peoples, however, did not start until India gained freedom in 1947 when a National Government was formed and an urgent necessity was felt by the Government to project the rich cultural heritage of India through the medium of short films. The Film Division, Government of India under the Ministry of Information and Broadcasting came into existence in the year 1948. It has been producing nearly 120 documentary films besides a number of news reels every year. So far, it has produced nearly 4000 films. The documentary films relate to a broad range of themes. Of all these films, those coming under the categories of Biographies, Arts, Festival, People of India and Experimental films are of special interest here. The Film Division has compiled a voluminous catalogue of its films made between the years 1949-72 and the films coming under the above categories numbered 51, 54, 13 and 30 respectively. The first category of Biographical films among others, show the Exponents of Performing Arts, Creative Artists at their work while the second category of Art films show some glimpses of the classical, regional and folk dances of India, Decorative Arts Drama, Music and paintings. The third category of films on Festivals present the glimpses of various all-India and regional festivals connected with different ethnic groups. However, as the figures indicate, films on Peoples of India also have a sizable number and they present short glimpses of some aspects of culture and life-style of Indian people from different regions of India—of tribal communities of north-eastern, central India, Cis-Himalayan region, Chotanagpur, Andaman and Nicobar group of Islands or elsewhere. Among them mention may be made of some more popular films produced in recent past like *Man in Search of Man* based on the life of some tribal communities of Andaman, *Chitrakathi* depicting the visual art of narrating stories from epics among the Konkani speaking people of West India which is on the verge of decline, *Nomadic Puppetteers of Rajasthan, Bhutan, Closed Centuries Opening Years, Manipur, Weavers of Sambalpur, Vanishing Tribe* and the like. A few films with a special emphasis on family life were also made, of which mention may be made of *House that Ananda built* depicting a typical Oriya family. It is significant that the Film Division, in collaboration with some talented artists, authors and intellectuals made a few 'experimental films' dealing with higher cultural philosophies viz., *Lost Child, Trip* and *Abid*. The *Lost Child* which runs into 25 minutes, is based on a famous allegorical story of the famous writer, Mulk Raj Anand. The story takes place in a fair where a child gets lost from his parents. The fair symbolizes the world while the child, man. *Trip* is the film running into just 4 minutes in which the pixilation technique has been used. The film depicts the transitoriness of life. *Abid* which runs into 5 minutes, depicts the life of a modern Indian painter. Most of the above mentioned films got national and international awards.

Besides the Film Division of the Government of India, a number of State Governments have also produced several short films through their Departments of Information, Publicity or Public Relations. Documentary film of the Governments of Assam, Meghalaya, Arunachal, Manipur and Tripura, West Bengal, Madhya Pradesh, Orissa, Himachal Pradesh may be specially mentioned in this connection. To give one illustration, the Department of Information and Pubiic Relations, Government of West Bengal has produced short films on *Bangaler Mela, Jatra Utsab, Kansari* showing Bell Metal Artisans of Murshidabad, *Dhokra* showing traditional crafts and the village of Dhokra tribe ($20\frac{1}{2}$ minutes), *Lodha Upjatir Bimukti-O-Bikash* (15 minutes) showing the life of Lodha—an ex-criminal tribe, *Pragatir Paschim Bangaler Adibasi* ($10\frac{1}{2}$ minutes), *Naya Gram*, the story based on Tribal development (20 minutes), *Pratibashi Oraon* showing culture and traditions of Oraon in West Bengal ($10\frac{1}{2}$ minutes), *Santal Samaj-O-Sanskriti* showing the life and culture of Santal community ($10\frac{1}{2}$ minutes) and *Ekti Mech Paribarer Kahini* showing the changing life of a Mech family (12 minutes). Besides, the Government of West Bengal produced a number of short films relating to the cultural and musical life in West Bengal, or those which come under the category of Biographical films. Here mention may be made of *Bangaler Majhi Bhai*, showing the boatmen of Bengal, *Bangaler Kirtan* showing devotional singing of Bengal, *Bauls of Bengal* showing the famous *Baul* singer of Bengal, *Chhati Ganer Dabi* showing six folk songs of Bengal. Similarly, films were made on *Chohow* dance of Purulia, story of *Ramayana* in dolls, cultural life in Shantiniketan, performance of folk music in the life of rural people, story of *Ramayana* in Terracotta and other media, dance-drama about the heroes of Sepoy Mutiny and others. All these films were produced between 1956 to 1970 and vary between 10 minutes to nearly half an hour in duration. Among the Biographical films mention may be made of the films on the life of Ostad Amir Khan, the singer, Ostad Allaudin and others. It is on special significance here that the famous feature film *Pather Panchali* directed by the great Master Sri Satyajit Ray was financed and produced by the West Bengal Government in 1953-54. By and large, the films of the Government of India and State Governments mentioned above are too small to depict a complete or systematic picture of even a single aspect of life or lack the scientific precision. Nevertheless, they give us some glimpses of the life and are important documents of culture.

Besides Government documentaries, some private agencies like Burmah-Shell, India, planned and produced 40 half-hour documentary films between 1954-68 for Burmah-Shell Oil Company with Indian production units for distribution in various language versions within India. Among those which are of special ethnographic interest, mention may be made of the series of *Village life in Travancore, West Bengal and East Punjab.* Another series relate to *Family in Andhra* and *Bangalore* and *Weavers of Maindargi, Tanners of Jharauta, Martial Dances of Malabar, Oraons of Bihar, Fisher Folk of Bombay, Himalayan Tapestry* and the like. The last film had won the President's Gold Medal award for the best documentary produced in India in 1957.

A definite advance was made in the field of Ethnographic films when the Anthropological Survey of India of the Government of India under the active supervision and guidance of Anthropologists produced as many as 40 Ethnographic films covering a very wide range of communities, regions and aspects of Indian life. Out of the total, 37 films are in Kodachrome (colour). The running time of these films varies between 8 minutes to 57 minutes, though in majority of the cases, they are of more than 30 minutes duration. These films mainly relate to the life of tribal communities from different regions of India viz. *the Abor of NEFA, the Onge of Little*

Andaman Island, the Nicobarese of Car-Nicobar Island, the Khasi of Khasi and Jayantia Hills, the Riang of Tripura, the Juang of Orissa, the Toda of Nilgiri Hills, the Gaddi of Himachal Pradesh, the Asur of Chotanagpur, the Birhor (of Chotanagpur), *the Olari Gadaba of Orissa, the Bison Horn Maria of Bastar, the Rabbari of Western Gujrat* and other films relating to the life of the *Monpa of NEFA,* the *Garo of Garo Hills, the Lanjia Saora* of *Orissa, Cholanaikan—the Cave Dwellers of Kerala.* Besides, some of the films also relate to the life and culture of the people in an area in general viz., the *Lahaulees* and *Spitiales, Garhwal Himalaya* or *Dussahra Festivals of Mysore. Rupkund Expedition, Arts and Crafts of Manipur, Potter's Craft of Poona, the Temples and Mathas of Puri, the Konark Temple, the Fisherman Community of Puri in Orissa, Hook-swinging festival of Singhbhum district, Ardha Kumbha Fair, Tons Valley Expedition* and *Gangotri, Gomukh, the Festival of Hemis Monastery, Inlay Crafts of Mysore,* and *Santiniketan* are some other interesting films made by the Survey. However, unfortunately, all these films are silent films and only single prints are available with the A.S.I. Of late, an attempt is being made for making extra prints and add proper sound and commentary to these valuable films.

Besides the Anthropological Survey of India, some of the Tribal or Cultural Research Institutes started by State Governments in early fifties, specially in Madhya Pradesh, Bihar and West Bengal, have made some Ethnogrpahic films relating to the life of tribal communities in their States. The Tribal Research Institute of Chindwara in Madhya Pradesh has made some films on the life of different types of Gonds while the Tribal Welfare and Research Institute of Ranchi in Bihar has made three films on the *Birhor,* the *Asur* and the *Oraon* communities of Chotanagpur. The Cultural Research Institute of Calcutta in West Bengal has so far produced 5 Ethnographic films on the *Birhor* (28 minutes), *Impact of Modern Education on the Tribals of West Bengal* (18 minutes), *The Oraons of Sunderban* (18 minutes), *Santals of Dohapara* (13 minutes) and *Annual Hunting Festival* (Santal; 9 minutes). All these films were produced by the Institute under the guidance of Anthropologists between 1964 to 1976. The Film Institute of Arunachal is also said to have produced some documentaries of ethnographic interest.

It is of interest that several universities in Western countries specially in U.S.A., offer courses on South Asia with the help of Ethnographic films. Such Universities have also produced some good Ethnographic films either independently or in collaboration with Indian anthropologists. Here mention may be made of the Department of South Asian Studies, University of Wisconsin-Madison, State University, New York and others. The former distribute a film series called "Contemporary South Asia". It consists of 7 films out of which six are from India viz., *An Indian Pilgrimage : Ramdevra* (26 minutes), *An Indian Pilgrimage : Kashi* (30 minutes), *Wedding of the Goddess, Part I* (36 minutes), *Wedding of the Goddess, Part II* (40 minutes), *Four Holy Men: Renunciation in Hindu Society* (37 minutes), and *Village Man, City Man* (38 minutes). Besides, the South Asian Area Center distributes two more films of ethnographic interest i.e., *A Musical Tradition in Banaras* (40 minutes) and *Banaras* (22 minutes).

The State University of New York by an arrangement with James Beveridge Associates produced a series of four Biographic films on 'Music of North India' which includes films on *Amjad Ali Khan*, the classical singer and *Vijay Raghav Rao*, the Flutist, a composer and a music director. These films, each running into 29 minutes present the style of teaching practice, and performance of the four musicians. Another series includes biographicals of 28 minutes each on *Bismillah Khan*, the famous *Sahnai* player and *Satyajit Ray* the well known Film Director.

The 5th Edition, 1972 of the publication on "Films for Anthropological Teaching" published by the American Anthropological Association includes in its list half a dozen of interesting films on India viz., *In India Sun Rises in the East* (14 minutes), *Mother Ganges* (1930s : 10-15 minutes), depicting Banaras City, its people the Holy Men, and very detailed cremation on the banks of the *Ganges*, *Mountain Community of the Himalayas* (11 minutes), *North Indian Village* (1958 : 30

minutes), *Tibetan Traders* (22 minutes), and *The Changing Rains* (1968 : 20 minutes). The last one depicts a poetic evocation of the life of the *Bhil*, a tribal group in the Gujrat of Western India.

One of the recent films to be mentioned in this context is *The Ho : The People of the Rice Pot* (70 minutes) by Dr. Michael Yorke of London who made this film during the course of his research work among the Ho tribe of Singhbhum in Bihar. This is an in-depth Ethnographic film backed by data sheets for class room discussion and analysis.

Besides the films made by individual Anthropologists or anthropological concerns as noted above, some professional film directors also either on the initiative of their own or sponsored by others, have from time to time produced or directed films on India some of which would be of significance to note. *Paul Zeals*, a German directed a film *Our India* some time in mid fifties which not only showed glimpses of contemporary life in India but depicted few scenes from Indian history as well. *Roberto Rosellini*, the famous Italian Director, came to India in late fifties and produced a film, *India*. But unfortunately, before it could have circulated in India, it was banned for reasons not known to common public. Satyajit Ray also made a documentary based on the life of Sikkimese people. A number of other names may also be mentioned of the people who made documentaries of ethnographic interest like K.A. Abbas, Shyam Benegal, Mani Kaul from Bombay and Barindra Nath Saha, Sushil Karan, Tarun Mazumdar, Ashish Mukerjee and Harisadhan Das Gupta from Calcutta. A number of other names may also be multipled.

It is felt that when we talk about ethnographic films, besides the short films exposed on real life situations and happenings of society which occur naturally and spontaneously, it may include under a separate sub-heading those few films which are not pure fiction but in a large measure present a faithful and vivid depiction of the typical life-style, problems, or the events connected with particular cross sections of the society. Here Satyajit Ray's films specially *Pather Panchali* which depicts life-like scenes from rural Bengal, Shyam

Benegal's *Ankur and Nishant* which depict the life style and exploitations of landlords, M.S. Sathyu's *Garam Hawa* which deals with the disintegration of a shoemaker's family in post-independent Agra and *Ghatsradha Samskara* which depicts the old values, caste conflict and some cruel aspects of the Hindu Society, and *Uski Roti* of Mani Kaul may be mentioned. However, feature films close to life is not a new thing. Many old day films made in early thirties and forties like *Achchut Kanya* dealing with the theme of untouchability, *Duniya Na Mane* dealing with the problems of conjugal life due to dis-parity in age, *Padosi* showing Hindu-Muslim relations, *Do Bigha Zamin* depicting the life of a farmer and his exploitation, *Dahej* dealing with the problem of dowry, *Chhota Bhai* made by New Theatres showing again, some typical features of family life, may be mentioned here. However, if, how and to what extent such films contribute to the body of ethnographic knowledge, remains an open question which this Symposium will take care to discuss in a separate session devoted to this subject matter.

NOTES

1. This paper was originally presented at the International Symposium on Visual Anthropology organised by the Commission on Visual Anthropology, IUAES at New Delhi, India in the second week of December, 1978 during the Xth International Congress for Anthropological and Ethnological Sciences.
2. This view is held by Firoze Rangoonwalla in his book *75 Years of Indian Cinema* (Indian Book Company, New Delhi, 1975) page 12. But Gaston Roberge in his book *Chitrabani*, Chitrabani 76, Rafi Ahmed Kidwai Road, Calcutta, 1974, page 140 says that the first film shows in Calcutta were made in January 1897.
3. The facts given in this section of the paper are mainly based on Firoze Rangoonwalla's *75 Years of Indian Cinema*, (India Book Company, New Delhi, 1975, pp. 9-25) and *Bhartiya Filmon Ki Kahani* (Hindi), by Bachchan Srivastava, Hind Pocket Books Private Ltd., Delhi, ND.

Chapter III

Visual Anthropology and Indian Fiction Films*

Visual anthropology is generally understood as studying man and his culture by employing Camera as its principal instrument of investigation that may produce either still photographs or moving images to be seen on a screen. Both these types of Camera works have received varying focus by different scholars. In case of the latter it is usually known as 'ethnographic' or 'anthropological' films. Visual anthropology may either be the result of joint effort of a filmmaker and anthropologist, or both may be combined into one. One finds divergence of opinion in this regard.

The Background

The importance of Visual data for anthropological inquiry was realized after Margret Mead and her colleagues like G. Bateson (1942) and F. Mac Gregor (1951) made pivotal use of film research to demonstrate culturally specific patterns of behaviour on Bali (Sorenson, 1974: 1079). Bateson and Mead used still photographs and movie films both in their study of Balinese behaviour. The methodological originality with which photography was used in *Balinese character* helped to establish it as 'a respected tool in anthropological research'[2] (Bateson and Mead, 1942). Earlier, in mid 1930's which was the "watershed between film's unimportance and its acceptability", to the scholars like W.D. Hambly, Melville Herskovits, Patrick O' Reilly and Marcel Griaule, film was just an illustration and not an integral part of research. But in contrast to it "Gregory Bateson and Margret Mead's decision to use cameras in Bali and New Guinea, in 1936-38, was dictated by the needs of

* Revised version of the earlier paper published in *Journal of Social Research*, Vol. 29, No. 2, September, 1986.

their research. They innovated both in the scale of their filming and photography (22,000 feet of 16-mm film, 25,000 stills) and in its aim, the description of the "ethos of a people" (Brigard, 1975 : 26).

Soon after R. Birdwhistell's (1952, 1960, 1970) discovered the subtle, visible components in human communication from film records which showed that films could be used as indispensable tool for detailed analysis of human interaction. This was further supported by E. Hall's (1959) demonstration of cultural difference in nonverbal human interaction (Sorenson, 1974 : 1079).

It was during the 1960's that the concept of producing anthropological film records as a permanent research resource began to take shape (Sorenson and Gajdusek, 1963). Initially, such research films were employed as a way to study child behaviour and development in primitive culture and subsequently it emerged as a way to study and retrieve data from changing cultures (Sorenson, 1966, 1967, 1968, 1975). By the early 1970's this development led to visual sampling strategies that were geared to naturally occurring behaviour and social situations (Sorenson and Jablonko, 1975). Alan Lomax (1968) and his co-workers were one of the earliest to make extensive exploitations of such film records for studying patterns of human movement in dance and work out their significance. The growing body of anthropological films contained retrievable data not necessarily sought or recognized by their film makers.

During the 1950's and 1960's anthropological film also emerged as a medium through which knowledge about culturally divergent peoples could be more generally disseminated. Following Robert Flaherty's *Nanook of the North* (1922), this movement took a new turn after world war II with the works of Jean Rouch (1955), John Marshall (1958, 1966, 1974), Robert Gardner (1974) and Asen Balikci et al. (1968). It was realized that anthropological films can better communicate the insights and knowledge of anthropological field workers to students and the public. This movement was further developed by Timothy Asch (1974) in his extensively detailed and documented film studies of the Yanamamo Indians and by the American Universities field staff's study of divergent paths to human adaptation in five modernizing cultures (Sorenson, 1974 : 1079).

In 1960's attention was also focussed on the influence of cultural difference in the construction of film presentations. Jay Ruby (1973) expressed that "all motion picture footage of human beings is anthropological in that it contains information which can become date for anthropological research and teaching".[3] This idea stems out from the pioneering works of J. Adair and S. Worth (1967, 1970) and in more general terms C. Metz (1971). Worth and Adair "showed that individuals in another culture reveal some of their differences in congnitive and perceptual organization in the films they construct. Such film productions are culturally marked forms of communication and may be studied as artefacts" (Worth and Adair, 1972).

While commenting upon anthropological film-making in general, Richard Sorenson (1974) talks of two distinct directions in scholarly enquiry: "(i) Films may be examined as 'windows on the past' preserving information from nonrecurring events or changing conditions in the form of data which can be abstracted, organized, and reviewed. (ii) Films may also be examined as 'mirrors of culture', which contain information on the cognitive organization, interests, and values of the film-maker and reflect culturally specific communicative parameters."[4]

Fiction Films: Significance and Pertinent Views

However, a fiction film, otherwise known as 'feature film', 'commercial film', 'popular cinema' and the like, though a most popular source of entertainment and a powerful means of communciation has been so far generally a neglected field of study. In India only casual writings of social scientist (Verma : 1981 : 333 - 46); Verma 1983; 283-86; Sharma, 1983: 275-82; Kakar, 1980; Das, 1980; Nandy, 1980) on content analysis of films have appeared from time to time. Some of the fiction films reflect in adequate measure various types of socio-cultural realities. While on the one hand these films may be considered to be a type of 'cultural document', on the other, a powerful medium of communication that wields considerable influence on socio-cultural norms of a society. The fiction films may also be used for ordering socio-cultural relations and promoting a harmonious intergroup and cultural relations.

John H. Weakland (1975) is of the view that in the broadest sense feature films are cultural documents by definition and examines what sort of cultural documents are such films and what significance can they have for cultural anthropology. He opines that feature films are fictional, and they are viewed as such in anthropological analysis. Although fiction films may at times portray aspects of behaviour accurately in a factual or documentary sense, this is not the main focus of their study. "Rather, these films are taken as projecting IMAGES of human social behaviour and these images are the first object of study. Such images, of course, may also be 'real' in important senses...., though differing from the reality of detailed records of actual behaviour. They may reflect cultural premises and patterns of thought and feeling. They may influence the behaviour of viewers and they may throw light on actual behaviour, whether similar or different from it. Again, all of these are potentials. Actual significances can only be determined, once film images are discerned by studying these in relation to the film makers, their audiences, and to other information about their subject matters." (Ibid., p. 233). However, the converse approach is also possible and "fictional films can be studied with a concern about actual behaviour, and documentaries..." (Kracauer, 1942).

Fiction films are specially useful in the study of general patterns of culture "because they are not factual" and present an interpretation of some segment of life by selection, structuring and ordering images of behaviour. Even the "real life involves the conceptualization, organization and punctuation of experience, and compared to daily life a fictional work represents a more highly ordered and defined unity, whose premises and patterns can be more readily studied." Besides, as field work in large complex and modern societies could cover an extremely limited fraction of actual behaviour, some such simplication appears an essential starting point. "And films specially, while more limited and manageable for study—particularly repeated study—than daily life, are still rich and relevant, with several advantages over other fictional materials such as novels" (Ibid., p. 246).

Films can project important cultural views. "Since films are a mass medium of communciation aimed for a wide popular audience, they are likely to present, relatively simply, quite basic and general themes rather than special or esoteric ones." Films are both rich and varied and each film offers a great deal of material for observation. Films as a group deal with a wide range of subjects which makes it possible to examine as to how general themes and specific social situations are interrelated. Besides as verbal and visual materials are jointly combined in films it provides an opportunity to compare what the players say they are doing with what the observer sees them doing in films. It may either clarify both or present revealing inconsistencies (Ibid, pp. 246-47).

Anthropological study of themes and patterns discernible on viewing feature films and attempts to relate such observations to wider areas of culture, began in the United States during the Second World War when extensive efforts were being made toward mobilizing the knowledge and skills of social scientists to develop better understanding of the nature of various foreign societies, "with the practical goal of better estimation or prediction of their members' behaviour, collectively or individually" (Ibid., p. 236-37). Ruth Benedict's study of the Japanese national character may be a case in point.

Since then, general themes and patterns have been sought by analysing films of Nazi Germany, Japan, India, France, England, the U.S.A., and China though "the surface has only been scratched".

"Comparative study of films from different culture coulc be applied to clarify cultural similarities and differences". This field is wide but so far approached only in the works of Wolfenstein and Leites (1950) and Weakland (1972). The idea that changes in film content could be used in studies of culture change is though explicit in Kracauer (1947) and implicit in some of Weakland's work on Chinese films, but "it has not yet been adequately tried out" (Ibid., p. 247).

The Present Context

Indian Fiction films which more popularly go by the name of 'Indian Cinema', "like any cultural expression, is a montage of diverse influences and many-layered set of aesthetic values". Cinema is the "new urban folk culture, dominant leisure activity, mass entertainment ......More than 700 features are made in almost a dozen languages every year. These are watched in about 10,000 theatres by an average of 12.5 million people every day and are exported to about 100 countries. It is the sixth largest industry employing over two million people....Its influence has spilled to other media: film music is broadcast 12 hours a day over 85 radio stations. Seven television centres show at least one film and two film-based programmes a week; advertising and fashions draw upon it and over six hundred fan magazines batten on the lives and loves of the stars" (Raina, 1983 : 3).

The Indian Cinema is almost 'omnipresent'. "The popular entertainment film has acquired a central position with respect to all other media, and sets the style for them. The values of film dominate other forms of visual communication...." (Bahadur, 1983 : 110-11) may it be calendar pictures magazine illustrations, labels of consumer goods, packaging, posters and advertisements, interior decorations, cover pages of school exercise-books, traditional iconography for religious worship, bhajan-kirtans, popular theatre, popular dance, popular music, dress and decorations, fashion, fictions in popular magazines, even crime pattern T.V. and what not. It raises some pertinent questions: whether a media which communicates so powerfully and wields such a pervasive influence on life be set aside by anthropologist merely as a non-serious thing to merit serious attention and just as a source of entertainment? Whether it is devoid of anthropological significance? It is these basic questions that inspired the present author to have a fresh look on fiction films and explore their utility for anthropological purpose.

Fiction films in the present context by and large refer to 'realistic feature films' known variously as 'new-wave', 'art', or 'avant garde' films, or 'new cinema', 'parallel cinema' against the popular variety of fiction or glamorous commercial films which have no use for realism. The new-wave movement in films is said to have originated from Italy in post-war years and influenced film-making in some other parts of the world like France and India. It was realized that films could be made cheaply and quickly by dispensing withconventionalitems like artificial and costly sets, established film stars. Such films used real locations and usually amateur artists but preserved the essential purity of art form (Ray, 1976 : 86).

Unlike ethnographic films exposed on real life situations and events that occur naturally and spontaneously, the new-wave films are shot on pre-arranged situations as in other variety of fiction films. But it is not just pure entertainment or grazing into the fancy world. In a considerable measure it attempts at presenting a faithful and vivid depiction of the typical life-style, problems and the events connected with different cross sections of the rural and urban society in a rich variety of cultural settings and multi-facet dimensions from different parts of the country that evoke considerable anthropological interest. Some of these films are based on novels and stories written by established or 'good' authors which provide mirror of the time and quite a number of which have bagged national and international awards.

Besides the new-wave films just discussed, realistic films also include several other fiction films that are very near to life and anthropologically useful.

Here it is significant to note that the types of fiction film referred to in the present context, can be best studied as supplementaries to conventional anthropological studies. Such films may also provide valuable illustrative materials to anthropological studies. Generally, no amount of fiction films taken from a culture are likely to give us an 'extensive' or 'complete' picture of the life and culture of the people we study though some specific and sporadic cultural materials may very well be culled out from these films to give us a general understanding of the society. But if adequate number of *suitable films* could be found out from a society for anthropological analysis, they can also very well constitute integral part of research relating to specific aspects of life.

Besides using camera as an instrument of investigation and research as in case of ethnographic films and the analysis of realistic fiction films as said for the understanding of man and his culture, visual anthropology may very well cover the study of fiction films from applied point of view i.e., the study of films in relation to society as discussed in the latter section of this paper.

Now it would be appropriate to present here the details of a *select number* of fiction films relevant to the present context as discussed.

New Wave Films in India

The new-wave films are usually based on regional themes. The new cinema is 'regional' as it speaks in terms of recognisable situations. It gives its characters a social identity and deals with such situations that are very close to life. "Exploring the growing contradictions of a traditional society seeking to modernize itself, it follows a different pattern of production too". The films are made on low budgets, shot on location, make experiment with new actors and in several cases are based on Indian literature. "Their thematic range is as large as life itself..." (Raina, 1983 : 16-17).

Regional cinema has been sometimes eulogized as the fountain-head of art. Regional films are generally more rooted in the culture of a people than the all-India Hindi films. Here the people are known by their surnames and are free to wear regional clothes without attracting ridicule. The films are very often based on literary works of quality with well-knit stories and characters. "The impression of their superiority over the all-India films is reinfored by the fact that first in Bengal, later in Karnataka and Kerala, outstanding films by Satyajit Ray and some quality work by Girish Karnad, Addor Gopala Krishnan and others in the south made their appearnace" (Das Gupta, 1983 : 40).

The new-wave movement in India is said to have started with Satyajit Ray's first film *Pather Panchali* based on a book by Bibhuti Bhusan Banerji released in 1955. It portrayed the life of a family in rural Bengal of old and the birth to childhood story of Apu. At the Cannes Film Festival it won the award for the "best human document". ".....Here was a film which reflected the Indian reality as no other film had done before. The story of the joys and trials of a Bengali village family in the 1920's appeared to many sensitive viewers in different regions of the country as truly Indian...." (Bahadur, 1976 : 102). It helped to establish Satyajit Ray as a director of international repute. Since then Ray directed a number of other films.

In fact Ray's films had demolished all the myths created by the advocates of 'popular cinema' that people wanted entertainment, that they did not want to see 'serious films' and that the box-office was an index of the needs of the audience (Raina, 1983 : 14).

In 1956, Ray directed *Aparajito* (The Unvanquished) made as a sequel to *Pather Panchali* with the same characters and some of the same actors continuing in the story. In this film Apu finds himself crossing the delicate stage of his life between two cities and a village and the film makes a beautiful study in the evolution of an adolescent. The rustic family has new experiences in the city life not devoid of its cultural shocks. There are hidden dangers in urban life and the film presents an interesting psychological situation. The film has a most natural shooting and this film also could bag big awards for Ray.

Ray's third film of interest here is *Jalsaghar* (The Music Room) released in 1958. It is a tale of the inevitable decline of a person and through him of the period and system which he represents. It is a sombre study of the slow decline of a feudal landlord pitted against a rich neighbour. Chhabi Biswas gave a masterly portrayal of the landlord who spends his last penny to keep high the traditional image of his family prestige of holding the finest musical session in his music-room. The thematic conflict between antiquity and modernity, feudal methods and mechanisation, between an aristocrat and a 'parvenu' was brought out in a very impressive manner in the film. This film also brought acclaims to Ray.

Devi, another film of Ray relased in 1960 and based on Tagore's story beautifully depicts some superstitious aspect of Hindu society and in reality attacks a certain religious dogmatism. The film depicts that a simple housewife is turned into a goddess to be worshipped when the venerable father-in-law sees a dream of her being an incarnation of Goddess *Durga*. The unfortunate daughter-in-law loses her peace of mind and keeps pining for her husband and a simple human existence.

Of the three parts of *Teen Kanya* released in 1961 and again based on Tagore's famous stories, the first i.e. *'Postmaster'* and the third i.e., *'Samapti'* (The Conclusion) are of special interest here. The theme of *Postmaster* is set against a typical rural setting and is an intensely moving story 'on the cycle of life's inevitability' and the emotional jerk of a little maid-of-all-work made to serve the changing postmasters in a village. 'Samapti' also presents a rich glimpse of rural life in Bengal centering round the delightful tale of a tomboyish adolescent who fails to be reconciled to a premature wedlock.

Mahanagar (The Big City) released in 1963 tells about the attempt of a housewife to become a career girl and the repercussions and estrangement caused by it in her domestic life. It also depicts the inner and other conflicts of this woman and some significant dimensions of the urban life.

Charulata (The Lonely Woman) based on a story of Tagore, released in 1964, tells about the story of a neglected wife, Charu in a wealthy Bengali household of the previous century whose husband is always busy editing his political journal and waging press-wars against the policies of the alien rulers. Like the ladies of the day, she cannot often stir out of the house. Her husband's cousin comes as if to provide the missing link in her scheme of life and 'his literary pursuits and bohemian ways' make him the centre of Charu's entire being. Circumstance makes the domestic nest thoroughly disorganised "yet there is a strong suggestion of the institution of marriage being upheld. Like Tagore, Ray emphasizes the morality theme. This is the indirect message of the film to a world where such a drama would have found an easy solution in elopement, adultery, divorce or perhaps even murder. That is why, apart from Berlin's best direction award, the international Roman Catholic office also gave it the prize for 'best serving spiritual progress" (Rangoonwalla, 1980 : 86).

Pratidwandi (Siddhartha and the City or The Adversary) released in 1970, has a problematic orientation and touches "the firm earth again, for the common folks, with a simple but extremely powerful and moving film on unemployment.....youths hanging on the bordering of existence as they travel hanging on the footboard edge of Calcutta's tram-cars every day, were portrayed in their true dilemma, through the sad state young man seeking a white-collar job through the choked channels of the Establishment. The city in which they grew up has become like a rival into whom they have to wrestle. The innocence of young days is forgotten and values have crashed all around. Sisters get jobs because of their looks and may go anywhere with that qualification. Brothers have become political activists. Friends have become vice-seekers.

Job interviews have turned into harrowing mockery. There is a place for the city's own youth, only away from the city, away from the place and persons he knows and likes. The film just depicts these realities in the life of an unemployed though does not find out a solution. However, the film leaves a question mark on "an inherited system which gives degrees to youths without giving them jobs, which leaves them shelterless in their own homes and strangers in their own city" (Ibid., pp. 89-90).

Jana-Aranya (The Middleman) released in 1975 also deals with the problem of unemployment of the educated Bengali youth and the deviation of his character in search of a viable alternative. "This time the throbbing non-Bengali business community in Bengal came in as a solution. Once again, the youth like a stranger in his own territory crowded with immigrants, tried to keep his head above water. This time he followed their example, became a businessman, got reduced to a middleman and ended up reconciling himself to bartering the flesh of his own friend's pretty sister for a fat contract. This film is of deep sociological interest and presents an intimate peep into the fast moving urban life. It shows that the intellectual middle-class Bengali was like a sad misfit. Times had changed and so too the traditional values. Economic power was in other hands and the youth's dilemma was either to compromise or to quit. (Ibid., p. 92).

Besides the impact of the films of Satyajit Ray some other significant developments in the 1960s like implementation of the various recommendations made by the Film Enquiry Committee like setting up of the Film Institute, National Film Archive, Film Finance Corporation, Indian Motion Picture Export Corporation, Directorate of Film Festivals besides political developments and upheavels like Indo-China and Indo-Pak wars, deaths of two Prime Ministers like Nehru and Shastri, politicalization of the masses owing to several General Elections, made this decade the most significant for Indian Cinema. These events led to an "introspection" and "critical re-examination, howsoever tentative, of the 'gains' of freedom as well as search for a national identity" (Raina, 1983 : 15). This introspective mood was adequately reflected in some of the films of Ritwik-Ghatak, another well-known film-maker from Bengal.

Ritwik Ghatak made eight major films between 1958 and 1978, *Ajantrik* (Man and the machine, 1958), *Meghe Dhaka Tara* (Star covered in the cloud, 1960) and *Suvarna Rekha* being some important among them. His experience of the war years in undivided Bengal and the final phase of the freedom struggle culminating into partition of Bengal deeply stirred his creative sensibility. As such, partition and its socio-psychological repercussions constitute the recurrent themes of his films.

Ajantrik is a human drama of exciting relationship between a man and machine and a study of apparent human obsessions, with subtle element of satire and a deep sociological analysis of the advent of industrialisation. *Meghe Dhaka Tara* is one of his films which depicts the awareness of the post-war refugee problem in Bengal. *Subarnrekha* is still another film making "a more brutal and frank depiction of the socio-psychological impact of partition on India" (Mukhopadhyay, 1978).

Shyam Benegal, another important director of new-wave films and very well acclaimed, produced and directed a series of films in the seventies, four of which deserve mention here. His first two films *Ankur* (Germination, 1974) and *Nishant* (End of night, 1975) depict the relations between the landlord and the villagers. The landlord in the two films, economically and sexually exploit his people. In the first film the story revolves round the son of a landlord and his deaf-dumb agricultural labourer and the beautiful wife of this labourer with whom the former has amorous relations in the absence of her husband who leaves the village in search of a job outside. When this labourer returns, he finds his wife to be pregnant. The landlord's son suffers with a guilty conscience and out of fear assaults this labourer very badly. It has an unpleasant reaction on some section of the villagers and the last scene depicts that while the window of the Zamindar's house gets closed, some village boys gather courage to hit it with a stone and flee away. The other film *Nishant* shows the state of panicky which the Zamindar, his brothers and their musclemen have created in the village. They are also very influential and close to the officials. Once they get the young wife of the villager-teacher kidnapped and keep her in their *Haveli.* This infuriates the teacher and his sympathizers in the village including the temple priest. The teacher knocks the door of Government officials but they do not pay any attention. Finding no better solution, the villagers work out a conspiracy to kill the Zamindar and wipe out his family during the occasion of an ensuing festival, and they actually execute it. Shyam Benegal's third film *Manthan* (The Churning, 1976) tells of the exploitations of a rich man trading in milk in rural areas who charges exorbitant rates. When a Milk Cooperative Society is opened in the village at the initiative of the Government, still the big businessman who commands great influence on the villages harasses them in many ways and once also commits arson through his men. The film shows the ultimate triumph of the villagers over the cunning and cruel businessman and strikes a note of optimism. Shyam Benegal's still another film *Kondura* (The Saga from the Sea, 1977) made in Hindi and Telugu depicts some old dogmas and superstitions of rural areas of the South.

The films of Shyam Benegal make a rich and vivid depiction of village life, politics, factions, exploitations of the landlord, his men or other influential men in the feudal setting, the tussel or conflict between them and ultimate triumph of the commoners over the evil forces, rural values and superstitions. The presentation is realistic and very near to life.

Mrinal Sen, another Bengali director is politically committed and generally makes problematic films. He used the "film as a pulpit for delivering......message". He feels that Marxism provides salvation for the economically oppressed masses of India. In his film *Chorus* he shows that it is only when the urban workers and rural workers unite in a movement against the exploitive system that they can hope to get out of the clutches of poverty. He does not only hold a mirror to reality but also interprets it. "He wants to show what causes this reality and how it can be changed. His characters are so real that if they step out of the screen they would be indistinguishable in the Crowd" (Narayan, 1975 : 26-27). His film *Bhuvan Shome* (1970) widely acclaimed and prized is the caricature of a bureaucrat at work. In *Interview* (1970) it is the absence of western attire that defeats the hero's purpose. We leave him in the last scene breaking the shop windows which raise the suit that might have made all the difference to his life. One of the most interesting features of the film is that Mrinal Sen has "captured the contemporary ambience of Calcutta superbly well. The overcrowding, the sea of hoardings which seems to fall on the spectator, the chaotic traffic, the incidental discomforts that constant strikes and inefficiency bring to the life of the average individual....all help to create an atmosphere of bubbling turmoil that characterizes the life of the average citizen of Calcutta in the seventies" (Sarkar, 1981 : 33).

"Calcutta '71" and "Chorus" are, in a sense a continuation of "Interview" but with an emphasis shifting from the individual to the general condition. 'Calcutta 71' has a larger canvas. It is an angry, more bitter, often cynical protest against man's inhumanity to man through the ages. The 'poverty, squalor and death' are illustrated in three short stories woven into the main theme" (Ibid).

Mrigaya (1976) another acclaimed film of Mrinal Sen is set against the Santhal tribal society of West Bengal during the British regime and tells of a close acquaintance of a young hunter with the British Commissioner in pre-Independent days. However, the theme has been viewed through contemporary values. The film in a very realistic manner depicts the exploitation by a rich money-lender of the tribals. The film-maker raises certain basic questions: "Wild animals are killed for destroying crops and the nationalist is killed for an alleged act of banditry. When a money-lender is killed by a tribal whose wife he had abducted, the tribal is put on trial and hung. Why, the film asks, if a bandit can be killed for one sort of offence, cannot a money-lender be killed for a worse offence?" (Ibid., p. 31). The merit of the film in the present context lies in a realistic depiction of some aspects of the tribal life, their relation with the Government, exploitation at the hand of money-lender and a people's reaction to it.

Garam Hawa (Hot wind, 1974), based on a story of Ismat Chugtai, is made by M.S. Sathyu. It relates to a Moslem family in Agra just after partition. The social and political pressure brought to bear upon it from the substance of the story. The central character is the gentle, dignified Salim Mirza, owner of a shoe factory at Agra, who keeps shrugging off the occasional signs of hostility as something which will 'pass off in a few days'. Mirza's optimism proves to be short-lived, with his daughter taking her own life, Mirza's hope vanishes. Father, mother and son pack their belongings and set off for the Railway Station. They intend to cross the borders like others. As soon as their *Tanga* pulls up, a procession appears with a red flag and crosses its path. The son makes a quick decision to join the procession and stays back for the communal harmony. Mirza too steps out, ponders a while, and decides to follow the suit. (Ray, 1976 : 100-101). This film makes an excellent human document showing the realities and the state of mind of certain section of Moslems in the days immediately after the partition.

Late Awatar Kaul's *27 Down* (1974) is a story of a middle class woman who is burdened with the support of her family. She does not marry as there is no other bread-winner in the family (Atma, 1977 : 38). However, she maintains affairs with married persons. Besides, the problems of a middle-class youth are portrayed within the framework of a personalized realism. The young man played by M.K. Raina is torn between obedience to a dominating father and the desire to lead an independent life (De' Monte, 1975 : 8). The characters of this film are appropriate products of the present day circumstances in many urban areas.

Kumar Sahni's *Maya Darpan* (1972) exposes feudal oppression through the subjugation of a young woman who is trapped in a classical feudal setting (Ibid., p. 9).

Mani Kaul's *Uski Roti* (1970) "Journeys into the loneliness of an uncared for wife in a village whose frivolous husband is a bus-driver returning home only once a week, spending rest of the six days with his kept in the city". (Jha, 1981 : 102).

Badnam Basti of Prem Kapoor based on a small novel of Kamleshwar and depicting the life and surroundings of a truck driver, *Rajnigandha* of Basu Chatterjee depicting the life of middle class woman and her love affairs, and *Saara Akash* (1969) directed by Basu Chatterjee showing alienation between husband and wife and the family life of a middle class family of Agra, and the most controversial film *Kissa Kursi ka,* a satirical film on the politicians of the day, may also be mentioned in this connection.

Duvidha (Dilemma, 1973) directed by Mani Kaul and based upon a haunting Rajasthani folk-tale dealing with spirits and exorcism is a significant film as it opens a new vista in cultural studies and enacts a folk tale.

Chakra (Wheel) directed by Ravindra Dharmraj makes a realistic and microscopic presentation of the life-style associated with slum dwellers of Bombay, while *Akrosh* (1980), another film by Govind Nihlani depicts the exploitations of a poor man (tribal) and his beautiful wife at the hands of a powerful and influential section of the society. He is so weak that he fails to fight for his legitimate right.

Albert Pinto Ko Gussa Kyo Ata Hai (What for Albert Pinto gets angry, 1980) is a film of Sayeed Akhtar Mirza and touches multiple aspects of life. The hero of the film, Albert Pinto, is a simple motor-mechanic who keeps aloof from political manouverings, stunts to weaken a strike, beautiful and young girls employed in service, exploitations of the economically weaker sections of the people and the like, which are the happenings around him. He is a simple hearted man and gets angry when the Boss of his bethrothed girl takes her to cinema, invites her at his residence on feasts and wants to exploit her. He gets angry when he knows the genuineness behind the strike call of his father serving in a Mill along with many other poor workers. He also gets angry when his brother being a good person could not progress in life. When he comes face to face with many social discrepancies and social evils, he is full of anger. He gets pained but is too helpless to change the situtation. The facts depicted in the film mirror what is happening in the modern society in contemporary times.

Estaphan directed by G. Arvindan of Malyali Cinema presents a powerful theme. It is a film made in the background of Christian fishermen of the coastal area and shows that merely a change of religion does not necessarily change the cultural affiliation and belief-system of the people.

Bhavni Bhavai (1982) directed by Ketan Mehta is another significant film based on a dying folklore of Gujrat known as *Bhavni.* It is through the medium of this folklore that messages of folk life are narrated. The theme of this specific film is based on *Achchuton Ka Vesh* (Get-up of untouchables) and implies the saga of the exploitation of the untouchables. According to this saga, the untouchables were obliged to wear a white turban like thing on head, a water-container suspended by the neck and a sort of broom-stick by the waist, with the objective that the road will be instantly swept clean when the untouchables passed through a road. It is in the form of narrative and when a group of children ask their grandfather as to how this practice was abolished, the latter replies in the typical *Bhavai* style that the people had to fight for their social right till last. It is a political film which makes an impressive use of comedy, satire and earthly iconoclasm inspired by the folk-theatre tradition (Shardeya, 1981 : 45-47).

The two films of Jabbar Patel viz., *Jait Re Jait* and *Simhasan* may also be mentioned here. The first is based on G.N. Dandekar's novel, and tells about 'cultural fatigue' or the disillusionment of a tribal boy as regards his belief in certain indigenous Gods is concerned. The second film was the exposure of an ugly system. It "went to the very grass-roots of political corruption, the infighting and toppling games politicians play to keep themselves in power" (Pradhan 1981 : 42-43).

Quite a few South Indian Film-makers like Girish Kasaravalli who in his Kannada film *Ghatashraddha* (1977) makes a strong protest against caste system and religious bigotry, Addor Gopalakrishna whose Malayalam film *Swayamvaram* (1972) highlighted in taxonomic details a 'yawning contrast between idealism and reality, so much discernible on the surface of our national existence', and Pattabhi Rama Reddi's *Samskar* (Last Rites, 1970) again set against the back drop of caste system and religious bigotry depicting Brahmin rituals and prejudices of earlier decades also contributed to the new-wave film movement. Though initially this film had some trouble with the censor, "it won wide admiration for its ethnographic authenticity, and set the tone for other such works" (Barnouw and Krishnaswamy, 1980 : 260) like *Vamsha Vriksha* (The Family Tree, 1971), *Kaadu* (The Forest, 1973). *Chomana Dudi* (Choma's Drum, 1975), *Ondanondu Kaladalli* (Once upon a Time, 1979) and the like. In *Kaadu* Girish Karnad depicted the details of a smoldering feud between two chieftains coming from the different villages separated by a forest, while B.V. Karanth's *Choman Dudi* was "a remarkable chronicle of a Harijan family of half century ago". Girish Karnad's other film *Ondanondu Kaladalli* related to the Karnataka area in early medieval times when chieftains vied for domination over sparsely populated forest areas and the men of that region were famous for their skills in the martial arts and its greatest exponents were sought far and wide as mercenaries (Ibid., pp. 260-61).

Of late, Aparna Sen wrote and directed a film on the life of Anglo-Indians of Calcutta showing some intimate glimpses of their life and pointing at their problems. In this film entitled *36 Chowringhee Lane,* she narrated the "saga of Miss Stonham, an Anglo-Indian school teacher, trying desperately to come to terms with her desolate existence. The role played with warmth and compassion by Jennifer Kapoor, has just the right nuances to reveal her loneliness, her despair and yet her final resolve to stay on in India" (Mirza, 1981 : 53). The film also points out the typical problem of Anglo-Indian community in India who even though have adapted themselves to the Indian environment, a larger section of the Indian people have failed to accept them in their society (Mehrotra, 1981 : 55).

Umrao Jaan, directed by Muzaffur Ali is "Probably the most glamorous art film yet, with the inimitable Rekha playing a legendary poetess and courtesan from the Lucknow of an earlier and more exotic period" (Saari, 1981 : 17). The film makes a descriptive presentation of the life-style associated with a courtesan and the love, pathoes and strife which come her way.

Some more recent films like *Ardha Satya* depicting corruption of Police Department and political interference much to the disadvantage of honest officers, *Bazar* dealing with the problem of purchase of girls by rich Arabian merchants and similar exploitations by their men, Prakash Jha's *Damul* dealing with exploitations of low caste people by higher castes in rural areas, *Mandi,* based on the life and feelings of prostitutes, *Party* delving into the life of urban elites and their values, and *Paar* depicting the poor lot and precarious existence of rural labourers, may also be mentioned in this context.

Other Realistic Films

As pointed earlier, it is significant to add here that besides the assortment of some relevant 'new-wave' films presented above, there are quite a number of fiction films directed and produced in early decades[6] or recent times which can also be said to be 'realistic' by any standard as they mirror in considerable measure the life, culture and some problems of their time and can very well be utilized for anthropological studies. It is interesting that some of these films even belong to the silent era. In fact, some people are of the opinion that these films in terms of themes belong to the same category of realistic films, though we do not use the appelation 'new-wave' for them (Ranjan, 1975 : 7 ; Bahadur, 1976 ; 97 ; Atma, 1977 : 37).

(i) Silent Era

Here, some of the films from Silent era may be mentioned as given below:

Two Little Untouchables (1925) made by N.D. Sarpotdar was probably the first film which made "a brave attempt to put before the then orthodox audience the sad plight of untouchables, who were totally neglected in a caste-ridden society and treated with disdain." Sarpotdar also made *Vilasi Kanta* (Flirting wife, 1927) and *Arya Mahila* (Ideal wife) (Dharap, 1980 : 34) which touched upon socio-cultural themes. Baburao Painter in the year 1925 directed a film entitled *Savkari Pash* (1925) dealing with the evils of money-lending which still plague our village economy to this day (Nadkarni, 1980 : 42). Bhalji Pendharkar launched in 1926-27 an important film named *Vande Matram Ashram* which showed a national ferver and strongly criticized British educational policies for "cultivating the clerk mentality" amongst Indians. This film, however, had got some trouble at the Censor Board (Kinikar, 1980 : 49). Dhiren Ganguly chose a subject with significant social comment for his film, *Bilaet Pherat* (England Returned), released in 1921. The film satirised the ways of England returned Indians in those days and was "hailed by the press as bold and contemporaneous in content" (Jha, 1980 : 58). Narayana's *Dharmapatni* (1929) had a theme explaining as to how addiction to alcoholic drinks could ruin domestic peace. This film set the tone for temperance propaganda in films—"which assumed the proportion of an obsession in later years." Raja Sandow's "The Elevation of the Down-trodden" (1930) was an adaptation of the drama *Nandan Charittram* by Gopi Krishna Bharti, himself a great protagonist for the removal of untouchability. It narrated the story of Nandan, a low caste devotee of Lord Shiva and loyal servant of a Brahmin landlord. He undergoes a lot of sufferings before he fulfils his ambition of worshipping Shiva at Chidambarm. Nandan preaches against superstition and alcoholic drinks and leads his fellow farm workers towards a better life. The landlord observing the result of Nandan's evangelistic work, has ultimately a change of heart and accepts the untouchable farm labourer as his religious mentor (Bhaskaran, 1980 : 66).

"Social injustice to women was another theme that was often touched upon in films with contemporary stories. By this time a number of reformist films had already been released in Bombay like *Mumbaini Mohini* or *Social Pirates* (1925). Sandow's own *Orphan Daughter* (1930) produced in Madras was about a girl who wanted to marry the man she loved and was therefore forsaken by her angry father; she suffered hardships and is eventually married to her man.....Another film of Sandow, *Rajeshwari* (1931), told the story of a woman driven to suicide by the ill-treatment meted out to her by her in-laws, focussed attention on the plight of women in society" (Ibid.). Another important film with a social theme was *Gun Sundari* (why Husbands go Astray) directed by Chandulal Shah in 1925-26. In this film, the wife was a simple domestic type while the husband, a westernized one and considered the wife socially and intellectually below himself. He begins to caste glances outside the house. The wife decided to win him over and started getting westernized. Eventually, they come together (Karnad, 1980 : 76). *Balayogini* (problems of Hindu widows, 1936), *President* (right of workers to participate in management, 1936), *Dharti Mata* (collective farming and mechanization of agriculture, 1937), *Adhikar* (economic and social disparities, 1938) were some other films that may be mentioned in this connection.

(ii) Talkie Era

After the advent of Talkie films in 1931 also the Indian Film Industry produced a number of realistic films which reflected socio-cultural dimensions of Indian life. Of special mention may be P.C. Barua's *Mukti* (showing class struggle), *Indira M.A.* (problems of westernization, 1934), F. Osten's *Achchut Kanya* (a Harijan girl in love with a Brahmin youth and attack on untouchability and caste system 1936), Shantaram's *Duniya Na Mane* (indictment of arranged marriage and the complications of disparity of age in a married couple, 1936), Moti Gidwani's *Kisan Kanya* (daughter of agriculturist, 1937), *Devdas* (indictment of arranged marriage, 1935), V. Shantaram's *Admi* (life of a prostitute and challenge to traditional ideas, 1939), B.N. Reddi's *Vande Matram* (a film on the praise of motherland, 1939), *Badi Didi* (dealt with the plight of widows in Hindu society, 1939), Master Vinayak's *Barandi Ki Botal* (Brandi's Bottle, showing the evil of liquor), Mehboob Khan's *Aurat* (showing the love, courage and valour of an Indian woman, 1940), Sohrab Modi's *Sikandar* (a historical film with an appeal to nationalism, 1940), Shantaram's *Padosi* (showing the destructive criminality of Hindu-Muslim antagonism), K.A. Abbas's *Naya Sansar* (exposed the pressure of business tycoons on the Press and struggle of a journalist, 1941), Devki Bose's *Apna Ghar* (own house—a revolutionary film which opposed tyranny and violence and propagated nationalism, 1941), G. Mukerjee's *Kismat* (depicting the life of a pick-pocket, 1943), Pancholi's *Khajanchi* (showing the life and conflict of a cashier, 1941), Mehboob Khan's *Roti* ('Bread', showing exploitations of the poor by a rich man in a modern industrial society symbolizing domination of Britishers in pre-independent India and preaching communistic philosophy), Prabhat Film's *Ramshastri* (showing the life of a patriot, 1944), K.A. Abbas's *Dharti Ke Lal* (a film on Bengal's famine, 1946), Kishore Sahu's *Sindur* (theme of widow-marriage, 1947), Jaimini Dewan's *Lahore* (a poignant tale based on India's partition, 1949), New Theatre's *Chhota Bhai* (Emotional bond between two brothers and family partition, 1949) and *Swayam Siddha* (story of a self-respected and courageous daughter-in-law), Heman Gupta's '42 (based on a real story of the attorcities of British officials on the Indians of Midnapore. It was so realistic that some viewers fainted in the hall and later it had to be banned), Jean Renoir's *The River* (based on the tale of a European family settled in rural Bengal, 1949), Shantaram's *Dahej* (depicting the ills of bride-price), *Shaheed* (a patriotic film showing freedom struggle), Rajkapoor's *Awara* (though a glamorous film, based on a powerful story of K.A. Abbas showing the impact of environment and exploitations of an unemployed youth, 1951), Fani Mazumdar's *Andolan* (showing freedom struggle, 1951), Zia Sarhadi's *Hamlog* (showing the weal and woe of a lower middle class family and the frustrations of an educated but unemployed youth, 1951); Bimal Roy's *Do Bigha Zamin* (showing the life of a poor agriculturist and his exploitations at the hands of a landlord, 1953), Prakash Arora's *Boot Polish* (showing the struggle of shoe-shine boy and girl and life in slums, 1954), Guru Dutt's *Pyasa* (showing the exploitation of an author by a publisher, betrayal by own men and some basic values of life, 1957), Raj Kapoor's *Jagte Raho* (showing private and clandestine activities going on in a mansion in one night, 1957), Shantaram's *Do Ankhen Barah Hath* (based on the theme of reform of hardened criminals, 1957), K.A. Abbas's *Sahar aur Sapna* (struggle of a young boy and girl in an urban centre and their dreams, 1964), Motilal's *Chhoti Chhoti Baten* (based on intra-family relations 1965), Tapan Sinha's *Hatey Bazarey* (showing the exploitations of a landlord, changing values and modernism, 1967), K.A. Abbas's *Bombai Raat Ki Bahon Men* (showing the night life in Bombay, 1967), *Saudagar* (depicting the life of a toddy-maker and petty businessman), Sunil Dutt's *Reshma aur Shera* (depicting the life-style in a desert area), K.A. Abbas's *Saat Hindustani* (based on the problem of National Integration, 1969), B.R. Isara's *Chetna* (showing the life of a Call Girl, 1971), Rajindar Singh Bedi's *Dastak* (showing life of outsiders in a Red Light area, 1971), Tapan Sinha's *Apun Jan* (present day unrest in the society) and *Call Girl* (life of call-girls and the circumstances responsible for it, 1972), Tarachand Barjatya's *Nadiya Ke Paar* (intimate glimpses of family life in rural areas (Roberge, 1974 143-59; Srivastava, N.D; Abbas, 1977: 71- 74) and Attenborough's widely acclaimed film on *Gandhi* (1983), *Desh Pradesh* of Devanand (dealing with the theme of illegal immigration of Indians in England, their life style and the way they are misled by dubious agents), *Aaj Ka M.L.A.: Ramavtar* (dealing with corruption in politics), *Aaj Ki Awaj* (dealing with the problem of crime, incompetence of Police and its 'probable' solution) and *Teri Kasam* (based on the problem of marriage of exchange (*Golhat*), may also be mentioned here.

To this list may be added films made from time to time under historical background but depicting socio-cultural life of the people. To give a few examples, *Pukar* of Sohrab Modi, and in recent years *Junoon* of Shyam Benegal, *Shatranj Ke Khiladi* (1977) of Satyajit Ray and most recently, *Mirch Masala* (1987) of Ketan Mehta may be mentioned here.

(iii) *Films on Television*

Besides, a number of films, being telecast in recent years on Indian T.V., Tele-films, or otherwise, like *Janam* dealing with the problem of concubinage and its impact on familial relations, *Ek Rooka Hua Faisla* analysing the process of decision-making by Jurymen in court and intricacies involved in it, *Party* pointing at the hollowness and artificiality of people living in higher urban societies, *Admi aur Aurat* showing the supremacy of human love above caste and creed and a moving human story contributing to the cause of national integration, *Andhi Gali* dealing with aspirations and problems connected with urban life, *Aadharshila* dealing with struggle and disillusionment of modern youths choosing film as a career, *Naadania* dealing with the themes of conjugal separation and its impact on child, *Nasur* depicting disorganization and vicious circle operating in medical profession and the trials of an honest doctor, *Agnidah* depicting the torture and consequent murder of a daughter-in-law by her in-laws for the greed of dowry and a retaliatory thought, *Aaghat* dealing with some of the intrigues of trade unionism, *New Delhi Times* (advertised but not telecast) dealing with the trials and risks in the career of Journalists, *Jane bhi do yaro* dealing with the 'conquest' of evil forces on goodness and truth, *Holi* dealing with degeneration of students in college campus, *Dhundhle Saye* dealing with corruption and vicious circle operating in a hospital and humiliations of an honest police officer on this account but his ultimate triumph in rounding up the culprit, *Massey Saheb*, making interesting study of an Indian Christian in British India who operates within a 'marginal culture' and behaves like a funny 'black Sahib', *Rao Saheb* showing disgraceful position of widows in traditional Brahmin society of Maharashtra, inevitability of tradition and its strong influence even on those who talk of change, besides entertaining the audience, mirror the events happening in our society and create an awareness of it compelling us further to think of viable solutions.

A number of 'regional films' made by regional film-makers and based on regional themes, a good number of them being award-winning films and shown generally on Sunday afternoon present before the audience a realistic picture of our national life which reflects unity in diversity. They show in adequate measure regional sub-cultures of India; style of life, problems and aspirations, dances and songs, dresses and decorations, practices and customs, manners and etiquettes of the people living in far flung areas of the country which the audience in general can hardly afford to know otherwise. It creates a sense of understanding and appreciation for 'others' culture' which helps to create an effective psychological condition for national integration.

Apart from regular or full-length fiction films shown on T.V. channels, a number of T.V. serials and T.V. features may also be broadly speaking included under 'fiction films' which are relevant to the present context. Technically they are not feature films but all the same 'short fictions' showing different episodes in series woven around focal themes. A T.V. fiction other than serials may be shown in a single sitting and called a T.V. feature. It may be small or sometimes unusually big. Though a large number of such T.V. fictions are meant primarily for the sake of entertainment showing casual realities communicating specific messages, some of them may specially be mentioned here that are anthropologically significant not only in terms of socio-cultural realities that they mirror but, also because they make us aware of some vital problems the society is faced with, with a slant on their plausible solutions. Some of the serials also attempt at reorienting traditional values and norms among the viewers or revitalizing them for the benefit of the larger society. *Nukkad* was one such serial that depicted the style of life, livings, aspirations and problems of common men on streets in urban areas. *Rajni*, another popular serial in all its episodes dealt with specific maladies of modern life which the society is presently suffering from and the way it may probably be solved. The solutions presented in the episodes are, however, debatable. *Darpan, Khazana* and *Katha Sagar* in many of its episodes usually based on depiction of Indian society, and the human society in general by well-known Indian and foreign writers respectively dealt with basic cultural and human situations that conveyed basic messages and wisdom relevant to our society making considerable impact on sensible viewers. *Rag Darbari* based on the award-winning literary satire aimed at capturing the crisis of post-independent rural India in its multidimensional and vivid form. *Hamlog* still another popular and a lengthy serial was woven round the realities of a middle-class joint family with a slant on unity in family life, inter-marriage and national integration. *Buniyad* in the same chain, was another family drama which began from pre-partition days, and made a case-study of the family of a businessman in historical perspective through three generations. Besides presenting historical materials relating to partition of the country, the serial apart from its shortcomings in a very engrossing manner dealt with the traditional and changing values of family life in pre-independent and independent India. *Chunauti* portrayed the vices of modernity that have crept in the campus life of teaching institutions which pose a serious problem before academic authorities. *Ramayan* based on the popular Indian epic not only depicts the exploits of Rama but also makes us aware of the higher ethical moral and spiritual values that play a vital role in the perpetuation of our society. Still another serial *Tamas* attempted to analyse the communal frenzy and some factors that led to it in pre-independent days ultimately leading to partition of the country though its thesis was hotly debated. T.V. features like *Anthin* and *Kath Ki Gadi* in a very powerful manner presented intimate glimpses of family life crumbling under the weight of poverty and trade-union activities of husband, and lives of lepers with a strong message respectively.

Typology of Films

The assorted list of fiction films given above are realistic in character and make an attempt to depict different dimensions of life and society rather in a faithful manner. Hence, they are of considerable educative and research value. They make a strong case for being studied under visual anthropology under the title 'Realistic Feature Films'. These films can be divided into three broad categories on the basis of main thrust of the film, though they may not be put under water-tight compartments. In fact, they form a continuum. These categories help us to make a meaningful understanding of the subject-matter, focus, and communicational and functional aspects of films in anthropological context.

These categories refer to: (i) films of ethnographic orientation which present socio-cultural realities as faithfully as possible, (ii) films of sociological orientation which are mainly problematic and may suggest probable solutions to given problems, and (iii) films which present either established, or changing models of life. Usually they carry some message and are inspiring. In case they depict established models of life, they reinforce tradition and uphold basic values and norms of a society. Now it would be desirable to make a few illustrations from each of these categories.

The first category of films showing ethnographic orientation may further be divided into two sub-categories viz. films which depict contemporary situations, and those set against historical background which relate to realities in the past. In the first sub-category may be mentioned the films like *Pather Panchali, Aparajita, 36 Chowrangi Lane, Jalsaghar, Estappen, Teen Kanya (Post-Master* and *Samapti), Saudagar, Badnam Basti, Rajnigandha, Admi, Jagte Raho, Ardha Satya, Mandi, Bazar, Damul, Paar, Nadia Ke Paar, Holi, Nasur, Aaghat* to cite just a few examples. These films are of contemporaneous interest. The other sub-category may be exemplified by the films like *Achhut Kanya, Two little Untouchables, Pukar, '42', Ankur, Maya Darpan, Umrao Jaan, Lahore, Satranj Ke Khiladi, Junoon, Mirch Masala, Gandhi, Massey Saheb, Ondanondu Kaladalli* and the like.

The second category of films on sociological orientation includes *Saukari Pash, Partidwandi, Do Bigha Jamin, Jan Aranya, Manthan, Interview, Calcutta '71, Garam Hawa, Akrosh, Albert Pinto Ko Gussa Kyon Ata Hai, Simhasan, Desh Pardesh, Dahej, Admi, Padosi, Aaaj Ka M.L.A. Ramavtar, Aaaj Ki Awaz, Nadania, Teri Kasam, Janam, Nasur, Aaghat, Ardha Satya, Bazar, Damul, Mandi, Party, Jait Re Jait, Bhavni Bhavai, Adharshila, Jane Bhi Do Yaro, New Delhi Times, Holi, Rao Saheb* and the like. Some of the films coming under this category deal with reformistic themes relating to widows (*Sindur, Balyogini*), untouchables (*Nandan Charittram, Achhut Kanya*), family life (*Rajeshwari, Gun Sundari*), crime (*Jis Desh Me Ganga Bahti Hai, Do Ankhen Barah Hath*), alcoholic drink (*Dharmpatni*) and the like. Some films produced during British times dealt with patriotic themes like *Vande Matram, Ashram, Roti* and *Saheed*. Interesting as it is, due to stringent censor enforced during those days some of them took recourse to symbolism and satire as reflected in *Roti*. In recent decades also a number of films, dealing with social or political themes used this approach. *Jalsaghar, Bhuvan Some, Simhasan, Kissa Kursi Ka, Admi aur Aurat* are some of the films that may be mentioned in this connection.

The third category includes the films like *Swyama Sidha, Gun Sundari, Nishant, Dharampatni, Aurat, Ramshastri, Saheed, Arya Mahila, Rajni, Ramayan, Duniya Na Mane, Do Aankheh Barah Hath, New Delhi, Ek Duje Ke Liye.* The religious or mythological films usually shown in picture-houses which reinforce the religious beliefs, values and sentiments of the viewers, also belong to this category.

Selection of Films

Coming to the methodology employed in the study of fiction films specially 'new-wave' and other realistic films (including T.V. films) that help us in culling out materials for anthropological use, the first question that confronts us is how to select an appropriate film relevant to visual anthropology, and whether it is possible to evolve some objective criteria for it? The answer is in positive and a set of six basic and objective criteria may be developed in the present context.

Here it would be significant to observe that before a visual anthropologist selects and analyses the fiction films to bear upon the culture of a people, he should preferably have some acquaintance with the people and their culture he is going to study as it will help him to make a correct choice of films. The criteria, for selecting relevant films are as follows:

Firstly, the theme of the film selected for study should be other than melodramatic and 'formula film'[7]. Usually such films are free from star cast, but it may not always be necessary.

Secondly, the main theme of the film should relate to any distinct and concrete aspect of life and culture in a society.

Thirdly, the script of the film should be based on literary work of quality in which one finds well constructed meaningful stories and characters.

Fourthly, a fiction film should preferably be an award winning film or in some way acclaimed or honoured. The award may be for the direction of film, its theme, presentation, problem it deals with, and the like. The award may be of the nature of local, state, all-India or international and come from governmental or private sources.

Acquisition of the copy of the film by National Film Archive, reputed institutions or government departments for educational or similar other purposes constitutes the fifth criterion in this connection.

The last criterion requires that the director (or producer) of the film should be a film-maker known for honesty, imagination and realism in the treatment of films. One may look for all these criteria together in a fiction film or just some of them depending on the situation.

T.V. serials and T.V. features which also broadly speaking come under fiction films, have a different format and they may be selected in the light of first three criteria given above. Besides, such T.V. fictions must convey some message to the viewers.

Analysis of the Films

After appropriate films have been selected, the next important question which confronts us is how exactly to proceed? How to analyse the film?

At the outset, it may be noted that film media is different from conventional anthropological study. In the latter case all the points of observation are substantially dealt with in writing. But in case of film, the researcher is expected to elaborate the 'spirit' and 'meaning' of a scene or sequence which may appear very briefly on the screen. A small shot may not necessarily diminish its significance.

There may be certain films the whole of which in terms of its constituent episodes and sequences seem to be realistic and relevant for analysis. But it may not always be necessary to accept a film in its totality; some of the constituents may be anthropologically relevant while others may be 'trash' and we can leave it out. So a film at the level of analysis, if necessary, may very well be fragmented into meaningful components and sorted out before making the content analysis.

Another relevant point is that in some fiction films, materials relevant to anthropological study may be too evident and explicit, while in others it may be implicit, or they use symbols and satire to convey its viewpoint. One has to go into analytic depth to grasp the true and underlying meaning of all of it and cull out the facts of anthropological significance. It basically relates to the realm of ideas and values.

Before coming to the analysis of films, it is necessary to provide its background information viz., credits, running time, dates of completion, release and the like.

A film may be divided into six major aspects for the purpose of analysis i.e., the script, setting, acting, presentation, music and message. The first point covers the story and arrangement of events while the second i.e. setting, relates to the surrounding, sets, environment or the total milieu in which the characters operate. Acting, besides proper action itself, will include costumes and get-up of actors and actresses. Presentation of the film will include photography, editing, dialogues and the style in which the story is presented. Music will include the lyrics and songs given in the film. Lastly, the message will include the moral of the story, symbolism, underlying meaning or whatever the story intends to communicate to the audience. One may also think whether or not the film contains any message and if there is one, whether it is explicit or implicit.

Some of the points mentioned above may seem to be 'technical' being connected with film making, but the visual anthropologist interested in the analysis of fiction films has no escape from it and he has no other way than to develop it. With what the visual anthropologist is concerned most is 'realism' or 'truth' in fiction films and he can very well manage to treat it as an index to assess the six components in question.

Keeping the above points, or totality of the film in view, the film may be further assessed in terms of a set of three criteria and one has to find out whether these criteria are met with or are absent in a film with reference to the society or culture the film projects. The first criterion is the 'conformity to traditional values, norms and standards'. It implies to which extent the components of the film or the totality convey, conform to or deviate from the traditional values, norms and standards prevalent in the culture or society to which the story relates. If one finds deviation, whether or not the film conforms to emergent realities of the society. The second criterion is 'naturality' and one has to see as to what extent the element of naturality gets reflected in the film. 'Justification' is the third criterion which will help us to check superfluous elements grafted in the film that are not well integrated and illogical to the total context.

Summary Observations

After a film has been analysed within the framework given above, finally, it would be necessary to understand the film in its totality and present major findings by way of summary observations. It will consist of various socio-cultural elements that get reflected in the film; the material culture, customs, practices, belief system, value system, ideals, other ethnographic materials, the real socio-cultural problems, significant message or any other point of anthropological significance.

By and large, the same procedure mentioned above need to be followed for the analysis of T.V. serials and T.V. features.

The methodology developed here analyses Indian films but they may also be relevant universally with minor modifications.

Films as Cultural Document and a Source of Awareness

After adequate number of films from a given culture are thus analyzed, they may be categorized on the basis of themes to have a proper understanding of the different aspects of culture. Film making is essentially a cultural activity and it can very well constitute a cultural document as said, not only showing traditional style of life and socio-cultural events but also the type of changes taking place in the values, ideals and different facets of the social and cultural life.

The films also give us an insight into the various problems and evils of the society. Such films are very significant as they help in creating a social awareness in the minds of the people which may make a necessary psychological base for moulding public opinion and effecting social reforms accordingly. Some such films also try to hint at 'plausible' solutions to these problems and one is always at his liberty to debate the workability of such solutions. Thus, fiction films not only just constitute cultural documents, but can be very well utilized in creating an awareness and stirring the conscience of the masses over a given issue, and raising their level of aspiration.

In 1965 while inaugurating the India's Third International Film Festival at Delhi, the then President of India S. Radhakrishnan (Shamim, 1965 : 13) said that films expose the basic contradictions in society. He further said that "Films can assist us in exposing our stupidities and follies, in bringing out the contrast between wealth and poverty, between prince and peasant, and make us feel that for human nature to manifest, itself in all its fullness, is essential for it to have its elementary needs and requirements met adequately".

M.G. Kamath (1976 : 22) similarly opines, "A visual medium like the film, if sensitively produced, has the potentiality of raising the expectations of the people, can take them out of a false sense of contentment and offer them a vision of a new life, a higher standard of living, and encourage experimentation. It can help bring changes in the values and attitudes traditionally clung to by the rural people."

Films are really a powerful means of communication and the most characteristic thing about it is that its effect is almost immediate and 'instant'. In 1955 the Prime Minister Nehru (Barnouw & Krishnanswamy, 1980 : 205) stated that the film medium was a "tremendous thing" with an influence in India "greater than the influence of newspapers and books all combined". But he had reservations about the "quality of influence".

Films as Powerful Agency of Change

Films have been a powerful agency of change though some opinions vary in regard to the nature and extent of such change. Some people may think that the impact of films works on the 'core aspect' of culture while others may be inclined to believe that it touches only 'peripheral aspects'. Again, the impact may work consciously or unconsciously.

Here it may be observed that by and large the impact may be felt more prominently in the non-material or ideational aspect of culture than the material ones. The impact on non-material aspect of culture may broadly relate to belief-system, value-system, ideals, attitudes, levels of aspiration, horizon of knowledge, awareness to the various problems or situations prevailing in the society, solutions to such problems and reform; while the material aspect may broadly relate to the areas like fashion, dress and decorations of all types, manners, etiquette and style of living, crime-pattern, material equipments and the like. But even though the impact may be greater in non-material aspect of culture that are subtle and not so apparently visible, it serves a significant purpose as any appreciable change in the society must precede a change in the non-material aspect of culture as elaborated earlier.

Dual Nature of Film's Impact

But it must be realized that the impact of realistic fiction films is of a dual nature. While it works as an agency of change on the one hand, on the other, irrespective of its non-material or material aspect it has a re-inforcing effect supporting the traditional and positive socio-cultural norm, values and ideals.

Here it is interesting to note that the all-India popular or 'commercial cinema' also reinforces traditional attitudes, but in a rather 'perverted manner' "after taking the audience on a detectable sin parade full of nudity, rapes and the whole spectrum of violence" (Das Gupta, 1983 : 40).

Films may also work as an effective instrument of revitalization. The traditional style of life shown in films may be used to inspire a people to revive its old but positive values and norms under the situation of culture change when loss of original culture is feared.

Positive and Negative Sides of Films

The impact of films has its positive and negative sides as well. On the positive side, fashion, modern style of dress and decoration, phraseology, style of living, ear for good music, sense of social integration, appreciation for other's way of life, awareness to social problems, re-orientation of positive values, few cases of intercommunity marriages, increasing number of marriage by mutual consent or marriage without dowry as reported from time to time from different areas, among other factors, have been also inspired by films.

On the negative side, morality is the worst casuality. Today, one of the reasons of violence and crime of all types, including that relating to sex, forgery etc. and their 'universalization' may be attributed to the influence of many such films which are freely showing violence and glamourizing it in spite of the existence of Censor Board. Films have also contributed its share to the draining out of some of our basic socio-cultural values which has led to all round deterioration and weakening of the social structure. In fact, one needs a thorough study of such films, their socio-cultural contexts, and the big way in which they have influenced our belief and value-systems. It has brought about further chain-reactions and various other types of changes in the society.

In view of this potentiality of the film-medium, if proper control could be exercised on the display of films, it can very well mould the taste of the masses of good ends. A number of films made by some 'good' and socially conscious film-makers in recent decades have gone a long way in moulding the taste of the public as reflected in their increasing interest in light-classical music and craze for 'clean films' with good story, realistic settings, natural acting, depicting real life situations or something indigenous upholding basic traditional values of the society and at the same time forward-looking, hinting at probable solutions to the various problems that our society faces today.

While inaugurating the Ninth International Film Festival at Delhi Sri N.K.P. Salve, the Minister for Information and Broadcasting, Government of India said, that the films were considered to be an important and universal medium of communication and entertainment that relieve us from tension for the time being that we have by living in the present day world full of various types of strain, conflict and fear. The messages that come through this effective audio-visual medium can be easily reached to every section of the society. Sri Salve further remarked that for the developing nations like ours the films have become a significant medium of moulding cultural values and influencing social standards of the changing society (Mishra, 1983 : 16)

U.G.C.'s Proposal for Film Societies

Of late, the Government has become aware of the potentiality of films and intends to use it in a big way. In 1984 the

University Grants Commission proposed a growth strategy for 'University Film Societies' or Clubs. The U.G.C. Report made a proposal for establishing Film Societies in Indian Universities with U.G.C. support. The objectives of the film societies were : "to increase the awareness of films as a modern art form and of the cinema as a 20th century medium of social communication and education by exposing students to international and Indian film Classics of various genres in a systematic manner; to organize discussions, symposia, lectures and courses on any aspect of promotion of film culture on the campus; and to attempt to relate films as a subject with other subjects which were being studied on the campus, and with the fine arts, and to expand the understanding of the relationship of cinema with the needs of individual growth and social development" (Khanna, 1984 : 1-9).

Bridging Peoples and their Culture with Films

When we talk of bridging peoples and their culture with films it presupposes the value of communiciation between different peoples. Sometimes we fail to appreciate others' culture because we are inadequately informed about them and their way of life. Since films reflect life and culture of a people, it can help bridging the gulfs among such different groups of people and promote a healthy mental outlook and tolerance that can lead to a better sense of mutual cultural understanding and appreciation.

In a heterogeneous country like India with diverse ethnic and linguistic groups coming from tribal, peasant, urban and cosmopolitan city backgrounds even though there are common points of unity among them, our knowledge about the other groups is desperately poor. In view of it the films shown either in Picture-houses or on Television to have a very significant role to play in bridging the gaps in our knowledge about diverse peoples, reinforcing a sense of unity amidst diversity and strengthening the sense of national integration.

Films have been considered to be a "reflection of national life and culture"[8] and as such, in the words of Mrs. Indira

Gandhi it constituted "the most powerful medium for the exchange of thoughts" (Shamim, 1965 : 13).

The films have their own usual channels of distribution outside the country through which one sees the films of other countries and learns about its people, but International Film Festivals provide special occasions which help to promote a better understanding among the people of different nations through films, acts as a stimulant to learn more and more about the cultural heritage and peoples of other nations and bring them closer.

While inaugurating India's Third International Film Festival at New Delhi in 1965 Dr. S. Radhakrishnan, the President of India stressed the role that films played in international cooperation and understanding. "The basic factors of human experience", the President said, "were the same everywhere and as they dealt with such universal aspects of life, films had a universal appeal". The President further said, "If he were given the choice of just one prayer to God he would pray, 'Give me the power to understand'. Since Cinema helped in promoting understanding in the world, films could play a very important role in the adventure of the human spirit and help us to move onwards" (Ibid.).

Beginning from 1952 so far Eleven International Film Festivals have been organized in India. These Film Festivals have drawn galaxies of distinguished foreign film-makers and provided unique opportunities to view the films of India and other countries. Over the years efforts have been made to expose foreign delegates and guests to glimpses of our own creative efforts through "Indian Panorama" that presents selected Indian films. The impact which our Film Festivals have made internationally can be measured from the fact that they have attracted a large number of outstanding films from foreign countries (Shamim, 1981 : 41). In the latest Eleventh International Film Festival held in January 1987 according to one estimate nearly 150 out of a total 200 feature films scheduled to be shown were films from other countries. These Film Festivals increased the international film traffic "which also moved in the opposite direction as more and more Indian film artists and their works were invited to foreign festivals, resulting in an inevitable cross-fertilization" (Barnouw and Krishnaswamy, 1980 : 246).

It resulted into some very big events for Indian Film Industry. A group of Indian film artists was invited to Moscow in 1951 on a good will mission and showered with hospitality. The next year another group of people from Indian Film Industry made a tour of U.S.A. which included a White House visit with President Truman and a lavish Hollywood banquet. In coming years such intercultural expeditions became more frequent and sometimes they generated international collaborations in film-making and also paved the way for future trade relations (Ibid., p. 246; Naik, 1965 : 33).

The rich cultural heritage of India and its beautiful locations in the light of the developments just mentioned, attracted several film-makers from abroad. On the other hand some Indian film-makers have also been keen about it and the idea of international co-productions was thus conceived. Roberto Rossellini, an Italian director of repute and a lover of India is said to have made few short films on India. *Pardesi* (The Traveller, 1957), an Indo-Russian venture was initiated by K.A. Abbas which involved Mosfilm. Another Indo-American project *Nine Hours to Rama* was based on the life of Gandhi and launched in 1962. The *Householder* (1963) and *Shakespearwallah* (1965) were the two successful Indo-American collaborations by Ismail Merchant and James Ivory. *Alibaba Aur Chalis Chor* was another film made in collaboration with Russia. *Gandhi* was a joint Indo-British production, while *Doordesh, Sohni Mahiwal, Clerk* and *Hena* are the other films of Indian film-makers being made or planned in collaboration with Canadian, Russian and Pakistani counterparts respectively.

Most of the co-productions which were successfully completed were not as popular among the masses as expected. Yet it does not minimise the significance as they were the outcome of collaborations between two nations, their artists and technicians had helped to establish some kind of cultural links and mutual appreciation.

It is said, Indian films have a very good market in near-east countries. The people there have a craze for Indian films. It is the same for the people of Pakistan. Rajkapoor, a matinee-idol of late forties and fifties became so popular in USSR through some of his films that people developed a craze for him and went to the extent of naming a street after him. Besides, a number of film stars and singers, music-directors and dancers connected with Indian films have frequently gone out on cultural mission to foreign countries and their programmes have drawn crowds and wider applause.

Politicians can very well use this situation to improve mutual understanding and foster harmonious political relations. The image of a country can be best projected outside through realistic films. Poor understanding of the life and culture of a group of people on the part of others breeds misunderstanding while an insight into other's culture through films brings the people of the two cultures together.

In spite of India's cultural image of a rich heritage and a peace-loving nation outside the country, barring some bigger nations, there are still some countries where the people do not know much about India. It is really funny that in some countries people confuse the 'Indians' with 'Red Indians'. What politicians could not do, probably Attenborough's *Gandhi* is doing in different countries of the world not only by propagating the message of Gandhi but also acquainting them with the India's great cultural heritage to which Gandhi belonged.

NOTES

1. This paper was developed on the basic idea presented in the International Symposium on Visual Anthropology of the Xth ICAES held at Delhi in December, 1978 in the form of a note. This is a revised and enlarged version of paper sent earlier to *Visual Anthropology*, an International Journal of the Commission on Visual Anthropology, Canada. The term 'fiction films' has been used here to denote 'non- ethnographic' and 'entertainment films'.

   In some western countries where visual anthropology has achieved a milestone people have started thinking also in terms of 'Visual Sociology'. The first European Newsletter on Visual Sociology edited by Leonard Henny at the Sociological Institute of the University of Utrecht, the Netherlands, is the outcome of a resolution adopted at the last assembly of the meetings of the programme "Audio Visual Productions in Sociology" at the World Congress of Sociology in Uppsala, August, 1978. Visual Sociology is supposed to cover the fields of sociology, social psychology, social welfare, history, filmmaking, mass communication etc. and the new term was coined as it was felt that "there was no term that appropriately covered all these areas of interest" (Sahay, 1980 : 1-2).

2. Although in scope, visual anthropology includes the study of culture or a society through still-photographs and movie-films both, many visual anthropologists concentrate only on movie films.

3. Emilie de Brigard (1975 : 13) also has to say a similar thing:

   ".......It is usual to define ethnographic film as film that reveals cultural patterning. From this definition it follows that all films are ethnographic, by reason of their content, or form or both. Some films, however, are clearly more revealing than others".

4. This brief account of the salient developments in anthropological film has been mainly taken from E. Richard Sorenson's paper on 'Anthropological Film: A Scientific and Humanistic Resource', SCIENCE, 20 December, 1974, vol. 186, pp. 1079-80.

5. One of the local contributing factors that expedited the development of new-wave films in India and also encouraged film culture was the films society movement. The objectives of film societies are to make good film from India and different other countries of the world, whether censored or uncensored, available to its member-viewers, and to "disseminate appreciation of film as an art" (Sarkar, 1975 : 156). The Calcutta Film Society was founded in 1947 by Chidananda Das Gupta and Satyajit Ray as "both were hungry to see and study films other than those appearing in Calcutta Theatres". Talking about the aims of the Calcutta Film Society, Chidananda Das Gupta said that it "established the idea that seeing good foreign films was essential to spread dissatisfaction with low, imitative standards of Indian films. The important thing was to develop a movement towards genuine national cinema" (Vasudev & Lenglet, 1983 : 68). Although the Amateur Cine Society and the Bombay

Film Society were already founded in Bombay in 1937 and 1943 respectively, they were "small societies, founded and sustained by individuals interested in seeing good films themselves without any further interest in starting a movement or spreading a film consciousness" (Ibid, p. 67). The Film Society movement had grown and is quite vigorous in Bengal and Kerala where there is an active interaction between the new film-makers and the film (Barnouw & Krishnaswamy, 1980 : 188). Some of the leading film-makers like Satyajit Ray, Tapan Sinha, Ritwik Ghatak, Mrinal Sen, Basu Chatterjee, G. Arvindan, Shyam Benegal and others were actively associated with Film Society movement before coming to films and it was the Film Society which inspired them to make good films relevant to the present context.

6. As this paper makes an exclusive study of 'fiction films', many Indian short films or documentaries of the early decades of silent era made by early pioneers which were by and large shot on real life situations and events occurring spontaneously in their natural settings, having broad resemblance with 'ethnographic films' (though obviously it lacked anthropological and methodological sophistication) and were the 'precursors' of the present day fiction films, have been deliberately excluded. For these films see K.N. Sahay's 'A Brief History of Ethnographic Films in India', *Visual Anthropology Bulletin*, vol IV, No. 1, 1982, pp. 2-7 and Ethnographic Films in India: Prospect, Priorities and Proposals', in Methodology in Anthropological Filmmaking, Papers of the IUAES-Inter Congress, Amsterdam by Nico C.R. Bogaart and Henk W.E.R. Ketelar (Eds.) 1983, pp. 49-59.

7. The 'formula films' consisted of songs, dances and contrived plots that became the vogue in 1940s. "Ostensibly, these were aimed at catering to the needs of a new class of audiences—industrial workers and others who had migrated to the big cities from rural areas, and the growing bourgeoisie—in search of 'entertainment' in an alien environment" (Raina, 1983 : 11). The well known formula of variety entertainment constitutes the pattern of popular Indian film i.e. "charming stars, songs, dances, fights, chase, spectacle, lavish sets and big locations, melodrama and humour, a bit of everything, all strung together along with fulfilling stories of fixed stereotypes viz. variations of the love triangle, the morality story of good vs. evil, the mythological with emphasis on miracle and magic, and the adventure story. Often these patterns may be skilfully woven in the same story......The entertainment film in India, as elsewhere, is concerned with reality but through a distorted mirror....." (Bahadur, 1983 : 110). Many of these films start with a real problem but go on to give a fantasy solution to the real problem. "This, of course, works as entertainment for the simple reason that this is the precise way people would like their problems to be solved if real problems could ever be solved by dreaming. This is the well known cathartic function of popular cinema" (Ibid).

8. It refers to a Symposium on "Films As a Reflection of National Life and Culture" held at Vigyan Bhavan, New Delhi in January, 1965 at the

occasion of the Third International Film Festival of India which was inaugurated by Mrs. Indira Gandhi. There were as many as eleven speakers on the list and the symposium was chaired by Dr. Mulk Raj Anand (Shamim, 1965 : 13).

REFERENCES CITED

Abbas, K.A., 1977: Mad, Mad, Mad world of Indian Films, Hind Pocket Books, Delhi.

Adair J. & Worth S., 1967: In American Anthropologist, 69, 76; 1970: In American Anthropologist, 72, 9

Asch. T. & Chagnon, N., 1974: The Yanamamo, Documentary Educational Resources, Somerville, Mass.

Atma, Hari, 1977: *Samanantar Cinema Men Nari Ke Kaun Se Roop Ubhre Hain? Pramukh Samanantar Filmon Ki Naikayon par ek Dristi (Hindi)*, Dharmyuga, 27 February.

Bahadur, Satish, 1976: The Context of Indian Film Culture in *Film Miscellany*, A Publication of the Film & Television Institute of India Pune 1, December,.
1983: Aesthetics: From Traditional Icononography to Contemporary Kitsch, Indian Cinema Superbazaar by Aruna Vasudev and Philippe Lenglet (Ed.) Vikas Publishing House Pvt. Ltd., New Delhi.

Balikci, A., Brown Q. & Young R., 1968: Netsilik Eskimo Series, Educational Development Corporation, Newton, Mass.

Barnouw, Erik & Krishnaswamy, S., 1980: Indian Film (Second Edition), Oxford University Press, New York.

Bateson G. & Mead, M., 1942: Balinese Character: A Photographic Analysis, New York Academy of Sciences, New York.

Bhaskaran, S.T., 1980: Silent Cinema in the South, *Cinema Vision India*, Vol 1, No. 1, January.

Birdwhistell, R., 1952: Introduction to Kinesics, University of Louisville Press, Louisville, Ky.
1960: Exploration in communications, E. Carpenter and M. Mc Lunan (Ed.), Beacon Press, Boston, pp. 54-56.
1970: Kinesics and Context, University of Pennsylvania Press, Philadelphia.

Brigard, Emilie de, 1975: The History of Ethnographic Film, Principles of Visual Anthropology, Paul Hockings (Ed.), Mouton Publishers, The Hague.

Chandavarkar, S.G., 1965: Problems of Export Promotion: Interview with Mr. A.S. Naik, *Filmfare*, February 5.

Das Gupta, Chidananda, 1983: The "New" Cinema: A Wave or a Future? Indian Cinema Superbazaar by Aruna Vasudev & Philippe Lenglet (Ed.), Vikas Publishing House Pvt. Ltd., New Delhi.

Das, Veena, 1980: The Mythological film and Its Framework of Meaning: An Analysis of *'Jai Santoshi Ma'* in India International Centre Quarterly, Special Issue, Vol. 8, No. 1, March.

De' Monte, Darryl, 1975: New Cinema, *Onlooker*, September 1-15, Vol. 37, No. 13.

Dharap, B.V., 1980: Some Important Film-makers of the Silent Era, *Cinema Vision India*, Vol. 1, No. 1, January.

Jha, Bagishwar, 1981: Mani Kaul: The Focal Point of Indian Film Renaissance, *in* Twelve Indian Directors by S.C. Ghosh and A.K. Roy (Ed.), People's Book Publishing, 50, Sitaram Ghosh Street, Calcutta.

Hall, E., 1959: The Silent Language, Doubeeday, New York.

Kakar, Sudhir, 1980: 'The Ties that Bind: Family Relationships in the Mythology of Hindi Cinema in *India International Centre Quarterly*, Special Issue, Vol. 8, No. 1, March.

Kamath, M.G, 1976: Films in Rural Development in *Film Miscellany*, A Publication of the Film & Television Institute of India, Pune.

Karnard, Girish, 1980: Glorious Gohar, *Cinema Vision India*, Vol. 1, No.1, January.

Khanna, Arun, 1984: U.G.C. Report Proposes Growth Strategy for University Film Club, *Screen*, June 22, pp. 1-9.

Kinikar, Shashikant, 1980: Bhalji Pendharkar: An early clash with censors, *Cinema Vision India*, Vol. 1, No.1, January.

Kracauer, S., 1942: *Propaganda and the Nazi war film*, Museum of Modern Art Film Library as quoted in 'Feature Films as Cultural Documents' Principles of Visual Anthropology by Paul Hockings (Ed.) Mouton Publishers, The Hague, page 233.
1947: From Calighari to Hitlar: A Psychological History of the German Film, Princeton University Press, Princeton.

Lomax, A., Bartenieff & Paulay, F. 1968: Folk Song, Style and Culture, A. Lomax (Ed.), AAAS, Washington D.C.; Res. Film 6, 505.

Marshall, J. 1958: The Hunters, McGraw-Hill Contemporary Films, New York.
1966-74: Kung and Gwi Bushman Film Studies, Documentary Educational Resources, Somerville, Mass.

Mead, M. & Mac Gregor, F., 1951: Growth and Culture: A Photographic Study of Balinese Childhood, Putnam, New York.

Mehrotra, Alok, 1981: *36 Chowrangee Lane: Suruchipurn Sashakt Abhivyakti* (Hindi), *Dharmyuga*, 18-24 October.

Metz, C., 1971: Language et Cinema, Larousse, Paris.

Mishra, Mangruram, 1983: *Cinema Sàmajik Mulyon ka Darpan Hai* (Hindi) Madhuri, 4-17 number, Vol. 20, Issue 478.

Mirza, Saeed, 1981: Aparna finds her Genius, *Sunday*, October 18, Vol. 9, Issue 18.

Mukhopadhyay, Durgadas, 1978: An Approach to the Study of Refugee Society Through Fiction Film—with Illustrations from the Films of Ritwik

Ghatak, A Paper presented to the symposium on Visual Anthropology, Xth ICAES, New Delhi in December, 1978.

Nadkarni, D., 1980: A Painter Called Baburao, *Cinema Vision India*, Vol. 1, No. 1, January.

Nandy, Ashis, 1980: The Popular Hindi film: Ideology and first Principles in *India International Centre Quarterly*, Special Issue, Vol.8, No.1, March.

Narayan, N., 1975: Mrinal Sen: Bringing the Hope of Freedom, *Filmfare*, September 5.

Pradhan, Shalini, 1981: Jabbar Patel: That Slickness has yet to be perfected, *Filmfare*, January 1-15, Vol. 30, No. 1.

Raina, Raghunath, 1983: The Context: A Socio-Cultural Anatomy, Indian Cinema Superbazaar, by Aruna Vasudev and Philippe Lenglet (Ed.) Vikas Publishing House Pvt. Ltd., New Delhi.

Rangoonwala, Firoze, 1980: Satyajit Ray's Art, Clarion Books, Delhi.

Ranjan, Girish 1975: *Samanantar Filmen: Kyon Aur Kiske Liye* (Hindi) Dharamyuga, August 10, Vol. 26, Issue 31.

Ray, Satyajit, 1976: Our Films Their Films, Orient Longman Limited, New Delhi.

Rouch, J., 1955: Connaiss. Monde, 1, 69

Ruby, J., 1973: Paper presented at the American Folklore Society Meetings, Nashville, Tennessee.

Saari, Anil, 1981: What the New Films are about, *Sunday*, March 29, Vol. 8, Issue 31.

Sahay, K.N., 1980: *Visual Anthropology Bulletin*, Vol. II, Issue I: 1.

1982: 'A Brief History of Ethnographic Films in India', *Visual Anthropology Bulletin*, Vol. IV, No. 1, June, pp. 2-7.

1983: Ethnographic Films in India: Prospect, Priorities and Proposals: Methodology in Anthropological Filmmaking by Nico C.R. Bogaart and Henk W.E.R. Ketelaar (Eds), Edition Herodot, Gottingen.

Sarkar, Kobita, 1975: Indian Cinema Today—An Analysis, Sterling Publishers Pvt. Ltd., New Delhi.

1981: Mrinal Sen's Films: Their bond is their Rebelliousness, *Filmfare*, January 1-15.

Shardaya, Jugnu, 1981: *Apne Sensar Se Jurta Hua Cinema* (Hindi) Dharmayuga, 15-21 February.

Sharma, Hari P., 1983: 'Rejoinder: Aakrosh: A Work of Art with Purpose' in *The Eastern Anthropologist*, Vol. 36, No. 3, July-September, pp. 275-82.

Shamim, M., 1965: Festival Bureaucratic Style, *Filmfare*, February 5, 1965, page 13.

Sorenson, E. & Gajdusek, D. 1963: Nature, London, 200, 112.

Sorenson E., 1966: "The study of child behaviour and development in primitive cultures: a research archive for ethnopediatric film investigators of styles in the patterning of the nervous system". Pediatrics 37 (Suppl., part 2), p. 149.

1967: In Current Anthropology, 8, p. 443.
1968: In Anthropological Quarterly, 41, p. 177.
1974: Anthropological Film: A Scientific and Humanistic Resource, Science, Vol. 186, pp. 1079-1080.
1975: Visual Records, Human Knowledge, and the Future, Principles of Visual Anthropology by Paul Hockings (Ed.) Mouton Publishers, The Hague.

Sorenson, E. & A. Jablonko, 1975: Research Filming of Naturally Occurring Phenomena: Basic Strategies, Principles of Visual Anthropology, By Paul Hockings (Ed.) Mouton Publishers, The Hague.

Srivastava, Bachchan, N.D.: *Bhartiya Filmon Ki Kahani* (Hindi) Hind Pocket Books Pvt. Ltd., Delhi

Tandava, G., 1983: The Documentary: Systematic Images. Indian Cinema Superbazaar by Aruna Vasudev and Phillippe Lenglet (Ed.), Vikas Publishing House Pvt. Ltd., New Delhi.

Verma, S.C., 1981: 'AKROSH as Liberation Anthropology' in *The Eastern Anthropologist*, Vol. 34, No. 4, October-December, pp. 333-46.
1983: 'Rejoinder: S.C. Verma Replies' in *The Eastern Anthropologist*, Vol. 36, No. 3, July-September, pp. 283-86.

Vasudeva, Aruna & Phillippe Lenglet, 1983: The Film Societies and the Film Press, Indian Cinema Superbazaar by Aruna Vasudev & Phillippe Lenglet (Ed.), Vikas Publishing House Pvt. Ltd., New Delhi.
1983: Indian Cinema Superbazaar, (Ed) Vikas Publishing House Pvt. Ltd., New Delhi.

Weakland, J.H., 1972: Conflict between Love and Family relationships in Chinese films, *Journal of Popular Film*, 1:290-298.
1975: Feature Films as Cultural Documents, Principles of Visual Anthropology, Paul Hockings (Ed.), Mouton Publishers, The Hague.

Wolfenstein, Martha & Leites, N. 1950: Movies: A Psychological Study, The Free Press, Glencoe.

Worth, S. & Adair J., 1972: Through Navajo Eyes: An Exploration in Film Communciation and Anthropology, Indiana University Press, Bloomington.

Acknowledgement

I am thankful to Sri Sushil Arora, Research Scholar for helping me with some relevant books and magazines while writing this paper.

Chapter IV

Visual Anthropology and Indian Fiction Films: Comments and Reply.

[*Abstract*: Visual anthropology studies man and his culture by employing Camera as its principal instrument of investigation. The importance of visual data for anthropological enquiry was first realized after Marget Mead and her colleagues made pivotal use of film research to demonstrate culturally specific patterns of behaviour on Bali. Fiction film, though a most popular source of entertainment and powerful means of communication, has been so far a neglected field of study. Fiction film in the present context by and large refers to 'realistic feature films' that are very near to life and anthropologically useful. Not only such films include 'new wave' films of contemporary times but many other films as well made during Silent and Talkie eras of Indian films and those being shown on Indian Television in the form of Regional films, Tele-films, or Serials. These films make a strong case for being studied under visual anthropology under the title 'Realistic Feature films'.

Such films may be divided into three broad categories on the basis of main thrust of the film viz., (i) films of ethnographic orientation; (ii) films of sociological orientation; and (iii) films which present either established or changing models of life. A set of six criteria has been evolved for selecting

---

The article, *Visual Anthropology and Indian Fiction Films* was published in Volume 29, No. 2 September, 1986 of the *Journal of Social Research* and being the Author and Editor, I circulated a *Special JSR Treatment* and requested for comments to twelve anthropologists, visual anthropologists and other scholars on social communication — India and abroad. However, the response was received from five of them and finally, the reply was made. As such, this Issue of the Journal (Vol. 31, Nos. 1&2, 1988) given in this Chapter, is being included.

relevant films for analysis which are as follows: Firstly, the theme of the film should be other than melodramatic and 'formula film' and preferably it should be free from star cast. Secondly, main theme of the film should relate to any distinct and concrete aspect of life and culture in a society. Thirdly, the script should be based on literary work of quality. Fourthly, the fiction film should preferably be an award-winning film. Acquisition of the copy of the film by National Film Archive constitutes the fifth criterion. Lastly, the Director of the film should be a film-maker known for his honesty, imagination and realism in the treatment of his films. One may look for all these criteria together in a fiction-film or just some of them, depending on the situation. A film may be divided into six major aspects for the purpose of analysis i.e., the script, setting, acting, presentation, music and message. Each of these aspects may be further analyzed in terms of a set of four criteria and one has to find out as to what extent these criteria are met within a film with reference to the society or culture the film projects. The first criterion is 'conformity to traditional values, norms and 'standards' while the other criterion is 'naturality'. 'Justification' is the third criterion while evaluation of a film from the angle of 'socio-cultural elements' would be the fourth one.

Films constitute a cultural document, a source of awareness and also a powerful agency of change. Films have a dual nature of impact on society—positive as well as negative. Films have great potentiality as a bridging mechanism among the people of different cultural backgrounds.]

Comments

Dr. V.S. Upadhyay
Professor of Anthropology, Ranchi University, Ranchi, India

A Science is known by its scientific methods used for analysing a problem. Anthropology is gradually enlarging its canvas of scientific analysis, incorporating various new dimensions. The present paper by Professor K.N. Sahay is such an example. Lately audio-visual aids have come to support the education system and its impact has formed an important field of research. The present paper is an effort in this direction. It is well known that pioneers are always to face brickbats and this attempt is no exception.

To begin with, Dr. Sahay has tried to 'analyse' what is Visual Anthropology. A full definition could have enriched the paper and attracted new scholars in this field. One could gather that the visually (including audio-visually) observable recording of anthropological data forms the core of Visual Anthropology. If not, a few questions come up before these recordings (fiction films) could form a part of Visual Anthropology. For example, whether Visual Anthropology is 'filming with a purpose' or 'purpose finding in a film'? Whether 'fiction' films have some anthropological authenticity (because they are not factual, p. 4)? To my mind Visual Anthropology should be 'filming a reality (real social situation), not the filming of 'a representative acting'. A fiction film, as the nomenclature justifies, is filming an 'acting based on social theme (and modulated according to the story of the film and likes/dislikes of audience). This paper here deals with (anthropological) 'fact finding' in the 'Fiction' films.

In the field of Anthropology, visual documentation has a long history of about half a century, starting with Mead in 1942 which Professor Sahay has well brought out. Perhaps the fear of the lengthening of paper has restricted the references to only a few. His experiences and data from France and Japan could have strengthened the paper.

While analysing the 'significance and pertinent views on Fiction Films', Dr. Sahay has commendably quoted various authors, whose "casual writings....on content analysis of films have appeared from time to time" (p. 3). Though one can hardly call a 'fiction film' a "cultural document", still there is every doubt whether they can be "used for ordering socio-cultural relations and promoting a harmonious inter-group and cultural relation" (p. 3). (Such an attempt by latest tele-serial

'Tamas' has generated social protests). The views of different authors like Weakland, quoted here still haunts one's mind whether "feature films are (not) fictional?" As has been pointed out, "studies of culture change (through films) has not been adequately tried out" (p. 5).

The various experts, giving an idea about on the 'Present Context' of Indian Cinema, has been well quoted by Prof. Sahay. His list of visual materials (p. 6) is really exhaustive. Again he has rightly pointed out that 'Fiction films in the present context......refer to.....new wave' cinema, as it presents "a faithful and vivid depiction of typical life-style, problems and the events". This statement of Professor Sahay is well supported by the long list and analysis of such films from page seven to page seventeen. A casual count brings out the names of 52 such films, which can "constitute integral part of research relating to specific aspects of life (p. 7). Though these 'art' films have well tried to picturise some social facts, they can only be used for analysis of the regional culture under Visual Anthropology, as they 'are usually based on regional themes' (p. 7). While the new-wave films are considered as of some anthropological value, one wonders whether "other Realistic Films" are really "realistic by any standard" (p. 17). Though the film stories are based on some "problems of their time", the research authenticity of the visual depiction is still in question. In all probability, the 'reality' must have been fictionalized for filming to attract the audience. In other words, those themes could have some anthropological value, but its presentation was quite unrealistic and fails to come up to the standard of visual anthropological documentation.

Similarly I have all reservations to include films on television as part of Fiction Films. All those, which Prof. Sahay has referred to, are purposeful depiction of some social facts meant for usually educated audience. There is no need of fictionalisation for commercial purpose in a tele-film. Similarly, with any amount of argument, even 'broadly speaking', the T.V. serials should not have been included under "Fiction Films". A 'FILM', as the connotation stands now, is a (audio) visual document to be presented from start to end for one sitting observation. Contrary to this, serials are serials, the art of keeping the audience under expectation for the next episode. (One should have liked to see the reference of AUR BHI HAIN RAHEN, TERAH PANNE, KAHAN GAYE WO LOG too).

After reading the first twenty two pages, one comes to know about the typology of films and selection of films made for this paper. One would have liked this to form a section of research methodology and be placed in earlier part of the paper. As Prof. Sahay has rightly pointed out that while categorising, the films "cannot be put under water-tight compartments" (p. 23). Still his categorization is quite meaningful which is based on "subject matter focus, and communicational and functional aspects of films" (p. 23). Coming to the methodology Prof. Sahay has taken "six basic and objective criteria" in selection of films. He could have further clarified whether anyone or all of these have helped to "select an appropriate film" (p. 24). For example, which is the "film serving 'Spiritual Progress' has been selected?" (p. 25).

The most remarkable part of the paper commences with 'Analysis of Films' from page twenty-five. Prof. K.N. Sahay must be congratulated to have made this pioneer effort in the field of Anthropology (with my reservations to call these Fiction Films as documents of Visual Anthropology). I am sure the author agrees with me that Visual Anthropology would not analyse the art of filming i.e. script, setting, acting, presentation and music (p. 26), rather would concentrate on the theme and message only. Prof. Sahay himself has discussed about the authenticity of the depiction of only social facts and realities in the films, referred in earlier pages of the paper. The first five aspects form the base of film technique, rather than anthropological technique. Similarly, each of these aspects may not fit in the criteria of "the angle of socio-cultural elements" (p. 26). As referred earlier, Prof. Sahay's analysis of Films as Cultural Document and a Source of Awareness (pp. 26-27) and as Powerful Agency of Change (pp. 27-28) strengthens their anthropological value. The impact and the positive and negative sides of films have been forcefully depicted. I am sure the U.G.C's. role in strengthening Film Societies will help in better analysis of impact study of these visual presentations.

Prof. Sahay's attempt to show the cross cultural value of film is really informative. It has made the world smaller and popularised Indian life and culture abroad and thus "had helped to establish some kind of cultural links and mutual appreciation" (p. 32). His reference to Attenborough's 'GANDHI' in concluding lines has brought in with full force, what impact a film can achieve among the human societies.

Thus the paper provides good food for thought on Visual Anthropology. The content analysis and visual impressions of a film make it a 'new-wave' or 'art' film, definitely above the 'fiction' in every standard and art of filming. If one compares them with the visual anthropological documentation made by NAV of Japan or Anthropological Survey of India, or even some filming by Public Relation Departments, one wonders about the visual anthropological value of these fiction films. Just as some writings in the literature may have foundations in social reality, it is not an anthropological document. Similarly filming 'fact' at one hand, and a fiction based on fact (?) on the other hand, must be faithfully distinguished. Therefore to my mind, the content analysis and impact study of films should come under social, rather than Visual Anthropology. The latter should be restricted to "the concept of producing anthropological film records as a permanant research resource" (p. 2). An anthropological film must be distinctive form of a fiction film.

Dr. A.R.N. Srivastava
Professor of Anthropology,
Allahabad University, Allahabad, India

Although it may not be helpful to treat films as a realistic presentation of entire facets of human life in any strict sense, an individual story, sequence of tales, or even a genre can be approached as a cultural corpus and analyzed in anthropological terms. Perhaps, this is the intention of the author of the essay under review.

The author has tried to study and evaluate the behaviour of people of distinct cultures utilizing information (data) presented in societal-theme-oriented fiction films. His model involves a careful consideration of selection of films in terms of six *basic and objective criteria,* analyzing data with respect to *six aspects* of film(s) under study; further, each of these aspects in terms of a set of *four criteria* (pp. 24-26, emphasis mine). The author appears to hold views if visual anthropologists follow this methodological scheme fiction films may offer valuable understanding of human behaviour.

I would like to briefly dwell on some methodological issues involved in the paper; and I do so in the role of academic anthropology not as a practitioner of visual anthropology.

The science of anthropology is basically a field oriented study of human society and cultural institutions. We are fully aware of the traditions in field work which virtually formed the integral part of the development of anthropological theory. The entire exercise in visual anthropology in above case appears to be tedious and futile. What eventually one would get after doing all this? Do we want to study a society at a distance what Benedict had set forth in early forties? If one does so that would be still treated as interpretation based on secondary source of data. Today cultural anthropologists cannot afford abandoning field work though they utilize available data of others but for comparative purposes.

I would argue keeping in view of the objectives of the paper, that criteria to select suitable commercial films are not objectively laid down. Any objective criteria should be universally applicable. Here some criteria carry subjective elements. Consider *criterion one:* a film should be free from 'star cast'. The fact is there are several realist films equally good for anthropological study starred by super star of film. What about Bimal Roy's *Devadas* in which title role was played by Dilip Kumar? Likewise *criterion three* is also problematic.

Scripts or realistic films are not always drawn from famous literary sources. Who wrote script of *Damul*? *Criterion four* is linked with *criterion three* which again may not be case always. Honesty, imagination and realism are dependent on one value judgement or wisdom (*criterion six*). It then appears that a visual anthropologist may select any commerical film which portrays human action and behaviour under given situation. All he has to have a *purpose*. His ultimate aim is to relate data to his own observations.

That the six aspects of a film and each of these aspects in terms of four criteria are to be analyzed, is again time consuming and repetitive. It is hard to follow that a visual anthropologist would do that in order to meet underlying assumption as "supplementaries to conventional anthropological studies" (p.7).

I am not, of course, suggesting that visual anthropology should abandon above noted variety of enquiry, but academic anthropology will fail its professional concern if it does not come up with a sound methodology to theorize issues relating to man and his behaviour.

Contrary to the point set forth in the essay I believe visual anthropology could offer distinctive insights that would make it worthwhile for those who are already in film industry.

With some reservations, however, I consider this paper an important essay, well researched and well told about Indian films. It is fascinating for both visual and professional anthropologists alike. I congratulate the author.

Dr. Binod C. Agrawal
Scientist,
Indian Space Research Organization,
Ahmedabad, India

I am happly to read your paper especially published in JSR wherein you have tried to bring together a lot of material on the Indian films. The unit of analysis both in lingustic and cultural terms is not clear to me. Film making no doubt is a

"Cultural Activity" but then the moot question here is whose "cultural activity"? Also I do not think that many anthropologists are well equipped to judge technical aspects of films. Some empirical research would be required before we can accept films as data base for analysis.

Dr. Timothy Asch
Professor of Anthropology & Director, Center for Visual Anthropology University of Southern California, U.S.A.

I read your very nice article......but didn't have any comments to add to it. You wanted critical comments but, in fact, I thought it was an excellent article as it is and I have few suggestions to change it. I did want to know on page 8, paragraph 4, when you mention Ray's third film of interest is *Jalsaghar* (and you have in parenthesis The Music Room) is that the film we know in America as THE WORLD OF APU? Also on page 29, paragraphs 1 and 2, I thought you should have some film examples.

Dr. B.B. Goswami
Joint Director, Anthropological Survey of India, Calcutta, India

The anthropological study of films has hardly taken any shape in India. In recent years, however, its usefulness has been stated on various platforms. The brief selected catalogue of (pages 7-23) prepared by you on new wave films in India, films of silent and talkie era, films on television etc. are welcome. More important from the professional point of view is the anthropologist's approach for analysis and understanding of films. I would propose that this aspect should be more discussed and an approach paper may be prepared by someone concerned with visual anthropology.

Anthropology in the West is considered largely as a subject which studies 'other cultures' specially non-western cultures. Visual Anthropology has also developed with this line of approach in the West. In India Anthropology is considered as 'self-study'. We are studying ourselves. We are in various cultural stages viz. hunters and food-gatherers, pastorals, agriculturists and also modernized. Therefore, our way of understanding ourselves, through films should be distinctly separate from the western models. We should bear in mind that construction of codes, symbols, markers etc. should not necessarily be dependent markers of the West. Being so much dependent on technology and methods of study this does not appear to be an easy task. Visual Anthropologists have to work very hard to develop proper methodological designs free from the methods used for other cultures.

Cinema as such is not an indigenous media of communication. The technology and other ingredients used in the cinema are the products of West; even the technique and ideas are borrowed from the West. But in the recent years Indian cinema has been using the indigenous ideas, values, cultural forms of narratives in presenting realities through ideologies and forms. Thus creativeness of the Indians in cinema has been recognized by the whole world. The task of the anthropologists in this situation is to either test their general theoretical formulations through the art forms to seek answers, questions concerning structure on processes of social change, social transformation, issues and the realities concerning deprivation and poverty.

This apart by and large I feel that Indian Visual Anthropology should concentrate on documentation and making of monographic films on transformation processes in India. From the point of view of physical anthropology, palaeo-anthropology and cultural anthropology, we must keep in mind that one of the important tasks of a teacher in Anthropology is to brief his students regarding existing bio-cultural realities of people of India. Visual anthropology can do a lot on this aspect. The subject of your paper, however, does not directly deal with this aspect. I thought that this point should be reiterated again for its pertinence.

Reply from K.N. Sahay

Dr. V.S. Upadhyay made indulgence to my article and pointed out a number of relevant points and criticism, though some of them have been repeated. My observations have already been made in the article and some points seem to be misunderstood. Instead of responding each, I would like to explain broad points which will cover them directly or indirectly.

Visual anthropology is known generally as the study of 'ethnogrpahic or anthropological films' which are based on real events. It is the latest development, and is still 'in trial'. But anthropology itself was not significantly developed before the early twentieth century or so. Recently, different dimensions are still adding like applied anthropology or action anthropology to mention a few. Similarly, visual anthropology particularly 'fiction' or 'feature' films is being further explored and fastly crystalising methodological ideas.

It was in connection with fiction-films, Ruth Benedict's study of the Japanese National Character through documentaries and other films, analysing other films from different countries, works of Wolfenstein and Leites, John H. Weakland and S. Kracauer (page 5), may be substantiated. Besides, it may be noted that while going to Tokyo and Paris in 1977 while planning the International Symposium on Visual Anthropology (ICAES), I discussed with the members of the Commission on Visual Anthropology and reached the consensus of opinion that Sri Satyajit Ray, the renowned Film-maker should inaugurate or be the Chief-guest in the 1978 Symposium. But unfortuately, it could not materialize. However, after the lapse of a decade, Dr. Asen Balikci, a Visual Anthropologist of Canada and the Chairman of the Commission on Visual Anthropology—a professional International Organization, in his own way honoured the *Honorary Chairman,* Sri Satyajit Ray of the Commission. It is for you to know the implication; the renowned Film-maker (and not an anthropologist) has a significant bearing connected with Visual Anthropology. Sri Satyajit Ray symbolizes the *genre* of the realistic or New-Wave films close to society like Ritwik Ghatak, Shyam Benegal, Mrinal Sen, Govind Nihlani, Adoor Gopal Krishna and several others from India.

What I intend to make clear is that the Indian fiction-films constitute an important part of *sub-type* within the visual anthropology. Fiction-film in contrast to the usual anthropological films, does not mean 'fiction' in real sense of the term, a 'cock and bull' story, or just 'trash', as it is probably supposed. As such, whenever we study fiction-films, there are *rational considerations, real situations* and backed by *appropriate methodology*. It should not be ignored.

Ethnographic data usually have a purpose for further analysis which need to be 'abstracted' for general proposition or models. On the other hand, specific type of fiction-films coming from real society similarly become abstracted for the purpose of anthropological models. No doubt, the two realities may be slightly of different types, but the content-analysis leads to similar models. Logically, the analysis of models either through ethnographic films or the fiction-films are certainly 'documents' connected with visual anthropology.

Ordering socio-cultural relations and promoting a harmonious intergroup and cultural relations (Page 3) as Dr. Upadhyay has contradicted, is not the fact as I have substantiated the 'Bridging peoples and their Culture with films' (pages 30-32). I did not thoroughly study the methodology from the point of view of *Tamas* and its 'protest'. But whatever I know of it, is that the facts of the films were certainly 'documents', though it was probably generalized. Secondly, protest to a film or emotional problem, does not necessarily mean that the facts based on a realistic story or fiction, are untruth. The case-study may be justified while studying the film, different newspapers commented on it.

Whenever a particular fiction-film is methodologically analysed at a particular time, it is generally 'not unique', but typical to a 'group of events'. Hence, it can very well constitute the anthropological model of study. Attracting the audience to fictionalizing the films, is not my purpose as Upadhyay is worried. I am just interested in methodologically checking a fiction-film and thoroughly selecting it with different criteria of studying under visual anthropology.

The New-Wave films are significant and have rationally structured or organised with methodology at par with ethnographic or anthropological films. So is the case with T.V. films though they have a different format. However, the *other* realistic films may be *somewhat* diffused, dramatic and without sophisticated methodology. Nevertheless, such films contain anthropological facts and may purposefully be scrutinized, culled out and make specific case-studies to analyse anthropological models.

If at all a fiction-film is relevant, and it does it, why should I exclude the Television? A Fiction Television film, either for commercial or non-commercial purpose, must be selected on the basis of merit. Yes, I do not mean 'fiction-film' as a serial. It was just a slip. I have noted the placing of the section of research methodology. The six criteria for selecting the relevant films should be checked by all such films for the study, particularly the first, second, third and the sixth. The fourth one cannot be exhaustive, or it may be just one award making the quality of a film. Similarly, the fifth one may be the National Film Archive, or a State Department, or any organization which makes a testimony of quality to the film. Again, the above last two criteria may be ignored if they are not available.

The 'Spiritual progress' (page 25) is connected with *Charulata* of Satyajit Ray (page 9). It comes under the *third category* of films (Typology of Films/page 23) which 'reinforce traditionality and uphold basic values and norms of a society'. Incidently, one of the articles i.e., *Portrayal of People: Analysis of Two Indian Fiction Films and a Model Perspective in Visual Anthropology* (Volume 31, 1988) of 'Journal of Social Research' is in process and is relevant to some of the points given above.

Even though it is known as visual anthropological connecting with large range of films, typology, technical points, analysis etc. (pages 23 to 26), by implication they are *multi-disciplinary;* anthropological, sociological (page 23), psychological, art-form, technology and different aspects of film-making.

Professor A.R.N. Srivastava bemoans that Visual anthropology is 'tedius' and 'futile'. It may be because visual anthropology is fastly developing specially in a number of rich western and other countries, having *generational gaps* in Indian anthropology relating to technical know-how, and rather biased with 'misunderstanding'. So it is not surprising if Professor Srivastava makes this remark. Before twenties, anthropology was still making ethnographic studies. But gradually, idea on 'man and his culture' further explored sophisticated tools, concepts and methodological theories. The discipline grew and made a number of useful ramifications and specializations. At the moment, visual anthropology developed specializations rolled into certain aspects like anthropological, sociological, art-form and congeries of film-making. They constitute multi-disciplinary potentials and break a new frontier of knowledge. Do you suggest that we should go back and put the horse behind the cart?

Ruth Benedict makes a reference to the study of a society at a distance in early forties. It was because exigency of the situation developed the making of content-analysis of documentaries and fiction-films, and Benedict duly justified and made the National Japanese character. Whenever another 'neutral situation' works, we may like to do once again, of course developing it further, either society at a distance, or otherwise, bearing the fiction-films.

Anthropology has a series of methods and different types of social situations suit the different methods. As fiction-films are powerful media, they influence the society. It is almost unexplored and there is a 'cultural vacuum' which must be explored in the interest of visual anthropology.

I do not mean abandoning primary data and field-work. A film-maker 'studies' or conceives some story or novel that seems authentic, 'close to life'. As such the 'good author' coming from the same society in his own way studies and collects basic 'real case-studies', facts and structures the story unless it is just imagination beyond the bearing of visual anthropology. Thus, I feel ethnographic data in conventional anthropology as well as the 'study' or 'exercise' of the story from the same society are somewhat similar, but come from different levels. Ultimately, they *abstract* on higher levels coming to anthropological models and the 'story models' respectively, which basically come close to the different sources. To illustrate the realistic fiction-films like *Pather Panchali, Postmaster, Samapti. Nishant, Manthan, Kondura, Garam Hava, Ardha Satya,* may be the story models mentioned above.

It is significant to note that fiction-films referred to in the present context, can be best studied as 'supplementaries' to conventional anthropological studies. Such films may also, provide valuable illustrative materials to anthropological studies (page 7).

My study has been made basically to the realistic type of fiction-films (pages 6 and 24 to 26) *combined with methodology* (pages 23 to 26) against the 'popular' commercial films. The latter are 'loose', or 'not properly structured'. As such, looking to the methodology, the commercial films are to be eliminated.

In regard to Professor Srivastava's remark, he is hurried and confused. I stick to the universal criteria given in the article. I never said that realistic films should be free from 'star cast'. If you see it properly, I meant '*preferably* it should be free from star cast'. Coming to the criterion three, it is not problematic. I did not say that scripts of realistic films always drew from famous literary sources. What I said was that, scripts should be based on '......established or good' author....(page 25). It did not contradict the *Damul*. Coming to criterion four, I mean just illustrations. They are not exhaustive. Coming to criterion six, I have given the background. I made clearly, the *term of reference* and the methods have been elaborated. Hence, it is not the question of value judgement.

As regards the six aspects and four criteria, supplementaries to conventional anthropological studies (pages 6 to 7) are a matter of opinion. I have explained my position as given above.

It may be a good idea in principle to interact visual anthropology with film-industry. Some of the new-wave films certainly come close to fiction-films in visual anthropology. But by and large, different people have different networks, backgrounds, professional ethics, values, and technical know-hows. As such, they have different limitations.

Coming to Dr. Binod C. Agrawal, I exclusively mean the New-Wave and other realistic fiction-films including some relevant T.V. films and serials/episodes as discussed. As more than 700 feature films are made in almost a dozen languages every year, and 12.5 million people watch the films from all over the country, it would be a colossal dimension of films. I have been closely involved and observing in touch with the films, Hindi, Bengali and casually other linguistic films through Film-Magazines and relevant literature. As such, certainly I do not mean a specific unit of analysis both in linguistic and cultural terms. But whatever I said above, I have just given a relevant select of films bearing with typology, selection of films, criteria or the methodology included above in the article for analysis. Thus sticking to the relevant points, other films may be added.

The cultural activity of films in the present context may be defined at least by four broad aspects viz., the films connected with different activities (pages 25 to 26) of film-industry culminating in the making of film for release; secondly, actively viewing the films by viewers in general; thirdly, though there may be some persons who do not view films, or some, or casually belong to the milieu i.e., awareness that the films influence the society, directly or indirectly, good or bad; and fourthly, visual anthropologists who look to all the different activities *interacting together* and analyse the models for the interest of the society.

By and large, I agree with the third point. It is highly specialized and visual anthropology must acquire technical know-how to deliver the goods. I am justifying to develop it for the last 17 years.

Similarly, I also agree to the view that some empirical research would be required. Incidentally, I have studied two fiction-films i.e., *Manthan* (Shyam Benegal) and *Admi Aur Aurat* (Tapan Sinha) in *Portrayal of People: Analysis of Two Indian Fiction Films and a Model Perspective in Visual Anthropology* as said above. Besides, Dr. Sushil Arora under my supervision submitted Doctoral Thesis on 'The Movie Films in India and its Socio-Cultural Context: An Anthropological Study' (2 Volumes), Mss., Ranchi University, 1989, and he was highly praised by examiners.

Dr. Timothy Asch favourably compliments my article. You are right that 'The World of Apu' is the third film of Satyajit Ray in the sequence. However, in my other context, i.e., the assorted of the Ray's films, *Jalsaghar* (The Music Room) is the 'third film'.

Though my thesis is seriously and specifically connected with realistic fiction (feature) films, the glamorous commerical Indian fiction-films have impacts more to the negative side (pages 28-29). The latter weaken the norms of social life involved with 'formula films', making 'absurd' or 'collective fantasies' in general.

There may be given a few examples, mainly or partly, connected with the themes like *Sholey, Deewar, Zanjeer, Mujhe Jine Do, Kachcha Dhaga* (glamourization of violence, crime and dacoity); *Chetna, Her Nights, Five Rifles* (censored scenes), *Satyam Shivam Sundram, Ram Teri Ganga Maili, Saat Bijiliyaan* (Sex and romance); *Call Girl, Do Raha, Insaaf Ka Tarajoo* (sex and rape); *Sampat, Delhi Ka Thag, Shaan, Jewel Thief, Ram Balram* (forgery, counterfeits); *Amar Akbar Anthony, Coolie, Kashmir Ki Kali, Muquaddar ka Sikandar, Bobby* (love triangle), *Sasural, Rajkumar, Love in Tokyo, Soley* (singing and dancing in public places); *Aaj Ka M.L.A., Swami Dada, Lavaris* (benevolent acts of supernatural powers); *Khush Naseeb, Deewar, Pukar* (quick gain of status); *Suhag, Trishul* (Lost and found); *Sambandh, All Rounder, Bidai* (funny college scene); *Amir Garib, Waqt, Bhai-Bhai* (funny court scene); *Mashal, Qayamat Se Qayamat Tak, Majdoor* (idiosyncratic hero-villain interactions); *Neel Kamal, Aan Milo Sajna, Teesri Manjil* (foolish comedy); and *Suhag, Mashal, Bhabhi, Dewar* (upmost idealism of family members) (Arora's Thesis).

Thus, the films in general and particularly the popular commercial themes given above, are powerful media of films. The latter are mostly connected with teen-agers crazy for films, and have 'day dreams' or 'fantasy'. The audience probably goes down to the level of 'sub-consciousness' which directly or indirectly, sooner or later, influence the people. Increasing crimes and sex, frauds, 'Romios' or adventures of the negative side, or just 'funs' at the inconvenience of others, have been *occasionally* confessed by people who were influenced by films. To note a few such films like *Kismat* (pick pocket), *Sholey, Deewar* (violence and crime), *Qayamat Se Qayamat Tak* (eloping teen-ager beloveds) may be given, while on the other hand, serious films connected with reforms in yesterdays may be mentioned like *Achhut Kanya, Duniya Na Mane* (page 19), *Dahej* (torture for bride-price) and the like.

The article from pages 7 to 17, increasingly a number of 'New Wave' films in early Nineteen fifties are by and large realistic, mostly authentic, moulding the refined and clean films catering generally to the educated, middle-aged and intellectual groups. Besides earlier, some other realistic films connected with Silent and Talkie eras, portrayed real and reforming lives (pages 17 to 21) although technically were not sophisticated at that time. Again, a number of films being telecast in recent years on Indian T.V., Tele-films, or otherwise (pages 21 to 23), are relevant and purposeful.

The New-Wave films whenever included, have appealing music background, but specially songs were rare. A few such films like *Manthan* and *Nishant* had enchanting music connected with folklore (pages 11 to 12). However, commercial films on the other side, have a number of hit music films since fifties like *Baiju Babra, Shabab, Jhanak Jhanak Payal Baje, Guddi, Chitralekha, Talash* and many others, wholly or partly, moulded certainly the taste of light-classical music of films.

The films have been given above for illustrations. Some others may be properly explored and further studied substantially combined with vital statistics.

Dr. B.B. Goswami makes certain observations but they do not raise questions. However, they are useful and I agree with him.

Thanks for your comments.

Chapter V

Visual Anthropology : An Approach to Cultural Documentation and Revitalization with Special Reference to India*

I

Visual anthropology which is precisely the study of man and his culture by using camera as its principal instrument producing either still photographs or movie films, not only provides 'illustrations' but "a respected tool in anthropological research" (Bateson and Mead, 1942). It is still under formulation in India. Heavy financial commitments, and lack of proper technical skill to handle camera and make film are the two great hurdles that come in its way. By and large, the conventionalists feel prejudiced; either they remain indifferent looking at its potentiality with amusing curiosity and distrust, or show a positive apathy to it. They talk of it but feel reluctant to promote its cause or include it within curriculum of an University. Many of them do not even consider proper to give it an independent status and view it as a part of mass-communication.

II

In India, cultures range from pre-farming and folk to complex urban and industrial stages and represent most of the levels in the evolutionary process of cultural development. A large variety of caste, creed and religious groups with varying racial, sub-racial and economic types along with rural, tribal, urban, cosmopolitan, and industrial styles of life coming from

---

* Revised version of the earlier paper published in *Journal of Social Research*, Vol. 30, No. I & II, 1987.

a wide range of ecological settings constitute the varied dimensions of Indian life and civilization. The civilization itself has an orthogenetic growth with a history stretching over five thousand years and in spite of evident diversities, its underlying unity adds to its conspicuousness and significance. This unity, among others, works through a host of religious centres situated in different parts of the country, and the institution of pilgrimage. The traditional channels of communications and dissemination of sacred knowledge through it, keep the rich religious and cultural heritage reinforced and alive.

On the other hand, exposure of Indian society to the western world since the advent of *Pax Brittanica* resulted into new administrative, police and judicial systems, opening of educational institutions on the pattern of western models, rail roads, bus routes, press, postal and telegraph services, electricity, radio, several industries, and the like. Independence of the country and promulgation of new constitution accelerated the process of modernization. Construction of dams, technological innovations in the field of agriculture, and other rural development programmes, T.V., Video, mass-communication, harnessing of atomic energy, space-research, several other advancements in science and technology, democratic processes and politicalization, have put the country on road to progress.

But probably we have been not so alert in our planning. In our anxiety to progress we have opened too many fronts without having a proper grip on the chain reactions that it generated. Some such reactions have adversely affected vital areas of our culture. In spite of spectacular progress and development we have witnessed in our country, it has created the problem of maladjustment. Generally, we have failed to fit in modernity in our traditionality. There has been large-scale draining out of our basic traditional values that were positive and we have been alienated from our own culture. Today many of us have the least understanding of our cultural heritage but somehow feel proud in criticizing it. There is blind race for aping the west. By and large, we are becoming individualistic and some even talk of crisis of conscience. Our life at many fronts is characterized by tension and conflict.

India being a heterogeneous country, very little do we know about other's way of life. This situation leads to misunderstanding, animosity and prevents integration which is the avowed goal of our national life. Besides, while on the one hand modernization has helped to develop the country as a whole and given its people a national awareness, on the other, paradoxically, it has widened the schism among its people owing to growing social and political awareness and large-scale politicalization.

In recent decades, specially after independence when our welfare programmes could not make much headway in spite of spending huge amount, our planners and administrators realized that there was something wrong with our approach. They learnt from experience the value of 'knowing' the people and their culture for whom they were planning and to whom they wanted to develop. Subsequently, provisions were made for giving orientation to those engaged in welfare programmes and the idea of 'welfare-oriented research' for the government was developed which could make the welfare programmes readily acceptable.

III

India has been rightly considered to be the epitome of the world. With its rich multi-ethnic and diverse cultural background it offers a vast scope to visual anthropology. But the vastness of the field is not matched by poor resources for ethnographic filming and documentation presently available in the country. Whatever work has been done in this field, remains negligible. It calls for making a planned and phasewise intensive documentation of its representative cultures. Besides, emerging developments and varied socio-cultural situations operating in the country need to be documented. With the fast rate at which the society is changing, we have to be careful and give top priority to document the life of vanishing communities and those who are under the process of rapid change. We are faced with the proverbial question of 'now or never'. A comprehensive filming and documentation programme for India has to be carefully evolved keeping in view these considerations.

The problems of draining out of positive traditional values, cultural alienation, atomization and the like are of a far serious nature. This situation appears to be partly caused because of gaps in our knowledge about the true nature and potentiality of Indian culture and lack of a definite idea as to which elements of culture we should retain and which others to drop in the modern context. The problem may have multi-pronged solutions and one of these relate to visual anthropology. Making of such ethnographic films which document the 'brighter side of culture' and positive traditional values, judged from the angle of basic needs of a society which still have relevance in the modern context,[2] should be encouraged.

Lack of knowledge about other's culture often breeds misunderstanding while a knowledge of it promotes mutual appreciation and trust among the peoples. It is felt more prominently in the heterogeneous country like India which is inhabited by a wide range of ethnic groups. It necessitates the documentation of basic cultural features of these different ethnic groups with a focus on cultural universals as well as those unique feature like arts and crafts of other characteristics for which these people are known to others. It may give us an insight into their values and ethos and evoke other's interest in them. Such films would also be useful to the planners and administrators providing them with a better understanding of the needs of various communities and at the same time help them to evolve a workable strategy for effective developmental work.

IV

Cultural documentation in visual anthropology apart from ethnographic films, has important bearing on some variety of fiction films generally known as, 'new-wave' films, other realistic fiction films besides some Tele-films, T.V. serials or T.V.

Features as well, which deal with themes very close to real life situations. Such fiction films may be put under three broad categories. The first category consists of films of ethnographic orientation which present socio-cultural realities as faithfully as possible. The second category includes films of sociological orientation which are mainly problematic. They may suggest probable solution to given problems and talk of reforms. The third category relates to films which present either established, or changing models of life. Usually they carry some message and are inspiring. In case they depict established models of life, they reinforce tradition and uphold basic values and norms of the society (Sahay, 1986:23). A proper methodology has been developed for the selection and analysis of fiction films for anthropological use.[3] The fiction films and the society act as a two-way process. On the one hand the films mirror the life and culture of people and constitute a sort of cultural document. On the other hand, the films influence the life of people in a significant way. They have the potentiality to create a powerful source of awareness and change and act as a bridge of understanding among the people of different cultures.

Many Indian short films or documentaries of the early decades of silent era i.e., towards the close of the last century that were made by early pioneers, were the 'precursors' of the present day fiction films. By and large, they were shot on real life situation and events occurring spontaneously in their natural settings having broad resemblance with 'ethnographic films' (Sahay, 1982 : 1986 : 34).

In the days to come in the talkie era which began in early thirties of this century, such films documented various facets of Indian life viz., social evils, problems and reforms that could be possibly effected, patriotic sentiments in British days, nationalistic feelings which integrate the country, ideals, positive values and norms relating to family life and social life, ethnic relations, modernization and westernization and the havoc it created on our lives, religious values which give sanction to many positive social acts, and the like. A systematic study of these film documents can help us in having a general understanding of the changes taking place in our society in time perspective.

A good number of 'regional films' are meaningful and document glimpses of regional sub-cultures of the country, style of life, problems and aspirations, dances and songs, dresses and decorations, beliefs and practices, manners and etiquettes of the people living in far flung areas of the country in the least adulterated form.

A number of Tele-films being telecast on Indian T.V. in recent years have been rather sincere in their approach and documented various realities from Indian life. To make a few illustrations: *Janam* dealt with the problem of concubinage and its imapct on familial relations; *Party* pointed at the hollowness and frustrations of higher class of people living in big cosmopolitan cities; *Andhi Gali* dealt with aspirations, struggle and problems connected with urban life; *Naadania* dealt with the themes of conjugal separation and its impact on child; *Nasur* depicted disorganization and vicious circle operating in medical profession and the trials and humiliations of an honest doctor; *Aaghat* showed the intrigues of trade unionism; *New Delhi Times* depicted the trials and tribulations of honest journalism in modern context; *Holi* dealt with degeneration of students in college campus; *Rao Saheb* depicted disgraceful position of widows in traditional Brahmin society of Maharashtra, inevitability of tradition and its strong influence even on those who talk of change, and the like. However, it is felt that some case-studies presented in these films like that in *Nasur* and *Holi* probably depict extreme situations, and it can not be generalized.

Technically speaking, T.V. Serials and T.V. Features may not be 'fiction films' but all the same 'short fiction' showing different episodes in series woven around focal themes. Though many T.V. serials are meant primarily to entertain showing casual realities, communicating specific messages, some of them are anthropologically significant not only in terms of socio-cultural realities that they construct, but also because they make us aware of some vital problems or other developments taking place in the society. As such, they have been also included under 'fiction films'. To mention a few of them *Nukkad* depicted the style of life, living aspirations and problems of common men on streets in urban areas. *Rajni,* another popular serial in its different episodes dealth with specific maladies of modern life which the society is suffering from. *Darpan, Khajana* and *Katha Sagar* in many of their episodes, usually based on depiction of Indian society or the human society in general by well-known Indian and foreign writers respectively. These serials dealt with basic cultural and human situations of universal significance. It put across specific messages and wisdoms relevant to our society making considerable impact on sensible viewers. *Raag Darbari* based on the award-winning literary satire aimed at capturing the crisis of post-independent rural India in its multi-dimensional and vivid form. *Hamlog,* still another popular serial and a lengthy one, was woven round the realities of a middle-class joint family with a slant on unity in family life, inter-marriage and national integration. It also documented generational gap and class of values. *Buniyad* in the same chain was another family-drama which began from pre-partition days in Lahore and made a case-study of the family of a businessman in historical perspective through three generations. Besides presenting historical materials relating to partition of the country the serial apart from its shortcomings, on the whole, documented the lives of patriots, refugees, westernization, changing values and the like. *Chunauti* documented the vices of modernity that have crept into the campus life of teaching institutions that pose a severe threat to institutional authorities. *Ramayan* based on the popular Hindu Epic, documented our cultural heritage. It did not only project the exploits of Rama, the cultural hero, but made us aware of the higher, ethical, moral and spiritual values which play a vital role in integrating our society (Sahay, 1986 : 22-23).

V

The documentation of certain traditional cultural values through films could be of immense help in cultural revitalization under the acculturative situation. They can help us in retaining the cultural identity and revigorating its positive potentials still relevant, and badly needed at the present juncture of time. Rapid secularization due to advent of western technology and western system of education struck at the very root of our ancient wisdom which were cloaked under ethical, moral, religious and spiritual teachings and injunctions to enforce a sense of compulsiveness among the masses. By conforming to these standards, to a great extent, life in the society could be made peaceful, worth living and the organic solidarity could be maintained. Such teachings by and large, were neither parochial nor specifically religious in usual sense of the term but of universal and eternal social significance and formed the *summum bonum* of every advanced religion. They did not go outdated but can very well be accommodated within the modern frame of things and may probably act as a panacea to most of the baffling problems with which our society is afflicted. Self-discipline, dutifulness, honesty, truthfulness, love for others, kindness, tolerance, contentment, purity, hard work and a sense of 'detachment', non-violence, sense of righteousness, social obligations are some of the basic virtues that may be mentioned in this connection. Even though in our personal lives so often we talk about disillusionment from these values and assume an indifferent attitude, paradoxically and most sensibly whenever we talk formally, we confess that it is the relative absence of these values in us which is causing so much of mutual distrust, unrest and tension in our society and we have to imbibe or revitalize them at any cost.

Films have a great feed-back value and it is hightime that these virtues are redefined in modern context and revitalized through films in the larger interest of the society. If necessary, new subsidiary values which support major traditional values that we want to revive, may also be created through a set of popular films.

Here, the author is well aware of the debate over 'popularity versus effectiveness'. A film rated to be 'popular' on T.V. may not necessarily be 'effective'. But the author does not wish to underrate the consequences of a popular film that works subtly on psychological plane. Nothing one sees or hears ever get lost. They are most likely to percolate down to behaviour if not immediately, any time later depending upon the working of unconscious factors. The theory of Indian *yoga* on *chitta* also confirms it. A value enacted through audio-visuals has a strong unconscious influence upon the viewers who in different degrees identify themselves with the characters on the screen. The first change even though one is unaware, occurs on mental plane and socialization level before it gets gradually expressed in action. Hence, one should not lose sight of this aspect whenever we talk about the popularity and effectiveness of films.

It is also to be realized that there is 'ideal culture' and a real one and there exists always a gap between the two. But the gap, even if we recognize an ideal, has much widened and revitalization of the virtues mentioned here will take care of it. Mutual appreciation and trust among different ethnic groups in a country like India constitutes another area in which revitalization is needed for a harmonious and integrated national life.

Ramayan is one of the T.V. serials which illustrates our point. Under the impact of modernization this epic fell in importance and people, specially the educated ones and elites considered it below their dignity to talk of *Ramayan* or quote it in their social talks. But since this serial was started on Television, reportedly, it has become immensely popular among all sections of the audience even some non-Hindus, and it has waded its way to the 'drawing-room culture'. *Ramayan* has begun to be appreciated not only as the legendary story of Ram and Sita but a source which re-acquaints us with the fundamental, ethical, moral, social, political and spiritual values and norms connected with different sectors of life which constitute the distinct hallmark of Indian ethos and cultural heritage. Here it would be significant to mention the sharp reactions of the Indian audience and unusual pressures on the government of the general public and even 'strike' in some part of the country against the termination of the *Ramayan* serial on *Doordarshan* in its 'incomplete' form and discussion on this issue even in the Parliament in July 1988. It is not only an ample proof of unusual popularity of this serial that is based on a highly popular Indian epic but in Durkheiminian terms reflects the working of 'collective mind' or 'collective consciousness' of the Indians.

Earlier, serials like *Dada Dadi Ki Kahani* for children and *Vikram and Vaital* were also reportedly popular and full of similar potentials which while providing entertainment put across serious morals to children-viewers and other sensitive section of the audience. *Kabir* and *Kabira Khara Bazar Me,* the latter repeated more than once on T.V., also recreate some of our social and spiritual values which integrate the society and exhort the people to be better human beings.

The telecast of *Festival of India* and *Apna Utsav* were other important programmes which may be mentioned here. These programmes were keenly watched by millions of Indians and were successful in arousing curiosity, sense of appreciation for other ethnic groups, and above all, a sense of national pride and common heritage which in turn revitalize the sense of national integration.

Telecast of a regular series of ethnographic films on the lives of different ethnic groups presented in an interesting manner, and of the duration of nearly an hour once a week or so, is likely to foster a sense of mutual understanding and create a necessary psychological base for integration, and revitalize our national life. Opening of a Cell of Visual Anthropology in High Schools and Colleges for the sake of creative hobby or as a part of the curriculum and encouraging the students to make 8 m/m or Video films on 'others' way of life' by giving prizes or fellowships for good films and organising local, regional and national film festivals of the amateures, will further help to fulfil the objectives just mentioned. It also embodies the idea of having a national body with four, five regional committees which will look into the interest and activities connected with visual anthropology in the country.

NOTES

1. It is a revised version of the paper presented at the International Seminar on Visual Anthropology (A Portrayal of People) held at Jodhpur, India from December 15 to 19, 1987 and sponsored by Anthropological Survey of India and INTACH.
2. This issue has been discussed in detail by the author (Sahay, 1985-86A, 1985-1986B) in his two articles: *Analysis of Some Ancient Cultural Models, Their Erosion and the Present Cultural Crisis in India and Dharma and Purusartha and Its Relevance to the Situation of Cultural Crisis in Modern India* published in *Journal of Social Research* from Ranchi.
3. The author (Sahay, 1986) discusses his methodology for the selection and analysis of fiction films for anthropological use in his article on *Visual Anthropology and Indian Fiction Films* published in *Journal of Social Research* from Ranchi.

REFERENCES CITED

Bateson, G. & Mead, M., 1942: Balenese Character: A Photographic Analysis, New York Academy of Sciences, New York.

Sahay, K.N., 1982: "A Brief History of Ethnogrpahic Films in India" in *Visual Anthropology Bulleltin*, Vol. 4, No. 1, June.

Sahay, K.N., 1986: "Visual Anthropology and Indian Fiction Films" in *Journal of Social Research*, Vol. 29, No. 2, September.

Sahay, K.N., 1985-86A: "Analysis of Some Ancient Cultural Models, Their Erosion, and the Present Cultural Crisis in India" in *Journal of Social Research*, Vol. 28-29, September, 1985-March, 1986.

Sahay, K.N., 1985-86B: "Dharma and Purusartha and Its Relevance to the Situation of Cultural Crisis in Modern India" in *Journal of Social Research*, Vol. 28-29, September 1985-March, 1986.

Chapter VI

Portrayal of People: Analysis of Two Indian Fiction Films and a Model Perspective in Visual Anthropology*

I

Ethnographic films portray the style of life of a people which is of considerable academic and applied interest in visual anthropology. But the portrayal of people also comes through such films which do not come within this or any of its allied categories. Nevertheless, they are significant in the present context and can be very well used for anthropological purpose. It is the realm of fiction films otherwise known as 'feature film', 'commercial film', 'popular Cinema' or also 'tele-film'. Cases are not lacking when anthropologists like Ruth Benedict, Wolfenstein and Leites (1950), Weakland (1972, 1975) and others studied people through such films but it never went beyond initial attempts and the field still needs to be systematically explored.

II

Recently I developed a methodology (Sahay, 1986) for the study of such fiction films and short films that are realistic and come close to life. They may be put into three categories viz., films of ethnographic orientation that present socio-cultural realities as sincerely as possible, films of sociological orientation that are mainly problematic and may suggest probable solution to given problems, and lastly, films that present established or changing models of life.

Revised version of the earlier paper published in *Journal o*
Vol. 31, No. 1 & 2, 1988.

There are certain films the whole of which in terms of theme, its constituents and episodes seem to be realistic and relevant for analysis. But it may not always be necessary to accept a film in its totality; some of the constituents or episodes may be anthropologically relevant while others may be trash and we can very well leave it out. Again, in some fiction films, materials relevant to anthropological study may be too evident and explicit, while in others it may be implicit in the form of symbols and satire that we have to interpret properly and cull it out.[1]

Selectivity of appropriate fiction films for anthropological analysis poses a question and we can employ six basic criteria for it. Before we point it, it is significant to observe that the visual anthropologist concerned should have some preliminary knowledge of the people and their culture he is going to study as it will help him to make a correct choice of films. The first criterion for the selection of fiction film for study is that its theme should be other than melodramatic and 'formula' film. Generally, it is free from star caste or 'unglamorous' in sense of the term. Secondly, the theme should relate to any distinct and concrete aspect of life in a society. Thirdly, the script of the film should be based on literary work of quality, or of such an author in which one finds well constructed and meaningful story and characters. Fourthly, the film should preferably be an award winning film, or in some way acclaimed. Acquisition of a copy of the film by National Film Archive, any governmental department or other institutions, constitute the fifth criterion. The last one requires that a director (or sometime, producer) of the film should be a film-maker known for his honesty, imagination and realism in the treatment of films. We may look for all these criteria together in a fiction film, or just some of them depending on the situation. T.V. serial and Tele-film may also come under fiction film, have a different and smaller format and they may be selected mostly in the first three criteria. T.V. fictions must convey some message to the viewers.

A Fiction film may be divided into six major components for the purpose of analysis viz., the script, setting, acting, presentation, music and message.[2]

Each of them or the whole film, may further be analysed in terms of a set of three criteria i.e., conformity to traditional values, norms and standards and the emerging realities; naturality; and justification.[3]

Finally, within the framework given above it is necessary to understand a film in its totality and present major findings by way of summary observations depicting socio-cultural elements as reflected in the film, problems, significant message or any other point of anthropological significance. These points have already been elaborated in one of the earlier writings of this author (Sahay, 1987 : 1-41) and some of it have been further revised in the present context.[4]

III

It is in this background that the author presents a 'model perspective' by analysing two recent Indian fiction films to show their relevance to visual anthropology. They are *Manthan* (The Churning, 1976) by Shyam Benegal, and *Admi aur Aurat* (A Man and a Woman, 1985) by Tapan Sinha. These films were telecast by the National Network of Indian Television (*Doordarshan*). The first film was full length feature film while the second one was a Tele-film or featurette sponsored and specially commissioned by the Indian Television. *Manthan* was telecast in 1986 while *Admi aur Aurat* in 1985.

IV

These films were selected as they were no 'formula films' and themes were other than melodramatic. Also, these films had actors but no star cast. Relevant details and analysis of these films are being presented one by one as given below:

(i) MANTHAN

Background Information:

Main Artists	*Charactars in Film*
Girish Karnad	Dr. Manohar Rao (Veterinary Doctor and leader of the Team)
Smita Patil	Bindu (Harijan Woman)
Naseerudin Shah	Bhola (Harijan Villager)
Mohan Agashe	Deshmukh (Team man)
Anant Nag	Chandavarkar (Team man)
Amrish Puri	Ganga Pd. Mishra (owner of a dairy)
Kulbhushan Kharbanda	Village Sarpanch
Sadhu Mehar	Mahapatra (an officer of Co-operative Deptt.)
Yashpal	Husband of Bindu
Abha Dhulia	Shanta (wife of Dr. Rao)
Produced by	Gujrat Cooperative Milk Marketing Federation Limited
Photography	Govind Nihlani
Running time	134 minutes
Film Completed	1976
Date of Release	1976

Selection of Film

Theme

The film tackles a problem that has hardly been touched in Indian Cinema. It refers to the process through which a tradition bound rural community where vested interests uphold the tradition, learns to redefine the relations of production and adopt new initiatives. Set in contemporary India, it brings a group of urban social workers to a village dominated by Harijans where they exhort the milk producing rural folk to organize themselves into a Milk Producers' Co-operative Society so that those who produce the milk should draw the gains. But the task is not easy. Traditions of exploitation and unquestioning submission to the age old system would not let the villagers to unite and take a stand. Ultimately, when it takes shape it creates a lot of complications and persecutions of the Harijans. The city group has its own equally inhibitory limitations, and they are also slandered. It all seemed to undo their efforts for some time. But as the latter retreat under the pressure of circumstances, the villagers discover their potential and try to collect their efforts once again.

Distinct and Concrete Aspect of Life

The main theme of the film relates to distinct and concrete aspect of life and culture. It concentrates on economic exploitation of poor villagers by a rural based dairy owner who purchases milk at very cheap rate and usurps the major share of profit. At the initiative of Government a team of experts is sent to this village with a view to mobilise the people to form a Consumers' Cooperative Milk Society. The film analyses the trials and tribulations of the villagers, their persecutions, power politics as well as the ordeals of the team members in the process of establishing the society. It presents a typical setting in the rural society of India and raises some typical issues that may not be palatable, connected with development that help to understand the Indian society and the processes of change.

Literary Work of Quality

The screen play of the film is written by the well known Marathi play-wright, Vijay Tendulkar on an idea developed by Dr. V. Kurien. Before writing his screenplay and fictionalising, Tendulkar studied the village situation closely and actually went to the project area in Gujrat and studied the things for himself (Bandyopadhya, 1984 : vi).

Award Winning Film

Manthan was given National Award in 1976 for best screen-play and best direction. It was honoured with *Rajat Kamal* and also got the Regional Award.

Acquisition of Film by Institutions

The film has been reportedly acquired by the National Film Archive of Poona, and the State Government of Gujrat for its viewing among the people as it depicts a realistic situation.

The Film Maker

Shyam Benegal, the Director of the film, is one of the exponents of 'new-wave' films in the country and is a renowned film maker known for his honesty, imagination and realism in the treatment of films. The film in question also reflects these qualities of Benegal.

Analysis

The Script

In the opening scene Dr. Manohar Rao accompanied by Mahapatra gets down from train on a platform in rural area located somewhere in Gujrat. Dr. Rao is the leader of the team sent by Dairy Board to set up a Milk Cooperative Society in a village as Government's dairy is 40 miles away. This village is dominated by the Harijans, then there are farmers, the potters, the shepherds, the Rajputs and a few barbers. Mahapatra being elderly and of old values, and an employee of the same Department, is sceptic of this scheme. He does not believe that a milk cooperative in that area could be successful. He already told it to his department but he felt, he was not listened to. But Dr. Rao is young in spirit, determined and enthusiastic. Rao gets down to work for his mission the moment he arrives in the village. In due course, his other colleagues like Desmukh and Chandavarkar come down from the city to join his team. Being city-bred, they, specially Chandavarkar experiences problem of adjustment. They educate the villagers on the concept and benefits of cooperative society most of whom are Harijans and try to win them over who suspect the activities of Dr. Rao. It is a tough job with many unpleasant experiences on his part. Bhola and Bindu who are Harijans initially suspect, resist and play tough but later cooperate with Dr. Rao in mobilizing other villagers to join the milk movement. These activities of the villagers bring them in confrontation with Ganga Prasad Mishra, a shrewd man who runs a personal dairy over there and buys milk of the villagers on cheap rate pocketing lion's share of the profit. Mishra initially discourages Dr. Rao from his work and advises him to look after the animals since he was a Veterinary doctor, their proper education, health and family planning. But Dr. Rao curtly reacts: "All because they won't touch your business at all. Isn't that so". Mishra contends that "the young people are great idealists. They are always dreaming of changing the world". Mahapatra also agrees to it and says that it is just foolishness. "All that idealism is nonsense". Bindu and many other villagers are well aware that Mishra is not a good man, and he cheats the villagers. The villagers are exhorted to unite together in their own interest to form a Milk Cooperative Society. When things take shape Sarpanch of the village, who has backed the efforts of the team and is a non-Harijan, stands for the post of Chairman of the Milk Producers' Cooperative Society. But the Harijans set up their own candidate, Moti, who contests and wins. It sparks off trouble. The defeated Sarpanch feels very bad and insulted. He joins hand with Mishra. Subsequently, arson is committed by the henchman of Mishra and Sarpanch and the houses of Harijans are burnt. It creates tension in the village. Mishra comes to the site of arson, sheds crocodile tears and pretends to help the affected families. In the meantime, many villagers including the Harijans and Bhola are arrested by the police. But later on they release the villagers on bail except Harijans. Mishra again pretends to be the well-wisher of Harijans and gets them released on bail with a view to win their favour and weaken the milk movement. But Bhola understands this design of Mishra and reacts to it.

Meanwhile, events move fast. Bindu's husband suspects the character of his wife thinking she is having illicit relations with Dr. Rao. It leads to a quarrel between them and the husband stealthily poisons the milching buffalo of Bindu with a view to torture her and see that her membership with the Society terminates. The Sarpanch sends his men to the city with the instruction to approach the people there and secure the transfer of Dr. Rao from that place. Chandavarkar develops amorous relation with a Harijan girl that leads to her pregnancy for which she is humiliated and beaten up by her father. When Dr. Rao comes to know of it he immediately throws Chandavarkar out of the village. With the connivance of Mishra and cooperation of her husband a fraud is played upon Bindu and Dr. Rao. She is called to Mishra's place on the pretext of helping her to get a buffalo and made to put her thumb impression on a plain paper. Later, a lier goes to tell Dr. Rao that Bindu has brought a charge of rape against him. It shocks Dr. Rao and he reacts sharply by saying that it was a white lie and the story was concocted to malign him. At one stage, the lier tries to 'bribe' Dr. Rao by saying that Mishra feels sympathetic to him, the latter will exert pressure on Bindu to retract it, and that he wanted to compensate for the mental agony that Rao had suffered on this account. Rao thrashes the lier with anger and asks him to get out. This development makes Dr. Rao dejected and indifferent to the work of his mission. In the meantime, Dr. Rao gets a telegram from head office of his transfer. It makes him happy and he feels a sigh of relief. He breaks this good news to his wife, Shanta, who is living for sometime with him in the village. He goes to meet Bindu for a moment before his final departure from the village but her husband does not allow him to do so and Bindu who is standing there, sobs. Dr. Rao leaves for the station. When Bhola comes to know of it he runs towards the station to meet Dr. Rao but the train steams off and he could not meet Rao. Now Mishra's men who had reduced the buying rate of milk to compete with the newly formed Society, raises the price of milk and the crowd of villagers with their milk including Moti, go to this booth of Mishra to sell their milk in sheer dejection thinking that the Society's folk have gone back. Bhola exhorts them by saying that they can run the Society themselves if they stand together. Gradually one by one the villagers join Bhola and Moti and walk up to the Society's Collection counter. The film ends here.

The Setting

The film has been shot in a real village of Gujrat and sponsored by 5,00,000 farmers of the Gujrat Cooperative Milk Marketing Federation, every farmer donating two rupees. Gujrat is one of the States where milk movement through cooperatives is working on an intensive basis and the situation depicted in the film bears credibility. The fact of sponsorship by five lakh farmers further substantiates it, for the simple farmers are not likely to get involved in a thing which is pure fiction. As the film has been shot on actual location, no artificial sets except probably those shown in the scene of arson, have been used. The story or the film-script which is well-knit and developed after actual field-work in the area, provides a real and convincing setting in which the characters operate.

The Acting

Manthan is a new-wave and small budget film having actors and actresses who are associated with such film movement. They are well known for their natural and lively acting free from dramatic elements. Besides, their costumes and get-up are such that give us an impression as if they are part and parcel of the local milieu and real characters.

Presentation of Film

Presentation of the film is equally good and significant. Of the many aspects, the film depicts encounter of city people with rural folk and presents many typical things. When Chandavarkar arrives in the village for the first time he enquires about lavatory and feels puzzled to know that he has to go outside in the field. He sits at a few places in the open but always finds some people passing by. Everytime, he has to change the place. Being urban-bred he is a real misfit in the village and always finds a pretext to leave the village, either by saying that there were mosquitos and he was going to get malaria, that he encountered a man who looked like murderer, or something had stuck in his throat and he would get sick. He does not stop at that. He is irresponsible as well. He develops amorous relations with a village girl who is too simple and easily enamoured by Chandavarkar. Staring at Chandavarkar when a narrator was explaining about artificial insemination and abruptly bursting into laughter shows her immaturity, innocence and adolescence. She is sexually exploited by Chandavarkar with the result that she conceives. When her father comes to know of it, she is humiliated and viciously beaten up. Bhola informs Dr. Rao of it and complains that the city people take advantage of his women. His friend had promised to marry her and take her to the city. Bhola is himself reminded to his mother who also was similarly exploited by a city man. It was this reason which had made Bhola bitter and explained his rough and tough behaviour to Dr. Rao and his team at the initial stage. After Dr. Rao knows of the incident, he is filled with anger. He goes straight to Chandavarkar's room where he was sleeping in the night, violently drags him, asks to collect his luggage and leave the village immediately.

Suspicions in the mind of villagers under the background said above, seems to be deeply engrained. In one scene, Dr. Rao goes to the door of Bindu to collect milk samples. Milk is kept there in a pot and Dr. Rao asks some of it as sample. Bindu bluntly refuses and walks out of frame. But Rao is bent upon collecting the sample and he does it. Bindu sees it and runs behind Dr. Rao accusing that he was a 'thief' and 'stole' her milk. A crowd is collected and the people interrogate him by saying being an educated man how did he stoop to stealing? Bhola remarks: "You steal milk today, who knows what you will steal tomorrow? Why didn't you set your buffalo on him, Bindu? Why did you let him come near you?" It also gets reflected from the behaviour of Bindu's husband with Dr. Rao. He fails to understand that his wife was cooperating with Dr.

Rao in a noble mission, and looks at their relation with suspicion. He calls Dr. Rao "the educated bastard, running after our women" and objects to their meeting. In one shot he blurst out: "Bastard ! Son of a bitch. She is no better either. I warn you, you dare look at her once and I will smash your society."

This suscipion tells upon his conjugal life. In one sequence it is night time and after Bindu's small son is asleep, his husband stealthily creeps up to her and touches her. She jumps, sits back and says "Don't touch me, I hate you". The husband calls her a whore. It leads to a browl. Next morning the husband acts revengefully and mixes poison in the fodder of her milching buffalo so that the buffalo dies. It was through milk of the buffalo that Bindu was affiliated with the Milk Society.

The film presents some rare human feeling and emotion in an impressive style. Bindu has started cooperating with Dr. Rao. Once while Dr. Rao was coming on his Jeep, he comes across Bindu at a lonely place and gets down. He asks where she was going and she replies that her buffalo was lost as his car gave it a scare. They talk about Bhola, the Society, the Sarpanch and move ahead. At one place while Dr. Rao stumbles, he keeps his balance by holding on to her arm. Bindu sits down at the mouth of a water-pipe innocently exposing her legs right up to the knees washing them casually while doing the talking. Dr. Rao looks intensely on her legs. Abruptly, Bindu asks if Dr. Rao had children. He replies in negative. Then she asks if he was married and his wife was beautiful? Dr. Rao sidetracks the question and asks as to where her buffalo had gone and did it vanish like this quite often. Bindu's mood gets a jolt and she sharply reacts : "It will come back, Saheb. You can go". This sequence subtly reflects the tender feelings of Bindu for Dr. Rao and probably also the latter's platonic attraction for Bindu with whom he had become close by that time. Next is the sequence when after Dr. Rao received his transfer order, goes to Bindu's house to say final good-bye. He comes across her husband to whom he says: "I am leaving the village today. I wanted to see Bindu for a moment before I went........". But the latter curtly says: "Bindu's not here. She is gone". He further remarks, "The great Lord himself comes and asks for Bindu." Dr. Rao goes out of shot, Bindu is seen sobbing against the wall who was already listening to the talk before the two. In another sequence, when Bhola comes to know that Dr. Rao had been transferred and left the village for station on way to the city, he runs to the station to meet Dr. Rao. He runs and runs but by the time reaches the station, the train steams off and he could not meet Dr. Rao.

Mishra's portrayal is that of a real exploiter and hypocrite. He tells Dr. Rao that it is he who had built the economy of that area. Ganganath dairy is his personal property. Bindu thinks that Mishra is a two-faced liar and cheats them. He pays less and less and asks them to come back next day for the price. He does not like the Harijans and other villagers to unite and form the Cooperative Society. He is an opportunist. He makes the buying rate of milk higher when the milk cooperative is formed and reduces it after Dr. Rao leaves the village. It was he who had burnt the houses of Harijans, through his henchmen. But thenceafter, posed himself to be the well-wisher of the villagers. When he visits the village settlement after arson, he is shown touching his ears, shaking his head and folding his hands as soon he alights from his car. Further, he is shown distributing clothes and packets to the homeless victims of fire. In another sequence, while Mishra is sitting among the victim women, he is seen dialling his telephone to the police official saying that he was prepared to stand bail for them. Subsequently, he 'welcomes back' these people including Moti, the Chairman of the Milk Cooperative. Mishra personally comes to raise Moti where he had been sitting on floor and takes him up to a chair. Bhola disapproves all this and understands this hypocrisy of Mishra.

While welcoming the villagers, Mishra speaks: "My dear brothers and sisters, you must have forgotton the old ties that have bound us together. But I haven't forgotten them. You know a true friend only at a point of crisis...........your sufferings have touched my heart. I think, I have a claim to a share in your joys and miseries. (At this stage a child weeps aloud and does not stop which interrupts Mishra's address and which symbolically shows the hypocrisy and hollowness of Mishra). You, all those whose houses have been burnt down, are requested to get their names registered at my office. I will try to help them the best I can.........All of you came under the influence of the city folk. But I won't hold that against you. For children will always make mistakes........and it is for the elders to overlook their lapses. For now you are wise enough to distinguish between the milk and the water, the genuine and the spurious." Bhola who does not tolerate the hypocritic words, interrupts by saying, "Are we here to listen to all this nonsense? He will give us money now, only to keep us in his clutches". But Mishra replies, "What are you saying? Have a little patience. Give it some thought. Anger is bad for health. Whatever I am saying now, remember that I have brought your welfare in mind. I speak with goodwill, for our relationship goes back to a hoary past." Bhola still challenges: "He will destroy the society". But the villagers' mind had been changed by that time. A villager says: "What have the Society folk done for us? It's Mishraji who got us free......" Another voice says "What's wrong with somebody giving loans?"

Similarly, at another occasion Mishra welcomes Bindu at his place addressing her time and again, "Sister Bindu". Further he says: "I am told you are in a bad state these days. Your man has left you. Your buffalo's dead. Why didn't you tell me? You know how concerned I am for all of you. It is my duty to stand by you". It is this sequence in which Mishra obtains her thumb impression on a plain paper in the presence of a lawyer and her husband, and later fabricates a charge of rape on Bindu by Dr. Rao.

The story has many other similar sequences and dialogues that reflect village politics, interrelations, high-handedness of the Sarpanch, resistant attitude of villagers, efforts to form the milk cooperative, village intrigues and so on which give us a deep insight into the working of Indian village as such.

Dialogues given in the text (within commas or otherwise) are relevant and develop the film. The editing is smooth and Govind Nihlani, the photographer, is renowned and makes a good job. The style of the story is realistic.

The Music

The film has a theme song containing meaningful lyric suited to the script sung in a folk song style that bursts forth in the opening shot showing Railway track and platform with rural surroundings simultaneously showing the credits on screen. This song which is most befitting to the theme and the total set up and conveys the profuse availability of milk and natural charm of the village, runs as follows:

My village on the river bank
With its rivers of milk
and the birds singing
You must visit our home
Hey, you must visit our home (Repeat)
My village is a whirl of fun
With peacocks dancing in glee
and milk flowing in streams
and cows grazing
under the shades of the peepal.
O come to our village, dear.
O come, come, come to our village
the finest village of all,
Hold it in mind, dear,
you must visit our home,
Hey, you must visit our home.
Stop for a spell in our village,
O Stranger,
O Stranger, Stranger, Stranger.

A few lines of the same theme song with variations of lines are repeated five other times in various sequences showing Bindu, Dr. Rao, or when Dr. Rao goes to meet Bindu before finally leaving the village and the husband refuses to allow her to meet Dr. Rao, and the last few shots when Dr. Rao is waiting for the train on platform, Bhola runs for the station, and villagers with pots full of milk first crowd before Mishra's dairy counter and then gradually moves to the Society's collection counter. The song makes the visual effect all the more impressive. Some other lines of the theme song are as follows:

I gaze on the path that should bring you,
My days and nights unending.
Who's there to cry my heart out to?
Oh, I am done up.
I no longer go to milk the cow
I no longer go to the well for water
I know neither peace nor rest.
Hey, you must visit our house.

The Message

The film is forward looking and communicates a significant message which is of topical interest at the present juncture of time. Till independence of the country, rural and illiterate section of the society remained neglected and exploited. It was more so with the Harijans. They suffered from social disabilities and were looked down upon by higher castes. Sharma and Sarpanch symbolize the group of exploiters who want to keep the Harijans under heels by crooked means and inspire fear so that the latter could never get united and raise their head. The film conveys the message of unity among the poor and expoited section of population and makes them cautious against their exploiters who have many evil designs and are always on the lookout to 'divide' and weaken the people so that they could serve their own vested interest. Though the film depicts the story of a particular village in the specific context of Milk Cooperative Society, it has deeper underlying meaning. The message it conveys has relevance to our whole countrymen and people in all walks of life. The film also depicts impediments coming in the way of developmental process and that there comes a time when those connected with development activities have to face grim situations and feel seriously discouraged. They are faced with serious limitations, but the initiative to improve the lot always rests with the people themselves.

The Three Criteria

Now the above points or the totality of the film may be assessed in the light of three criteria given below:

Confirmity to Traditional Values, Norms and Standards

By and large, the script of the film shows traditional situation and circumstances prevailing in the village viz., caste feelings between clean and unclean castes, caste dominance of upper caste, meek submisison and fear of the Harijans from higher caste to which Sarpanch belongs, economic exploitation of the poor Harijans by Sharma, feuds and factions, evil designs of Sarpanch when he gets Bhola arrested for his alleged aggresive behaviour or when their henchmen put the huts of Harijans on fire. The rural folks by and large do not have the awareness that they are being exploited. They feel that Sharma helps them during needs, or may it be the feeling of helplessness even though they are aware of it, initial resistance to developmental programmes, suspicious attitude towards people coming from city and that they corrupt village women, all conform to traditional values, norms and standards from the standpoint of villagers. Similarly, the setting, acting of characters, presentation, as well as music also conform to or match the traditional standard of an Indian village. The message of the film as elaborated above makes a departure from traditionality and infuses a sense of modernity for the betterment of the village community as envisaged by Government. This refers to the emerging reality.

Naturality

The turn of events depicted in the story of the film have a natural flow. The setting, acting of characters, presentation and music also fulfil this criterion. The message, in the background of the theme and the story of the film, looking from human angle, seems to be the most natural outcome.

Sexual indulgence with young Harijan girl, or Chandavarkar who is in the position of a responsible member of the team of Dr. Rao, may seem to be somewhat unnatural, but, he is city-bred—who looks at village life in a special perspective, a *junior employee* and a misfit to his job as reflected from the few pretexts that he makes to go back to the city. Looking from this angle, the incident may not be considered to be unnatural.

Justification

The story of the film is realistic, logical and justifiable. It is well-knit and does not seem to have marked superfluous elements.

Summary Observations

The film does not intend to present a systematic picture of rural life in Gujrat. But mainly speaking, it makes a problem-oriented study and is of adequate sociological and applied interest. However, it does present to us many important glimpses of Indian rural life and village organization, and tells what happens when there is an encounter with the outside world.

It tells us about caste dominance, caste politics, politics of violence, village factions, conditions of Harijans and their persecution at the hands of higher and dominant castes to serve their own vested interest. The Harijans who constitute the majority, suffer from fear complex and do not dare to stand against the Sarpanch when election for the chairmanship of milk cooperative takes place. It was only after Dr. Rao educates them on this point that they are ready to contest the election.

Sharma who owns a private dairy farm and economically exploits the villagers is known as a cheat but people have no courage to defy him. Sharma is selfish and hypocrite, combines with the headman who has lost the election, plays fraud with Bindu and Rao, harasses and persecutes the Harijans in several ways and still wants to impress them that he was their well-wisher so that the people may not get rid of his clutches. Sharma detests the efforts of opening the milk cooperative in the village which will affect his interest and that is why plays all kinds of prank to futile this effort.

The headman who is dissatisfied, also on his own level tries to throw out Rao from the village and ultimately succeeds.

The villagers, specially the Harijans are biased with the team workers who are city people and look at their activities with suspicion. They have a definite reason for it. Bhola's mother was sexually exploited by a contractor coming from the city and he was born out of this illicit union. The same thing was repeated by Chandavarkar who is consequently thrown out by Rao for his bad act. On the other hand, Chandavarkar's behaviour specially his romance with the Harijan girl symbolizes some city people's attitude towards rural folk. The lavatory sequence and his other pretexts speak that he was insincere, irresponsible, and failed to adjust himself in the village.

The film presents some intimate glimpses of village election and things that go behind it. The dialogues that go on between the headman and Dr. Rao at the time of election clearly spells it out. After the result of election is announced and the headman is defeated, the latter says: "Doctor, Doctor, this can't be. This just cannot be. I have never lost an election in my life till now. You have razed my reputation to the ground. You don't know me, Doctor. The big leaders have come here to canvass for me when I stood for the Panchayat elections. And now for this joke of a Society of yours, you have dragged me into disgrace. But.......in the village it's the Panchayat that is supreme. You know very well that your

Society cannot take over its functions. Arrange the draw again and this time I must win", Dr. Rao tells him that it would be against the law. At it, the headman exclaims "The law? What law? Forget it. Just for once announce that I've won. I'll resign voluntarily immediately, I promise you." Dr. Rao again expressed his helplessness. The headman retorts "If I had known, I wouldn't have contested. You have brought my village into disrepute. I'll see to it that your tricks don't work here. They won't work here." It depicts a clash of ego, prestige value, canvassing, politics of power, threat, revenge and all that which constitute typical features that get free play in village elections in our country.

The film is informative and gives us a lot of informations on the objectives and functioning of Milk Cooperative Society, conservatism of the rural folk and resistance to change, orthodox values so far mixing of men and women is concerned, and generational gap in attitude towards development that gets reflected in the dialogues that go on between Mahapatra and Sharma on the issue of opening the milk cooperative in the village.

On the whole, the film makes a vivid case-study of a specific developmental programme in a rural setting of the country and acquaints us with typical problems that come in its way, moments of frustration, failure and success, aspirations of people, leadership and all that which give us a deeper insight into the understanding of development process in the Indian rural society in general.

(ii) ADMI AUR AURAT

Background Information

Main Artists	*Characters in Film*
Amol Palekar	Bansi (Male Traveller)
Mahua Roychoudhury	Aurat (Female Fellow Traveller)
Produced by	Doordarshan, India's National T.V. Network

Photography	Kamal Naik
Running time	One hour
Film completed	1984 (13 days of shooting)

Selection of Film

Theme

When Tapn Sinha, the Director of the film was asked to make one hour long featurette for *Doordarshan* which an estimated four crore of people were expected to watch, the theme that he chose to depict was human endurance for that was something universal. The film was "a moving human story told in an unusually tense, taut and yet warm style. With no frills at all, it follows the course of a journey relentlessly, and lets the strain and concern of the journey itself change the characters in a subtle metamorphosis" (Bandhopadhyay, 1986 : 69).

Distinct and Corncrete Aspect of Life

The film focusses on finest sentiment of compassion and human love for those in distress above all mundane considerations.

Literary Work of Quality

The story of the film is by Prafulla Roy while its script and dialogue have been written by Tapan Sinha, the director of the film himself. It is a literary work of quality with well constructed story and characters.

Award Winning Film

The film was honoured with a National Award for its contribution to the cause of national integration.

Acquisition of Film

As the film is commissioned and produced by Doordarshan, it is naturally acquired by it.

The Film maker

Tapan Sinha is a renowned director of West Bengal well known for his many realistic and off-beat films which won many laurels to him.

Analysis

The Script

The story of the film focusses on a single event of life i.e., a man and a sick woman, unknown to each other set off on a course of journey from a rural area to a neighbouring small town, and depicts something lofty that happens on the way.

The film starts with the opening scene of a highway in a village of Bihar where a few villagers are waiting for a bus that could take them to Vakilganj, a neighbouring small town. Black clouds are looming in the sky and there is a possibility of rain, the place being surrounded by hills and forests. A young woman who is in her advanced stage of pregnancy (discovered later on), is also seen sitting among the passengers with *Sari* covering her body completely and anxiety writ large on her face. Several trucks pass in a row and then a bus comes but it is so crowded that the woman fails to board it in spite of her frantic efforts. She and few other villagers who also could not get into the bus, decide to go on foot through a short cut way that passes through fields, jungles and vunerable hills—some part of it infested with robbers and wild animals. The young woman who looks despairingly at the surrounding hills, gets off with a bundle in her hand.

On the way, a man known as Bansi, who looks like a ruffian and shown keeping such things like *bhoojali* (sharp weapon), knife, and a few yards of rope in his bag, also leaves for Vakilganj. From the talks that go on between Bansi and other wayfarers, it is obvious that Bansi runs after young girls, he is a dubious character and a poacher. At one place a young girl 'invites' him from a bush and he promises to go to her next day. Presently, he is going to Ragunath Singh of Vakilganj, a wealthy man, to assist him in a hunting expedition.

The journey is difficult and other fellow travellers who follow her one by one go ahead. At one stage it starts raining. The young woman falls behind. When she comes across Bansi, the latter takes causal interest, stares at her and smiles. The woman feels apprehensive and rearranges her clothes in proper order. Gradually, Bansi comes to know that she was physically 'indisposed' owing to pregnancy and was going all alone. Bansi feels slightly concerned and asks the fellow travellers not to part company with her as she was falling behind. But they are in a hurry. The scenes that follow, show the woman steadily becoming more and more weak who finds the journey much arduous and exhausting. Bansi helps her in many ways, bucks her up and narrates stories and incidents of robbery and his own hunting expeditions etc. to divert her attention. But the woman gets gradually weaker and more than once, collapses. Bansi helps her and checks her fall holding her tightly. The women who was so long careful and particular to arrange her clothes properly, gets dishevelled and disorganized. The sense of distance between the two under the circumstances, gets dissolved. She, out of breath, pants and groans from the pain in stomach.

The film uses two flashbacks and shows that the young woman had lost her child and was taken seriously ill at its birth. Her husband felt much worried on knowing that she had conceived for the second time. But this time he had decided to send her to a hospital at Vakilganj. The woman had expected her husband to accompany her as she was in her advanced stage of pregnancy. But he just gave her forty rupees and a letter of village headman in the name of the doctor of the hospital and asked her to go alone by bus. The woman had set off on this journey reluctantly in a tense and worried mood.

After going to some distance, the young woman groans in pain till she cannot walk any logner. Bansi shakes her vigorously and drags her along. But she faints. Bansi feels nervous. He shakes her and shouts but the woman does not respond. He now drops her gently on the muddy ground. It has started raining again. Bansi, panting, sits down beside her and covers her up properly with her *Sari*. The young woman slowly opens her eyes and says that she cannot walk any more. Now Bansi lifts the woman, carries her along but after a distance finds it too much and sinks to the ground gasping, the woman resting against him. The pain starts again and the woman moans. Bansi holds her hand tightly. The woman says, "Hey, man, don't leave me alone."

Bansi makes a bamboo cart without wheels. He lifts her gently and places on the cart. He keeps his bag under her hips and starts pulling at the cart. As the cart has no wheels, Bansi has to strain to his utmost to make it move with the young woman on it. He has to bend double to pull the cart. The young woman holds her stomach with hands, her eyes shut. Bansi pulls desperately and asks the woman to chat and keep awake. He does bits of chatting narrating his own events of life. After going some distance Bansi finds that the woman was lifeless. He shakes her vigorously, puts his ear to her chest, panics and shouts "Hey woman, hey......" The young woman folds her knees and starts crying in pain. Bansi in sheer desperation runs here and there in the forest shouting for help. He finds a forest-guard who suspiciously looks at him and tiasks whether he was there in the forest for poaching. Bansi explains the situation and the two persons carry the bamboo cart up to a distance. Then the forest-guard leaves by saying that he was to go on duty. Bansi finds himself standing before a hill rivulet which blocks the way flowing with a strong current from the rain water.

Bansi now holding the woman to his chest pleads with her to get strong and get up as they have to cross the rivulet. He binds her to himself with a rope and moves towards the stream. Bansi struggles hard with the rushing water and carries the young woman through. He stumbles and falls on the way several times, but manages to recover every time. At one point the woman is drifted away by the current but Bansi pulls her and places her on his back and carries her along. He says, "Think of the baby that's coming........Times are changing. That child of yours will bring a new light to the world......Come, show a little strength." Struggling frantically with the swirling water, ultimately, he reachs the other bank with the young woman.

Bansi finds a bullock cart on which he places the woman and it speeds up. The jerk hurts her. She bites her lips, her face twisted with pain. After sometime they reach the hospital and the woman is placed on a bench. Bansi pleads the clerk over there to admit her fast as she was going to deliver a baby and there was not much time left. But the clerk informs that no bed was vacant. Bansi loses control over himself. In a flash he lifts the clerk up by his neck and goes on threatening him, drawing out a sharp weapon from his bag at one point. Bansi shouts, "I have carried this woman on my shoulder for ten miles across hills and woods, and now, you son of a pig, you tell me you don't have a bed for her. Isn't the hospital for poor folk like us or is it for your father? You tell me. Tell me, you bastard, or I will tear your heart out". The Doctor rushes there and intervenes. The woman receives immediate attention and she is taken to labour room.

In the meantime Bansi goes to meet Raghunath Singh who postpones the hunting programme as he was going to Patna and asks Bansi to stay over there and return the next morning.

Next morning Bansi goes to the hospital and meets the Doctor. The latter directs him to the woman who has already delivered the child. Bansi enters the ward where the woman was lying with her new child. She looks at Bansi with a tired smile and shows her child. Bansi says that he would be going back to his village and in the way he would pass by her village. He may carry any message to her husband. For this purpose Bansi asks the name of her husband. "Anwar Hussain", the young woman replies. "It takes Bansi some discomfiture and sometime to get used to the idea that it was a Muslim woman he had been carrying. He had never imagined that she could be a Muslim woman". The woman gives some landmark of her house. Bansi is to leave the place. The young woman raises her both hands while lying and says, "I will pray to *Allah* for you and ask for His blessings". Bansi smiles and leaves. The young woman keeps looking in that direction for a while, then she looks away. The film ends.

The Setting

The whole film has been shot on actual locations: the village, forests, hills, place of a hunter and hospital.

The Acting

Acting of the two main characters, Bansi and the young woman is convincing and their get ups also look appropriate to the milieu and the characters of the script.

The Presentation

Dialogue is simple and in tune with the story. Photography has a scenic beauty in rural areas, hillocks, forest and rivulet. Elements of suspense, pathos, benevolence, sincerity, reaction, and integration have beautiful editings and keep us engrossed till the last.

The Music

The film has no song. However, there is a simple music.

The Message

The film gives a very important message relevant to our society. Ours is a composite society with different ethnic and religious groups. In actual life, there appears to be a schism among these groups the manifestation of which ranges from indifference to marked animosity and conflict. Under this background a man and a woman quite unknown to each other, who are off to a common destination get unusually close to one another under exigency of the situation. The woman is initially apprehensive of Bansi, apparently looking like a ruffian. On the other hand, the man did have the reputation of chaser of young woman and initially might have romantically felt inclined towards this woman. But the situation changes. The woman in course of the journey gradually weakens, moans in pain, collapses, faints and becomes immobile. It rouses humanly feelings in Bansi. He identifies himself with the sufferings of the woman who is utterly helpless and lonely. He does his utmost and leaves no stone unturned to carry the woman to Vakilganj in spite of all hurdles—quite oblivious to the fact who she was and to which background did she belong. For him, she was just a human being in distress who was to be helped by all means. He even goes to the extent of assaulting the clerk when the latter tells him that there was no seat in the hospital. As on the part of the woman, as she gradually becomes more and more sick and weak, becomes mentally and physically completely dependent on the stranger forgetting to care her clothes, or any other inhibitions that is natural between a woman and an unknown man. At one stage she pleads the man not to leave her behind. It is only in the hospital when the man comes to know that the woman was a Muslim, that he is 'apparently shocked' for a moment but recomposes himself and smiles. The scene when the man is about to leave the hospital for his village and the woman says that she will pray to *Allah* for him, is touching. In all, the film enacts a human situation which belongs to the realm of ideal and the highest human value which constitute a part of Indian cultural heritage. Besides, the film contains the message of human endurance, and social integration so much needed at the present moment of time.

The Three Criteria

Conformity to Traditional Standards

This point does not have much relevance except the fact that it is not unusual for the village folks to cover the distance of ten miles or so on foot. Initially, the young woman, like any other Indian woman is shy and has traditional inhibitions while interacitng with a male stranger. But the circumstnaces under which she comes close to Bansi is exceptional and cannot be judged by a fixed standard. Rather, helping a woman under the circumstances depicted in film reflects greater traditional concern of rural people for those in distress in contrast to many city people. The film conforms to the traditional Indian values of compassion and *'manav dharma'*.

Naturality

The film seems to have some dramatic element when it initially creates the impression of Bansi as a cruel, dubious person and a debauche who later proves to be a man so magnanimous and exemplary. However, if it intends to convey that a 'bad man' also under certain circumstances becomes gentle and kind hearted, it is also not unnatural. A wife in her advanced stage of pregnancy is advised by her husband to go to the neighbnouring small town by bus all alone, seems somewhat unnatural for many of us, though from the point of view of lower strata of people, negligence of wife may not be an uncommon phenomena. However, this fact could have been made explicit in the film. He could have been shown at least securing her a seat in the bus. Carrying a pregnant woman on a make-shift bamboo cart without wheels in a hilly and forested area even for a kilometre does not sound very natural. And even after such great physical strains and exertions which the young woman undergoes on her way to hospital, she delivers a normal child, may be a matter of surprise.

Justification

So far main thrust of the film is concerned, it is justifiable and realistic. The film is well-knit and it does not have superficial graftings.

Sumamry Observations

The film as a whole depicts a brilliant human situation and makes an important psychological study. It conveys the message of human values that are above all other considerations. It has significant bearings on social and national integration so relevant to our present day society.

The film reflects a negligent attitude of certain lower section of people towards women. In the film, the wife who is in her advanced month of pregrancy, is left on her own to go to the neighbouring small town. But it may be a way of life for such rural folk.

It also makes a brief hint to the ill treatment meted to the poor people in institutions like hospital and an attitude of negligence towards them. At times one has to fight for it as Bansi did it.

Continuity of the feudal tradition in the form of hunting, and poaching has been also pointed out even though there are forest guards to prevent it.

NOTES

1. A film media is different from conventional anthropological study. In the latter case, all the points of observation are substantially dealt with in writing. But in case of film, the researcher is expected to elaborate the 'spirit' and 'meaning' of a scene or sequence which may comparatively appear briefly on the screen. A smaller shot may not necessarily diminish its significance.
2. The first point (script) covers the story and arrangement of events. The second i.e., setting, relates to the surroundings, sets, environment or the total milieu in which the characters operate. Acting, besides proper acting itself will include costumes and get-up of actors and actresses. Presentation of the film will include photography, editing, dialogues and the style in which the story is presented. Music will include the lyric and songs relevant to the film. Lastly, the message will include the moral of the story, symbolism, underlying meaning or whatever the story intends to communicate to the audience. One may also think whether or not the film contains any message, and if there is one, it is explicit or implicit.

   Some of the several points mentioned above may be somewhat 'technical' connected with film-making. But the Visual Anthropologist interested in the analysis of fiction films must become aware of the different aspects of film-making and develop it.
3. One has to find out whether these criteria are met with or are absent in a film with reference to the society or culture the film projects. The first criterion is the 'conformity to traditional values, norms and standards'. It implies to which extent the components of the film or the totality convey, conform to or deviate from the traditional values, norms and standards prevalent in the culture or society to which the story relates. If one finds deviation, whether or not the film conforms to emergent realities of the society. The second criterion is 'naturality' and one has to see as to what extent the element of naturality gets reflected in the

film. 'Justification' is the third criterion which will help us to check superfluous elements grafted in the film that are not well integrated and illogical to the total context.

4. The same procedure for selection of fiction films mentioned above, need to be generally followed for the analysis of T.V. serials and Tele-films. Further, the methodology of analysing Indian films developed here, may also be relevant universally with minor modifications.

REFERENCES CITED

Bandhopadhyay, Samik, 1986: Introduction to Admi aur Aurat (A Man and a Woman), The Complete Film Script in *Splice*, July, page 69.

Sahay, K.N., 1986: "Visual Anthropology and Indian Fiction Films" in *Journal of Social Research*, Vol. 30, March-September, pp. 1-41.

Sinha, Tapan, 1986: Admi aur Aurat (A Man and a Woman), The complete film Script, in *Splice*, July, pp. 69-79.

Tendulkar, Vijay, 1984: Shyam Benegal's The Churning (Manthan), Screenplay, Script reconstructed and translated by Samik Bandhopadhyay, Seagull Books, Calcutta.

Weakland, J.H., 1972: Conflict between Love and Family relationship in Chinese films, *Journal of Popular Film*, 1 : 290-298.

1975: Feature Films as Cultural Documents, Principle of Visual Anthropology, Paul Hockings (Ed.), Mouton Publishers, The Hague.

Wolfenstein, Martha and Leites, N., 1950: Movies: A Psychological Study, The Free Press, Glencoe.

PART - TWO

Chapter VII

The First International Symposium on Visual Anthropology at New Delhi*

A Symposium on Visual Anthropology, sponsored by the Commission on Visual Anthropology, I.U.A.E.S. (1973-78) was held at the National Council of Educational Research and Training, Ring Road, New Delhi, on December 7-9 and 11 & 13, 1978. Participants came from 10 different countries Japan, Korea, Tunisia, Australia, France, Austria, The Federal Republic of Germany, Canada, and the U.S.A. as well as India. Originally, the Symposium was to last three days, but the participants found it so useful that it was extended for two days more. A total number of 20 Abstracts of papers were received and circulated among the participants. Selected papers of this Symposium would be published in book form in near future.

In addition to the Symposium, there was a screening of some three dozen enthnographic films for participants in the Xth ICAES; Marielle Delorme of Paris organized this programme on behalf of the Commission.

This Symposium consisted of seven sessions as given below. A meeting of the Commission was also held.

Opening Session (December 7, 1978)

1. Welcome and Address— Dr. K.N. Sahay, India

2. Tribute to Late Margaret Mead—Miss Yasuko Ichioka, Japan

---

* This proceeding is based on *Visual Anthropology Bulletin*, Volume 1, No. 1, June, 1979, Pp. 3-6 and *Current Anthropology* (Newsletter), Volume 21. No. 2, April, 1980, Pp. 271-73.

3. 'Portrait of a Friend: Dr. Margaret Mead' (Film) —Dr. Jean Rouch, France

History of Ethnographic Films (December 8, 1978)

1. A Brief History of Ethnographic Films in Korea—Dr. Duhyun Lee, Korea

2. L' Anthropologie Visuelle in Afrique du Nord (Visual Anthropology in North Africa)—Dr. Sophie Ferchiou, Tunisia

3. A History of Ethnographic Films in India—Dr. K.N. Sahay, India.

Use of Films in Teaching & Research (December 8, 1978)

1. Programme Development of the National Anthropological Film Centre—Miss Gay C. Neuberger, U.S.A.

2. Phenomenological Data in Human Understanding—Dr. E. Richard Sorenson, U.S.A.

New Trends in Visual Anthropology (December 9, 1978)

1. The Development of Ethnographic Film by Videotheque in Museum—Dr. Yasuhiro Omori, Japan.

2. Mechanical Maps: The Problem of Presentational Form—Dr. Roger Sandall, Australia

Fiction Films and Anthropology (December 9, 1978)

1. An Approach to the Study of Refugee Society through Fiction Films with Illustrations from Films of Ritwick Ghatak—Dr. Durgadas Mukhopadhyay, India

Urgent Need in Visual Anthropology (December 11, 1978)

1. A Note by Dr. Anna Hohenwart-Gerlachstein, Austria

Future of Visual Anthropology (December 11, 1978)

1. A Note by Dr. K.N. Sahay, India

Meeting of the Commission on Visual Anthropology, IUAES, 1973-78 (December 13, 1978).

Apart from these sessions, 28 films were screened and thoroughly discussed. The opening session was chaired by Dr. Masao Oka of Japan and Dr. K.N. Sahay of India (Chairman and Co-Chairman of the Commission, respectively), and the next four sessions and the film screenings were chaired by Dr. Jean Rouch of the Musee de l'Homme, Paris. The sessions on urgent needs, and the future were chaired by Dr. Roger Sandall of Australia and Dr. E. Richard Sorenson of the U.S.A. respectively. A meeting of the Commission was held on December 13.

The opening session started with a welcome address by K.N. Sahay in which he described the aims of the commission, its activities and the progress made since its last meeting in February 1977. That meeting had discussed cooperation with other organizations connected with ethnographic films, financial support, a catalogue of bibliographies on ethnographic films, the production of films on themes especially relating to Third World countries like India, and a symposium at the Xth ICAES. Of a number of international and Indian agencies approached for funding, only the Finance Committee of the IUAES was able to grant a modest sum to help organize the symposium. It was found that nearly two dozen organizations throughout the world had prepared indices of ethnographic films. Under the circumstances, what seemed most needed was a bibliography of such indices. Rouch was requested to undertake this task through his institution, while Junichi Ushiyama of Tokyo was requested to prepare an index of ethnographic films on Asia and Oceania. Anna Hohenwart-Gerlachstein of Vienna argued for cooperation with the Commission on Urgent Anthropology, of which she is the chairman. The commission also took up with the officials concerned the matter of the proper preservation of the valuable ethnographic films of the Anthropological Survey of India. Sahay then mentioned the death of Margaret Mead, who had been a member of the commission and had promised an opening paper and participation in the symposium. He pointed out that she had been one of the pioneers of Visual Anthropology and had given him the benefit of her wise counsel. Yasuko Ichioka of Japan spoke of the achievements of Margaret Mead in the field of Visual Anthropology and offered condolences on behalf of the commission and participants in the symposium. This was followed by a film on Mead's life by Rouch, who explained its background and offered his own tribute to Mead.

In the session History of Ethnographic Films, Duhyun Lee reported on the history of ethnographic films in Koera. He said that film was introduced to Korea by a Japanese in 1904. Korea's first documentary, *Overview of Seoul,* and its first entertainment film, *Fights for Justice,* were made in 1918. Since these films, hundreds of movies have been made by and for Koreans. Under Japanese rule, however, only entertainment films were made, and films stressing Korean culture were forbidden. After the liberation from Japan in 1945, Koreans began making ethnographic films to preserve and transmit Korean culture to coming generations. The history of ethnographic films proper begins only at this time. Lee showed two of the films referred to in his paper.

Sophie Ferchiou of Tunisia, in her paper "Visual Anthropology in North Africa", said that, as in the Third World countries in general, the North African countries are more concerned with problems of national independence and economic development than with their cultural identity and safeguarding their heritage. The young North African cinema aims at being politically committed and avant-garde and turns its back completely on the traditional past. Ferchiou further said that ethnographic films as they are conceived in the West, particularly in France, are rare in North Africa, but the history of Visual Anthropology would be incomplete if one were to content oneself with an inventory of so-called ethnographic films. There is a kind of cinematographic production which, without any scientific intention, supplies rich materials to Visual Anthropology. Taking these materials into consideration, one will have to find a new definition for the ethnographic film, one better adapted to the situation in North Africa and the Third World in general.

Sahay, in "A History of Ethnographic Films in India", said that Indian cinema began in 1896, when the Lumire Brothers of France showed a number of films to the people of Bombay. The earliest known Indian film of any ethnographic value was *The Wrestlers*, produced and screened in 1897 by H.S. Bhatvadekar. Some of the short films produced by foreign and Indian agencies presented glimpses of native life and culture in India. A systematic and meaningful approach to ethnographic films did not begin, however, until India gained freedom in 1947, when a national government was formed and an urgent need was felt by that government to project the rich cultural heritage of India through the medium of documentary films. A government film division was established in 1948. Awards and recognition by national and international organizations have also attracted many talented Indians to produce some outstanding documentary or realistic fiction films of ethnographic interest. A number of documentary or ethnographic films have also been produced by anthropologists or other scholars from foreign universities who have done fieldwork in India or have been associated with courses on Asian studies. Burma-Shell Oil Company, the Anthropological Survey of India, and the tribal research institutes of the various States have also produced ethnographic films.

In the session "Use of Films in Teaching and Research", Gay C. Neuberger of the United States discussed the programme of the National Anthropological Film Centre at the Smithsonian Institution. She reported that the Center was founded to take advantage of the potential of film records as a tool of inquiry into vanishing and changing ways of life and culture. Since 1975, progress has been made in obtaining and preserving, as a permanent research resource, synchronous-sound film, records of human behaviour and social interaction in isolated and rapidly changing cultures. Some 600,000 feet of research footage is now housed in a temperature and humidity-controlled film vault especially designed for long-term preservation.

E. Richard Sorenson, in "Phenomenological Data in Human Understanding", said that what separates human science from natural science is that the subject of inquiry—the human condition—requires that humanity examine itself. When one people looks at the culture of another, an epistemological situation is created that cannot be divorced from human values. This takes us beyond the usual natural-science methodology. Because of this it is useful to obtain facsimiles of the phenomenological situation that go beyond the researcher's culturally patterned ability to identify, understand, perceive, or appreciate. The phenomenological data-gathering quality of film and tape provides a means to penetrate this cultural barrier. Sorenson substantiated his points with three ethnographic films, one of them shown with a slow and controlled-motion device.

In the session "New Trends in Visual Anthropology", Yasuhiro Omori of Japan spoke on the development of ethnographic film through "Videotheque" in museums. He said that the Japanese did not recognize the meaning of ethnology until the opening of the National Museum of Ethnology in November 1977. One of the most interesting exhibits, called "Videotheque", displayed films on the life and culture of different ethnic groups throughout the world in 37 viewing booths. Omori presented the results of questionnaires administered to more than 2,500 visitors six months after the opening of the museum. His paper was supported by a film on the National Museum.

Roger Sandall of Australia, in his paper "Mechanical Maps: The Problem of Presentational Form", posed the basic question "Is there any difference between 'a film' and 'footage'?" Though everyone knows the difference, often what is called a film is all too plainly footage. Sandall further observed that false names—"shots", "takes", and "scenes"—abound in the everyday vocabulary of film makers, a vocabulary inherited from other walks of life and no longer serving the purpose for which it was designed. This general problem, he said, was strikingly present in the field of what have come to be called "observational films." The established presentational forms had been narrative and dramatic: the new ones were not. Internally, at the structural level of the shot, they were identical with research films, and despite some atavistic straining in traditional directions the research model seemed to be gaining the upper hand. Sandall contended that "raw data", "footage", or uncut and unsullied archival material did have a form, but this form was not presentational. Rather, it was that of a map. Just as aerial photographs mapped geographical topography, the new technology, with its long camera runs and its ever deeper fields, mapped the topography of social action—each frame, each picture a coordinate of sorts, each intact shot having the unique descriptive accuracy of a continuously plotted representational field. He further stressed the importance of the diagram, which may be worth a thousand shots, and said that the task of explanation, which is central to presentational forms, is precisely what has been overlooked or underestimated.

The session "Fiction Films and Anthropology" attempted to explore the extent to which fiction films help viewers to understand the life and culture of a people. In his paper "An Approach to the Study of Refugee Society through Fiction Films, with Illustrations from the films of Ritwik Ghatak", Durgadas Mukhopadhyay of India presented a framework for the analysis of a refugee society based on eight feature films by a renowned film-maker from Bengal. Sahay opined that some fiction films, for example, those of Satyajit Ray, Shyam Benegal, and Mani Kaul, faithfully depicted the life of a certain element of Indian Society or certain aspects of Indian culture. Such films might well be considered valuable cultural documents. At the same time, he said, criteria will have to be developed for judging which films faithfully depict the culture if such films are to be used in the scientific study of the society. Sorenson remarked that he did not know why Visual Anthropology had so far neglected fiction films. Rouch said that the relation between fiction films and reality was very important, but reality in the presence of the camera is not the same as reality in its absence. Pierre Amado of France said that a film made on an aspect of culture might dilute reality.

During the session "Urgent Needs in Visual Anthropology", Sandall said that the topic confronted us with three problems—priorities, funding, and organization—but that tremendous contributions had been made in the past 15 years (notably by Ian Dunlop in Australia and others). Hohenwart-Gerlachstein stressed the need for training of anthropologists in film making; many communities are being filmed without producing much of scientific value. Rouch said that in France students of anthropology were being trained in Super-8 film-making and that Ph.D.'s were being awarded in anthropological film making. Sahay said that in speaking of Urgent Visual Anthropology we have to think not only in terms of filming the cultures of small-scale and "dying" communities, but also in terms of filming rapidly changing aspects of culture, covering geographical regions in which filming is not well developed, and preserving films already produced but in poor condition because of the lack of proper storage facilities. Rough agreed that the latter was a particularly important problem.

Sorenson raised the question whether film makers who lack any background in anthropology should be included in the field of Visual Anthropology; he felt, however, that all sources of ethnographic films should be explored. Sahay reiterated that any film that is a faithful record of a culture should be considered relevant, whatever the background of its maker, though criteria for judgment will have to be developed. Upadhayay asked whether Visual Anthropology was an independent discipline. He and Sandall argued that films should be accompanied by notes by anthropologists who are experts on the culture in question. Sahay and Engelbert Stiglmayr of Vienna agreed.

The session "The Future of Visual Anthropology" opened with some remarks by Sorenson on the use of computers in connection with the materials of the National Anthropological

Film Centre. Sahay then discussed the organizational aspects of planning for the future of Visual Anthropology. While many advanced and affluent nations had made remarkable progress in the field, he said, the Third World countries by and large had insufficient funds, facilities, and technical know-how to do so. It should be our urgent task, he argued, to see that local talent is encouraged and proper facilities, expertise, and funding are provided so that film makers in these countries can produce films from their own viewpoint and understanding of the cultural situation. Further, the organization of Visual Anthropology should become truly worldwide, with centres in all the major countries and even in smaller ones. Such centers could help create a pool of local talent and resources for concentrated effort in the field and also provide assistance and guidance to film makers from abroad. Though they might include persons from many different backgrounds, anthropologists should be in the majority. Such centres would assume real importance if they also served as clearinghouses for information on visual anthropology and disseminated that information through bulletins or journals. In addition, they could encourage research and experimentation in Visual Anthropology. They could also act as liaison between the government and film makers and take the steps necessary for the preservation of existing films. Finally, they could be affiliated with other centres in the region for intensive cooperation and mutual guidance and, beyond this, with a world body.

Rouch spoke of the technical and ethical aspects of the development of visual anthropology. On the technical side, he mentioned synchro-sound filming and the availability of sophisticated light-weight cameras. On the ethical side, he said that the problem was more than that of the duty to show the films to the people on whom they are based; their permission should be sought before showing the films to outsiders. There was general agreement on this point. Mukhopadhaya said that the question of ethics entered into the selection of themes as well, mentioning cases in which screens were destroyed and projectors confiscated by the audience on seeing a film that injured their feelings.

A Meeting of the Commission: A meeting of the Commission held on December 13, 1978 in the presence of Professor Masao Oka (Chairman), Dr. K.N. Sahay (Co-Chairman), Dr. Jean Rouch (Member), Dr. Anna Hohenwart-Gerlaschestein (Member), Mr. Junichi Ushiyama (Member), Miss Yasuko Ichioka (Member), a few invitees like Dr. E. Richard Sorenson, Dr. Roger Sandall, Dr. Pierre Stevens, and a number of observers. The following resolutions were adopted:

Whereas the increasingly rapid loss of cultural variety in the world has intensified the need to prepare permanent researchable illustrative records of vanishing ways of life and culture; and

Whereas the visual potential of film makers is well suited to presenting and preserving multicultural viewpoints in records of human heritage; and

Whereas humanistic film studies heighten national and international awareness of the needs of ethnic groups by presenting in accessible and understandable form information vital to their social, cultural, and political life;

For these reasons it was resolved:

1. That the Resolution on Visual Anthropology passed at the IXth International Congress of Anthropological and Ethnological Sciences, Chicago, September, 1973, be hereby reaffirmed and emphasized.

2. That film studies be undertaken which go beyond the particular belief system of a single culture to present multicultural viewpoints.

3. That new kinds of humanistically oriented centres be created to take advantage of the multicultural potential of the visual media for furthering human understanding.

4. That the technologically advanced nations be encouraged to lend resources, training, and effort to developing nations, particularly those with broad independent cultural traditions, to develop local talent and expertise in Visual Anthropology.

5. That, since much of anthropology is in the Western cultural tradition, a new type of humanistic orientation be developed in which the nonverbal potential of film is employed in cross-cultural studies and documentation.

6. That freer international movement of educational, cultural, and scientific film materials be encouraged.

7. That a joint international commission on ethnographic film and urgent anthropology be formed to bring together from time to time the existing Commission on Urgent Anthropology and the Commission on Visual Anthropology.

8. That, in pursuit of the goals delineated above, a global network of regional and national centres in Visual Anthropology be established to coordinate the filming, indexing, educational, archival, and research activities required.

Screening & Discussions

7-12-1978

1. *Heaven on Earth: Pilgrimage to the Ganges, from Ocean to the Sources, 1957-1977: Tradition to Modernity (India)*—60 Mts. (Pierre Amado, France)
2. *The Straw Tomb* (Korea)—27 Mts. (Duhyun Lee, Korea)
3. *The Seaside Village* (Korea)—24 Mts. (Duhyun Lee, Korea)
4. *Traditional Fishing in Tunisia* (Tunisia)—30 Mts. (SophieFerchiou, Tunisia)

8-12-1978

5. *Growing up as a Fore*—26 Mts. (E. Richard Sorenson, U.S.A.)
6. *Intersibling Affect in Micronesia* (Micronesia)—4 Mts. (E. Richard Sorenson, U.S.A.)
7. *Individuality and Solidarity among the Canela Indians of Brazil* (Brazil)—12 Mts. (E. Richard Sorenson, U.S.A.)

8. *Forgotten Head Hunters* (India)—10 Mts. (Jayasinhji Jhala, India)
9. *Apa Tani Sacrifice* (India)—10 Mts. (Jayasinhji Jhala, India)
10. *Afterlife*—7 Mts. 12 Seconds (Pierre M. Stevens, Canada)
11. *Bali: Island of Gods* (Indonesia)—50 Mts. (Yasuko Ichioka, Japan)
12. *A Film on Africa*—40 Mts. Appr. (Jean Rouch, France)
13. *A Film on Africa*—25 Mts. Appr., (Jean Rouch, France)
14. *The Toda of Nilgiri Hills* (India)—43 Mts. (S.K. Chattopadhyay, Producer : A.S.I. India)

9-12-1978

15. *Animation from Cape Dorset* (Baffin Island)—18 Mts. 52 Seconds, Pierre Stevens, Canada
16. *Cree Way* (James Bay)—26 Mts. 18 Seconds (Pierre Stevens, Canada)
17. *A Film on Africa* (Jean Rouch, France)
18. *The Chenchus of Andhra Pradesh* (India)—28 Mts., R.N. Datta (Producer : Barin Saha), India
19. *The Toto* (India)—12 Mts., R.N. Datta (Producer: W.B. Govt., India)
20. *A Film on Osaka Museum* (Japan)—30 Mts., Yasuhiro Omori, Japan
21. *The Onge of Little Andaman Island* (India)—51 Mts. (S.K. Chattopadhyay, Producer: A.S.I., India)

11-12-1978

22. *Black Island* (Japan)—37 Mts. (J. Ushiyama, Japan)
23. *A Film on Africa*—15 Mts. (Jean Rouch, France)
24. *Sanghai* (China)—75 Mts. (J. Ushiyama, Japan)
25. *Ekti Mech Parivarer Kahini* (India)—12Mts. (R.N. Datta, Producer: W.B. Govt., India)

13-12-1978

26. *An Afghan Family: Sons of Haji Omar* (Afghanistan)—60 Mts. (Asen Balikci, Canada)
27. *Mort du Hegan* (Africa)—(Jean Rouch, France)
28. *The Wedding Ceremony of the Ainus* (Japan)—33 Mts. (Tadayoshi Himeda, Japan)

Chapter VIII

Films of Ethnographic Interest on India

Ethnographic film is a focal point of Visual Anthropology as it is the study of culture through film. Even though we use the name as 'Ethnographic film', there may have somewhat different strands within it.

We have serialized relevant ethnographic films on India in the Issues of the *Visual Anthropology Bulletin* (Volumes 1 to 4) culling from different sources like anthropological institutions, Universities, State and Central Government Departments, Film division, Film makers, other Media people, —India in itself and coming from International organizations. They are given as below:

Films of Ethnographic Interest on India

(a) Contemporary South Asia Film Series, South Asian Area Centre, University of Wisconsin-Madison, 1242 Van Hise Hall, 1220 Linden Drive, Madison, Wisconsin 53706, U.S.A. (Film makers: Mira Reym Binford and Michael Camerini).

1. *AN INDIAN PILGRIMAGE: RAMDEVRA*—Colour — 26 minutes—16 mm. The film follows a group of Hindus on a folk pilgrimage from Bombay to the grave of Ramdevra, a medieval martial hero and saint of Rajasthan.

2. *AN INDIAN PILGRIMAGE: KASHI*—Colour 30 minutes—16 mm. The film follows two Telugu speaking brahmans and their wives who come from South India to the sacred City of Kashi (Banaras, Varanasi) on the Ganges river to perform classical ancestor rites.

3. *WEDDING OF THE GODDESS: PART I*—Colour—36 minutes—16 mm. The film provides the historical background for the annual *Chittirai* festival in the South Indian City of Madurai and illustrates the basic process of exchange between the temple deities and their worshippers and the importance of festivals in re-establishing order between humans and gods.

4. *WEDDING OF THE GODDESS: PART II*—Colour—40 minutes—16 mm. The film places the viewer in the midst of the annual *Chittirai* festival, providing an intimate picture of the day-and-night proceedings of the nineteen-days festival.

5. *FOUR HOLY MEN: RENUNCIATION IN HINDU SOCIETY*—Colour—37 minutes—16 mm. The film focusses on four different individual sadhus (holy men); (i) the administrator of a Ramakrishna Mission hospital, (ii) a traditional guru who heads a monastery, (iii) a recluse with no organizational ties, and (iv) a scholar who is also founder of a national political party. Although each sadhu has severed his personal ties with the secular world, each maintains sacredly—articulated relationships with the secular world.

6. *VILLAGE MAN, CITY MAN*—Colour—38 minutes—16 mm. The film shows the life of a young mill worker in an industrial section of Delhi and follows him on a return visit to his village in Uttar Pradesh. Changes and continuities in his life are documented by conversations with his friends at the mill and by observations of how he works and spends his leisure time in both city and village. The question whether this mill worker is a village man or city man remains unanswered.

(b) The Cultural Research Institute, Government of West Bengal, New Secretariat Building: 1, K.S. Roy Road, Block-B, Calcutta 700001.

1. *TOTO*—B/W—1955—16 mm.—12 minutes—Bengali (I and P.R.D., Government of West Bengal). The film depicts some aspects of socio-economic life of the smallest tribal group living on Bhutan border of Jalpaiguri district.

2. *EKTI MECH PARIBARER KAHINI*—BW—1956—16 mm.—12 minutes—Bengali (I and P.R.D., Government of West Bengal). The film depicts some aspects of change among the Mech through generation.

3. *BIRHOR*—Colour—1964—16 mm.—28 minutes—Bengali. The film depicts the socio-economic life of a nomadic band of the Birhor of Purulia district in West Bengal.

4. *ANNUAL HUNTING FESTIVAL (SANTAL)*—BW—1967—16 mm.—9 minutes—English. It is a film on ceremonial hunting of the Santal on full moon day of April. The occasion is also marked with the sitting of special type of traditional court for giving decision on different social offences kept pending throughout the year.

5. *THE ORAONS OF SUNDERBAN*—BW—1969—16 mm.—18 minutes, Bengali, The film depicts the socio-economic life of the Oraons inhabiting Sunderban area of 24 Parganas district of West Bengal.

6. *IMPACT OF MODERN EDUCATION ON THE TRIBALS OF WEST BENGAL*—BW—1973—16 mm.—18 minutes—Bengali. The film focusses on the type of modern education received by the tribals with the assistance of Government. Shots have been taken from Midnapur district and Calcutta.

7. *SANTALS OF DOHAPARA*—BW—1976—16 mm.—13 minutes—English. It is a film on Santal migrants from Indian enclave of erstwhile East Pakistan who were settled in Dohapara, a village in West Dinajpur, West Bengal.

(c) Barindranath Saha, 18, Bipradas Street, Calcutta-700009, India.

1. *THE CHENCHUS*—B/W—1971—35 mm. and 16 mm.—26 minutes 28 seconds, English. The film depicts socio-economic life of the Chenchus, a tribe in Andhra Pradesh. Changes due to modern education have also been shown.

(d) M.K. Jayasinhji Jhala, 108 Malcha Marg, New Delhi-110021, India.

1. *APATANI SACRIFICE*—Colour—1977—16 mm.—10 minutes. This film depicts the *Mlaka* ritual among the Apatanis of Arunachal Pradesh when they sacrifice for the fertility of their fields.

2. *THE FORGOTTEN HEAD HUNTERS*—Colour—1977—16 mm.—10 minutes. This film depicts the spring festival of the Ozziale celebrated by the Wangchus of Arunachal Pradesh.

(e) Dr. Durgadas Mukhopadhyay, Chalchitra Workshop, K-5/8, Model Town, Delhi-110009, India.

1. *PENANCE, PERFORMANCE AND PROTEST*—BW-1974—35 mm.—15 minutes. A film on Gambhira—a socially conscious folk-theatre of North Bengal.

2. *THE BAULS*—B/W—1978—16 mm.—20 minutes. A film on the life and music of the Vaishnava mendicants of Bengal.

3. *RAMLILA OF RAMNAGAR*—Colour—1978—16 mm.—50 minutes (appr.). A film depicting the Ramlila of Ramnagar in Benaras which lasts for 30 days during September-October.

(f) Dr. Michael Yorke, 12 Belsize Park, London NW3 4ES

1. *THE HO: THE PEOPLE OF THE RICE POT*—Colour—16 mm.—70 minutes. This is an indepth anthropological film on the life of the Ho tribe of

Chotanagpur in Bihar. It is an intimate observation of a man and his family over a year of their lives in a Ho village. It falls broadly into two parts, the first depicting seasonal changes and activities, and the second focussing on specific issues such as dispute settlement and the effects of wage labour and nearby mining operations on a particular village community.

(g) Dr. Frits Staal, Department of South and Southeast Asian Studies, Unviersity of California, Berkeley, California 94720, U.S.A.

1. *ALTAR OF FIRE*—1975—16 mm.—45 minutes. This film is a detailed record of the World's oldest surviving ritual, the Agnicayana, a Vedic ritual of sacrifice dating back some 3000 years, performed in a village in Kerala.

(h) Dr. Pierre Amado, CNRS, Ferolles, 77330 Ozoir—la—Ferriera, Paris, France.

1. *HEAVEN ON EARTH: PILGRIMAGE TO THE GANGES, FROM OCEAN TO THE SOURCES*—1957 1977—TRADITION AND MODERNITY— Colour—60 minutes—16 mm. By surveying and re-surveying Ganges pilgrimages for the last 20 years, the filmmaker shows through his film as to how alive the tradition is, what kind of changes it does undergo and how the most sophisticated modern techniques have to be used in organizing the largest congregation of people in the world.

(i) Anthropological Survey of India, Government of India, 27, Jawaharlal Nehru Road, Calcutta 700016, India (All Films are Silent and 16 mm.)

1. *ABOR OF NEFA* (Adi of Arunachal)—Colour—1954—31 minutes—751 ft.—16 F.P.S. The Abor of Siang Division of NEFA live in the spurs of Eastern Himalaya. The film describes the life of the Abor. It includes basketry, weaving of colourful shirts, cotton

rugs, preparation of local drinks, Mithun sacrifice, ironsmith at work, funeral procession, dance, etc.

2. *ABOR DANCE* (NEFA)—Colour—1954—14 minutes—338 ft.—16 FPS.

3. *THE ONGE OF LITTLE ANDAMAN ISLAND*—Colour—1955—51 minutes—1,231 ft.—16 FPS. This film depicts the life of the Onge, a nomadic negrito tribe of little Andaman Island. They number about 150 souls. They live on food collecting, hunting and fishing. The film gives an ideas about some aspects of their culture viz. collection of food articles, community hut, fishing, turtle hunting, preparation of food, painting and decoration of body and dance.

4. *GARHWAL HIMALAYA*—Colour—1955—36 minutes—869 ft.—16 FPS. This film is based on the journey of Kedarnath and Badrinath, the famous Holy places of Garhwal Himalaya.

5. RUPKUND EXPEDITION—Colour—1956—38 minutes—922 ft.—16 FPS. The Rupkund lake is located at about 16,000 ft. altitude in the high mountains of Garhwal Himalaya. A large number of human skeletons and frozen shattered bodies were recovered by the members of this Survey from the frozen lake of Rupkund. This film covers the entire journey of the expedition from Kathgodam Rly. Station to the mysterious Rupkund lake and documents the vivid picture of the frozen lake.

6. *SANTINIKETAN*—Colour—1956—45 minutes—1,100 ft.—16 FPS. Santiniketan is situated in the district of Birbhum of West Bengal and is about 150 K.M. from Calcutta. The Visva-Bharati University at Santiniketan was founded in 1918 by the famous poet Rabindra Nath Tagore. This University has centres for general education, arts and music, teachers training and a centre of rural construction at Sriniketan. This film

has recorded the activities of different centres at Santiniketan and Sriniketan.

7. *DUSSERAH FESTIVAL OF MYSORE*—Colour—1956—12 minutes—392 ft.—24 FPS. This picture illustrates the ceremonial parades starting from palace, and colourful illuminations on Dusserah day at Mysore during the regime of the Maharaja.

8. *THE KHASI OF K & J HILLS*—Colour—1957—35 minutes—1267 ft.—24 FPS. The film depicts a general survey of different towns and villages in Khasi and Jaintia Hills, including their daily activities, dance, and recreation. Their monoliths, stone cairns, hand-made pottery and a local market are also shown in this film.

9. *POTTERS CRAFT OF POONA*—Colour—1957—24 minutes—849 ft.—24 FPS. A group of potters known as Khat Kumbhar live in the village of Wagholi near Poona City. They manufacture three types of black pottery, two of which are wheel-made and one is hand-made. This film gives a clear idea of their techniques of manufacturing black pottery.

10. *GARO*—Colour—1957—16 minutes—584 ft.—24 FPS. (Pile Dwelling).

11. *THE TEMPLES & MATHAS OF PURI*—Colour—1957—28 minutes—835 ft.—24 FPS. This film is documented on the old temples and *mathas* of Puri Distt. in Orissa.

12. *THE RIANG OF TRIPURA*—Colour—1959—56 minutes—1,345 ft.—16 FPS. The Riang are a scheduled tribe of Tripura. They are said to have migrated from the Shah States of Burma. This film portrays the activities of their daily life, shifting cultivation, rituals, social customs and funeral ceremony.

13. ARTS & CRAFTS OF MANBHUM—Colour—1959—50 minutes—1,198 ft. 6 FPS. This film is taken on the

following artisan groups and their crafts of Manbhum Distt. in Bihar, viz., Potters, Black-smiths, Brass-workers (using lost wax process), basketry makers, mask makers, weavers and oil-press workers. The Chchow dance of Manbhum is also recorded in this film.

14. *THE JUANG OF ORISSA*—Colour—1960—57 minutes —1,367 ft.—16 FPS. The Juang live in Keonjhar Dist. of Orissa. The film covers the major activities of their daily life. Even to-day they live on hunting, collection of wild roots and tubers. They practise shifting as well as wet cultivation. Festivals, communal feast and dance are also documented here.

15. *THE TODA OF NILGIRI HILLS*—Colour—1960 & 1965—43 minutes—1,025 ft.—16 FPS. The Toda once well known as a polyandrous tribe, live in the blue-mountains of South India. The Toda, a pastoral tribe, do not subsist on agriculture. Their economy centres around tending of buffaloes and selling milk and milk products. Their bow and arrow (marriage) ceremony, construction of hut, funeral ceremony and other activities of their daily life are delineated in this film.

16. *THE GADDI OF HIMACHAL PRADESH*—Colour—1962—49 minutes—1,766 ft.—24 FPS. The Gaddi are a semi-nomadic tribe of Chamba Distt. in Himachal Pradesh. In winter they migrate from higher region and return to fixed villages in summer. Some migrate to Lahaul and other higher regions of Himalayan ranges in summer for grazing the sheep and goats. In this film their village life, agricultural activities, migration to Lahaul with the flock of sheep and goats are shown.

17. *THE ASUR OF CHOTANAGPUR*—Colour—1962—18 minutes—435 ft.—16 FPS. Asur, the iron smelters of Palamau Distt., Chotanagpur in Bihar have their own

indigenous process of extracting iron from ore. This film records the techniques of using their foot bellows, blast furance, melting iron-ore and shaping of ploughing share.

18. *THE KONARK TEMPLE*—Colour—1962—8 minutes — 280 ft.—24 FPS. The famous Konark temple or the Sun Temple is situated at the seashore near Puri in Orissa. This film is a document of the Konark temple.

19. *TEMPLES & CAVES OF BHUBANESWAR*—Colour—1962—20 minutes—707 ft.—24 FPS. This film is documented on the Udaigiri, Khandagiri caves and on the Mukteswar, Rajarani and Lingaraj temples of Bhubaneshwar.

20. *THE INSTALLATION CEREMONY OF THE RAJA OF PURI*—Colour—1962—8 minutes—282 ft.—24 FPS. Every year during the month of *Magh* (January-February) a formal coronation of the king of Puri is perfromed with splendour and amidst a chain of rituals. The Brahman priests who are associated with the temple of Lord Jagannath, play an important role in presiding over the rituals, and the king is given a golden sacred thread on the occasion. The day's festivals are ended by carrying the king in a palanquin in the evening to the temple of Lord Jagannath.

21. *THE BIRHOR*—BW—1965—35 minutes—1,264 ft.—24 FPS. The Birhor, a nomadic tribe, live in Chotanagpur in Bihar. Their main stay of economic life is based on making ropes from bark fibre of *Mahulan* creeper. The film portrays their daily activities in their temporary settlement and also depicts hunting, bark collection, bird trapping and ritual.

22. *THE OLARI GADABA OF ORISSA*—B&W—1966—31 minutes—1,108 ft.—24 FPS. The Olari Gadaba live in Koraput Distt. of Orissa. Their source of economic life depends on agriculture. The film covers the activities of daily life, marriage ceremony and dance.

23. *FAIR AT DARRANGA*—*BW*—1966—21 minutes—751 ft.—24 FPS. Every year in the month of February a fair is held at the side of Darranga river at the border of Assam and Bhutan. The Bhutanese come to this annual fair to sell their indigenous articles, mainly colourful clothes. They also purchase many articles from plains people. This film records the activities of Darranga fair.

24. *MONPA-TAWANG*—1966—Colour—10 minutes—377 ft.—24 FPS. (NEFA).

25. *THE NULIA OF PURI*—Colour—1967—17 minutes—612 ft.—24 FPS. The Nulia (fishermen group) of Puri in Orissa live at the seashore in the Puri town. Their main profession is fishing in the sea. This film portrays the daily life and activities of the Nulia.

26. *THE NICOBARESE OF CARNICOBAR ISLAND*—Colour 1967—47 minutes—1,632 ft.—24 FPS. The Nicobarese of Car-Nicobar Island are a Mongoloid people subsisting on trading, hunting and fishing. The film shows the daily life and activities of the Nicobarese and also the canoe-race, wrestling dance, pig fight, fishing and funeral ceremony.

27. *HOOK-SWINGING (CHARAK) FESTIVAL OF SINGHBHUM DIST., IN BIHAR*—B&W—1967—28 minutes—1,006 ft.—24 FPS. Hook swinging (Charak) festival of Singhbhum Dist., is one of the important festivals of the area, which takes place between the last day of the month of *Chaitra* (March-April) and the last day of the month *Jaistha* (May-June). This festival is performed by the villagers on different dates in different villages and continues for five to six days. The central theme of the festival is the worship of Lord Shiva. The main attractions of the festival are the Chhow dance, the Acrobatic (Natua) dance, the Hook swinging by the devotees who

observe severe penance and the fair. This film has recorded all the diverse activities of the festival.

28. *FISHERMEN OF FRAZERGANJ*—B&W—15 minutes—555 ft.—24 FPS. This picture depicts the life of fishermen who migrate from different places of West Bengal and settle here only during the season.

29. *ARDHA KUMBHA FAIR*—Colour—1968—22 minutes—795 ft.—24 FPS. In April, 1968 the *Ardha Kumbha* fair was held at Hardwar in Uttar Pradesh. This film gives an idea about the assembly of the Sadhus of different organisations, ascetics and peoples' belief about the Holy-Bath.

30. *THE LAHAULEE OF HIMACHAL PRADESH*—Colour—1968—40 minutes—1,427 ft.—24 FPS. The Lahaulee a scheduled tribe of Lahaul & Spiti Dist. of Himachal Pradesh, live at the altitude of about 10,000 ft. The Rotang pass altitude about 13,000 ft. connects the Lahaul & Spiti Dist. with the rest of the country. This high pass closes on account of heavy snowfall to all traffics (November to April) and thus this area remains cut off for a period of about six months. Everyday life of the Lahaulee during summer season and the dances of Lahaulees, Tibetans and Spitialee are delineated in this film.

31. *THE RABARI OF WESTERN GUJARAT*—Colour—1969—20 minutes—707 ft.—24 FPS. The Rabari, a nomadic tribe, live in Bardo Hills of Jamnagar Dist. in Western Gujarat. Their main source of economic life is based on milk and milk products. They are a pastoral tribe and do not subsist on agriculture. This film portrays the daily life of the Rabari.

32. *THE SPITIALEE OF HIMACHAL PRADESH*—Colour—1969—36 minutes—1,264 ft.—24 FPS. The Spitialee, a hill tribe of Lahaul & Spiti District of Himachal Pradesh, live at the altitude of about 11,000 ft. Due to heavy snowfall at Kunzam pass, altitude

about 16,000 ft. this area becomes isolated from the rest of the country for a period of about nine months. Their daily life, agricultural activities and the devil dance by the Lamas of Ki Monastery are recorded in this film.

33. *THE BISON HORN MARIA OF BASTAR*—Colour—1969—27 minutes—952 ft.—24 FPS. The Bison Horn Maria of South Bastar in Madhya Pradesh, who are distinguished from the other tribes of Bastar by their splendid head-dress which they use during their dance, live to the south of the Indrawati river of Jagdalpur. Their main source of livelihood is agriculture. The surroundings of the village, the daily life activities, the exciting cock-fight and the dance are delineated in this film.

34. *THE KINNAUREE OF HIMACHAL PRADESH*—Colour—1970—37 minutes—1,328 ft.—24 FPS. The Kinnaurees live in the Kinnaur Dist. lying in the high Himalayan ranges of Himachal Pradesh. Their main occupation in the Sutlej valley is terrace agriculture. Other occupations like sheep breeding, weaving, silver and blacksmithy, carpentry are supplementary. Their daily life activities and the Behri or (Boring) Nag festival and dances are recorded in this film.

35. *TONS VALLEY EXPEDITION & GANGOTRI, GOMUKH*—Colour—33 minutes—1,100 ft.—24 FPS.—1972. The Tons valley is situated at the North Western part of Uttar Pradesh in Garhwal Himalaya. The Rawin, a scheduled caste, live in this area up to the altitude of 9,000 ft. They consider Durjodhan and Karna as their patron gods. In this film the glimpses of their life are recorded during a journey of the expedition to Dhumdharkandi pass altitude about 18,400 ft. The famous pilgrim spots Gangotri and Gomukh (the source of the Ganges) are also documented and spliced at the end of this film.

36. *THE LANJIA SAORA OF ORISSA*—Colour—1973—29 minutes—1,039 ft.—24 FPS. The Saora is one of the most numerous Scheduled Tribes of India. Their main concentration is in Orissa. Though the traditional Saora Culture has undergone substantial change and modification in the recent years the Lanjia Saora, shown here, may be considered as one of the most primitive sections of the community. It appears that they have retained many of their traditional customs even today. The main source of their livelihood is agriculture. They practice both shifting and wet cultivation. This short film gives an idea about the village environment, agricultural activities, domestic life, mortuary practices and dance.

37. *THE ARTS AND CRAFTS OF MANIPUR*—Colour—1974—28 minutes—1,000 ft. Manipur is studded with charming crafts. These either subsidise the economy of the people or happen to be the mainstay. Tradition of such artistic talents has been built up through ages. This documentary attempts to portray some of the brilliant pieces of arts and crafts, the technology and typology. The coverage includes weaving (cotton and silk), blacksmithy, hat-making, pottery (clay and stone), mat weaving and doll-making.

38. *THE FESTIVAL OF HEMIS MONASTERY*—Colour—1975—36 minutes—1,286 ft. The famous Hemis Monastery is situated at the altitude of about 12,000 ft. in Ladakh district of Jammu and Kashmir State. This monastery is the biggest monastery in the northwestern part of India. Every year in the month of June the yearly festival of the monastery is observed with much pomp and glory. This short film has recorded the yearly festival, the general environment of the Hemis monastery and the route to Hemis.

39. *CHOLANAIKAN, THE CAVE DWELLERS OF KERALA*—Colour—1976—20 minutes—700 ft. Cholanaikan, the cave dwellers live in the dense

forest of Kerulai in Malappuram district of Kerala. The inhabitants number only 281, live in natural rock-caves on the river beds. They are food gatherers as well as collectors of minor forest products for barter. In this film their life activities and the general environment of the area have been recorded.

40. *INLAY CRAFT OF MYSORE*—B&W—1977—11 minutes—400 ft. The Inlay work in Mysore is a traditional art. This art is made through the modern machines and hand crafts. This film has recorded the entire process of Inlay craft. At the end of this film the art of sculpture in Mysore is added in a short length.

(j) Department of Information and Public Relations, Government of West Bengal, Writers' Buildings, Calcutta (All B/W with Bengali commentary unless otherwise indicated).

1. *PATHER PANCHALI*—35 mm. and 16 mm.—1953-54—120 minutes (Bengali and English Subtitled) The famous film of Satyajit Ray based on rural life of Bengal.

2. *PRATIBESHI ORAON*—35 mm.—1954-55—10 minutes 30 seconds—The film depicts the culture and traditions of the Oraon of West Bengal.

3. *BANGALER MELA*—35 mm.—1955-56—10 minutes—The film depicts various fairs which are held throughout the year in West Bengal.

4. *NILBARNA SRIGALAKATHA*—35 mm. and 16 mm. —1956-57—21 minutes 30 seconds—It is a film on dance drama of Nilbarna Srigala Katha.

5. *RAMAYAN KATHA*—35 mm.—1956-57—26 minutes 30 seconds—It is a story of Ramayana in dolls.

6. *SURYA JAKAN PATEY NAMEY*—35 mm. and 16 mm.—1958-59—20 minutes 30 seconds—It is a film

depicting the performances of folk music in the life of rural people of Bengal.

7. *KANSARI*—35 mm.—1959-60—9 minutes—It shows the activities of Bell metal artisans of Murshidabad.

8. *SANKHO-O-SANKHARI*—35 mm. and 16 mm.—1960-61—10 minutes 30 seconds—It depicts the conch shell products of West Bengal.

9. *INDOR-KA-GHARANA*—35 mm.—1960-61—16 minutes —It is a film on classical music of the Indor Gharana style by Ostad Amir Khan.

10. *BRAMANANDA KESHABCHANDRA*—35 mm. and 16 mm.—1960-61—24 minutes—It depicts the life of Keshabchandra as the preacher of Brahmo Samaj.

11. *OSTAD ALAUDDIN*—35 mm. and 16 mm.—1960-61—20 minutes 30 seconds— It is a film based on the life of the famous musician Ostad Alauddin.

12. *SANGIT NAYAK GOPESWAR BANDHOPADHYA*—35 mm.—1960-61—20 minutes 30 seconds—The film shows Gopeshwar Bandhopadhya as a singer.

13. *BANGALER KIRTAN*—35 mm.—1961-62—20 minutes 30 seconds—It depicts the performance of *Kirtan* songs of West Bengal.

14. *LOKE-SHILPER TERRACOTTAI RAMAYANA*—35 mm.—1962-63—10 minutes—It is a film based on story of Ramayana in Terracotta and in other media.

15. *PASCHIM BANGLER GAJADANTA SHILPA*—35 mm. and 16 mm.—1962-63—10 minutes 30 seconds—It depicts the Ivory crafts of Murshidabad.

16. *CHHATI GANER DABI*—35 mm.—1965-66—20 minutes 30 seconds—It is a film on six folk songs of Bengal.

17. *SAHID SMRITI*—35 mm. and 16 mm.—1966-67—30 minutes 30 seconds—It is a film depicting dance drama about the heroes of Sepoy Mutiny.

18. *LODHA UPAJATIR BIMUKTI-O-BIKASH*—35 mm.—1967-68—15 minutes—The film depicts the life of Lodha—an ex-criminal tribe of West Bengal and their development.

19. *DOLL MAKER OF KRISHNANAGAR*—35 mm.—colour—1968-69—20 minutes—It shows the activities of clay modellers in a colony at Krishnanagar.

20. *AJKER SHILPI PARITOSH SEN*—35 mm.—1968-69—10 minutes 30 seconds—It is a film on the life of the artist Paritosh Sen.

21. *BAULS OF BENGAL*—35 mm.—1968-69—20 minutes (Enlish)—It is a film on the famous Baul singers of Bengal.

22. *BANGALER MAJHI BHAI*—35 mm.—1969-70—20 minutes 30 seconds—It depicts the life of boatmen in Bengal.

23. *PURULIAR CHHOW*—35 mm. and 16 mm.—1969-70—20 minutes—It is a film on the famous *Chhow* dance (mask dance) of Purulia.

24. *JAMINI ROY*—35 mm.—1969-70—20 minutes 30 seconds—It is a film showing the artist and his work.

25. *PRAGATIR PATHEY PASCHIM BANGALER ADIBASI*—35 mm. and 16 mm.—1972-73—10 minutes 30 seconds—The film shows that the tribals of West Bengal are marching towards progress.

26. *SANTAL SAMAJ-O-SANSKRITI*—35 mm.—1972-73—10 minutes 30 seconds—The film shows the development of Santal community and their social manners and culture.

27. *SHANTINIKETAN*—35 mm. and 16 mm.—1973-74—14 minutes 30 seconds—It is a film on Shantiniketan—a famous centre of culture of West Bengal.

28. *JATRA UTSAB 1973*—35 mm.—1973-74—13 minutes—It is a film on *Yatra* festival organized by I. & P.R. Department, Government of West Bengal.

29. *PAHARER HATCHANI*—35 mm. and 16 mm.—1975-76—11 minutes—(Bengali and Nepali)—The film shows the cultural development and customs of hill tribes.

(k) Some Noteworthy Films of Film Division, Government of India, 24, Dr. G. Deshmukh Marg, Bombay-400026, India

1. **Birju Maharaj:** B/W, 35 mm/16 mm, 22 mts., 1972; Produced through M/s Chidananda Das Gupta Productions, Calcutta.
   The film gives a brief account of the achievements of the famous Kathak dancer, Birju Maharaj. It also brings out some interesting glimpses of Birju Maharaj's personal life.

2. **Damayanti Joshi:** Colour, 35 mm/16 mm, 21 mts., 1973; Production: G.P. Asthana; Script and Direction: Hakumat Sarin.
   This film deals with the life of the famous Kathak Dancer Damayanti Joshi.

3. **Heart Beat:** B/W, 35 mm/16 mm, 30 mts., 1973; Production: Shanti Varma; Treatment & Direction: K. Vishwanath.
   A 30 minute TV programme wherein Miss Vija Vetra—dancer-cum-choreographer expresses her earthly philosophy through interviews and dances. Her dancing repertoire ranges from all classicial, modern and ritual ones in the occident to traditional classical in the orient, and a combination of both.

4. **Kathakali:** 35 mm/16 mm, Colour, 22 mts., 1959; Production: Ezra Mir; Direction: Mohan Wadhwani.

   This is a description of the unique dance drama of Kerala. In this pantomimic form of stage-show, a lot of drilling and self-discipline being necessary, the documentary takes us to the school where the pupils are taught the essentials of this particular genre and later to the 'green-room' where various characters are made up for the performance.

5. **Kuchipudi Dance Part I (Ancient & Modern)** and **Kuchipudi Dance Part II (Bhamakalapam):** Part I—Colour, 35 mm/16 mm, 19 mts., 1973; Part II—Colour, 35 mm/16 mm, 16 mts., 1973; Production, Script & Direction: T.A. Abraham.
   The first part traces the original history of Kuchipudi Dance (taken its name after the village of its birth) and shows in detail the Ancient Dance Drama of Bhakta Prhalad and the modern trends in the choreography of staging Kuchipudi dance items.
   After briefly tracing the days of Siddhendra Yogi and his compositions the second part of the film presents the Bhama Kalapam rendered by the famed dancer Padmashri Vedantam Satyanarayana Sharma. The drama of Bhama Kalapam presents Satyabhama, the consort of Krishna, in varying moods, as an ardent lover, a jealous wife and uncompromising critic.

6. **Tandava:** Colour, 35 mm/16 mm, 7 mts., 1970; Production & Direction: G.K. Gokhale. In his abode the Holy Himalayas, Lord Shiva comes to know that Sati, his consort who was humiliated at Daksha's Yagna (Penance) has burnt herself. Infuriated, Shiva opens his third eye and bursts into 'Tandava'—the dance of destruction. This animated film has no commentary but music only.

7. **Chhow Dances of Bengal:** Colour; 35 mm/16 mm, 17 mts., 1971; Purchased from M/s Film Orientalia, Calcutta,

   The film is on the famous Chhow Dances of Bengal. 'Chhow' reflects both an artistic achievement and a way of life.

8. **Dances of Assam:** Colour, 35 mm/16 mm, 16 mts., 1965; Production: Mushir Ahmad; Direction : Dilip Jamdar.
   The film deals with the colourful dances of Assam. Depicted in it are the Wangla, Bau and Laho Dances performed by the Garos and the Jaintias. The Assamese spring dance depicts the gaiety of the season.

9. **Odissi Dance:** Colour, 35 mm/16 mm, 21 mts., 1972; Purchased from M/s Konarak Films Pvt., Ltd. Cuttack.
   This is an educational and informative film on the subject of Indian dance 'Odissi' originated in Orissa many centuries ago but has now become most popular throughout the country and abroad.

10. **Folk and Tribal Images:** B/W, 35 mm/16 mm, 11 mts., 1970; Production: Gopal Datt, Direction: Shanti Varma.
    The film presents the works of folk and tribal artists of India which were displayed at an exhibition organised by the Lalit Kala Akademi in New Delhi. The uncompromising faith of the tribal artists and their belief in the supernatural finds solace in protective deities and other symbols.

11. **Rangoli:** Colour, 35 mm/16 mm, 15 mts., 1968; Production: Mushir Ahmad, Direction: Dilip Jamdar.
    A colourful depiction of various Rangoli patterns in the different parts of the country. Along with charming patterns, the film unfolds the way of Indian women folk in their day-to-day rituals and festivals.

12. **Ahmed Jaan Thirakhwa:** B/W, 35 mm/16 mm, 14 mts., 1971; Production: G.P. Ashthana, Direction: L. Shankar.

    The film is based on the life and performance of the Tabla player Ustad Ahmed Jaan Thirakhwa.

13. **Music of India (Classical):** B/W, 35 mm/16 mm, 16 mts., 1966; Script, Direction & Production: A. Bhaskar Rao.
    Indian classical music is the theme of the film. It shows the two styles of music of North India or Hindustani, and South India or Karnatak school. The film explains the *ragas* or the basic note in Indian Music and reveals the difference between both these types.

14. **Music of India (Drums):** B/W, 35 mm/ 16 mm, 12 mts., 1953; Production: M. Bhavnani, Direction: A. Bhaskar Rao.
    This short film shows the variety of drums used in the music and dance of this country. Presenting the intricate *bols* played on the Pakhawaj, Mridang and Tabla by renowned artists, this documentary shows the other types of drums used with the folk-music and dances of India.

15. **Music of India (Instrumental):** B/W, 35 mm/16 mm, 11 mts., 1952; Production: M. Bhavnani, Direction: A. Bhaskar Rao.
    This documentary shows the rich variety of instruments used in Indian music, which virtually provide the 'looms of sound' on which the musicians weave a rich pattern of melody and rhythm. The film presents some well-known instruments such as the *Been,* popular in North India, the *Veena,* an instrument of the South, the *Sarangi,* the *Sarod,* and the *Sitar.*

16. **Music of India (Santoor):** Colour, 35 mm/16 mm, 12 mts., 1971; Purchased from Blaze Film Enterprises,

Bangalore.
Santoor is an Indian instrument which has got its origin in Kashmir. The artist Pandit Shiv Kumar is also from Kashmir. He is playing 'Raag Mishra Khamaj' on Santoor. The basic mood of this Raag is romantic. This piece is rendered in a happy and playful movement. While the artist is playing the instrument, he imagines the snowcapped mountains, the beautiful gardens, the lakes, the Shikaras, waterfalls and the flowing of the rivers. Some paintings have also been shown to depict his mood.

17. **Ravi Shankar:** B/W, 35 mm/16 mm, 27 mts., 1970; Production & Direction: Pramod Pati.
'Ravi Shankar' is a film portrait of the Sitar Maestro, depicting through a series of interviews and recitals his versatile personality as a well-known classical performer and a creative composer of Indian Music (Also available in shorter version titled 'Moments with the Maestro').

18. **Lost Child:** Colour, 35 mm/16 mm, 25 mts., 1974; Production: Jagat Murari, Direction: Dr. Mulk Raj Anand, Co-direction & Photography: B. Khosla.
'The Lost Child' is a famous allegorical story written by Dr. Mulk Raj Anand. The story takes place in a fair where a child gets lost from his parents. The fair is the symbol of the world and the child, a symbol of man.

19. **Then the Rains:** Colour, 35 mm/16 mm, 13 mts., 1969; Script, Direction & Production: Ramesh Gupta, Co-Direction, Photography: B. Khosla.
This documentary brings to screen the pictorial depiction of the monsoon season. The film has been built entirely on music and the visuals. The highlight is 'Megh Malhar' *'raag'* associated with clouds and rains. This composition builds up the mood of formation of the clouds before the rains and bursts into a joyful 'Bhupali' *raag* welcoming the rain. Although

the *raags* are purely Indian, use of western instruments gives a greater depth and volume to these *raagas.*

20. **Trip:** B/W, 35 mm/16 mm, 4 mts., 1971; Production & Direction : Pramod Pati.
This is an experimental film in which the pixilation technique has been used. The film depicts the transitoriness of life.

21. **Apostle of the Indies:** Colour, 35/16 mm, 21 mts., 1964; Production: Mohan Wadhwani, Script & Direction: T.A. Abraham.
The film shows in detail the ceremonies connected with the exposition of the sacred remains of St. Xavier in Goa in December, 1964. It also gives glimpses of the history of Goa and the secular character of the Indian Nation.

22. **Bhutan (Longer Version):** Colour, 35 mm/16 mm, 41 mts., 1971; Production: Promod Pati, Direction: P.N. Kaul.
In the film, an attempt is made to project Bhutanese culture, traditions, manners and customs with an accent on progress made during the last decade with Indian assistance.

23. **Bhutan (Shorter Version):** Colour, 35 mm/16 mm, 20 mts., 1971; Production: Pramod Pati, Direction: P.N. Kaul.
(Synopses as above)

24. **Closed Centuries Opening Years:** Colour, 35 mm/16 mm, 11 mts., 1966; Production: Mohan Wadhwani, Script & Direction: Arun Chaudhuri.
The film presents myriad aspects to Naga life and the intense efforts now going on to raise the living standards and to build the framework of community and individual welfare.

25. **Elephat Lore:** Colour, 35 mm/16 mm, 18 mts., 1971: Produced through D. Bhakta, Calcutta.
Amongst most of the animals, elephant has figured in our culture more prominently. This film depicts the elephants within its proper perspective through the span of our religious, historical and social life.

26. **Festival Time:** Colour, 35 mm/16 mm, 19 mts., 1971; Produced through M/s Bhardwaj Films, Bombay.
This coloured short depicts the various festivals in Madhya Pradesh and also tries to impart the message of emotional integration between different communities.

27. **Glimpses of India-I (Eastern Region):** Colour, 35 mm/16 mm, 15 mts., 1967; Production: Mohan Wadhwani, Direction: Arun Chaudhuri.
The film shows the life, culture and the economic development of the people of the eastern region of India, which comprises of Assam, Bihar, West Bengal, Nagaland, NEFA and Manipur.

28. **Glimpses of India-II (North Region):** Colour, 35 mm/16 mm, 13 mts., 1974, Production: Mohan Wadhwani, Direction: Krishna Kapil.
The film deals with the way of life of the people in northern India in brief.

29. **Glimpses of India-III (Southern Region):** Colour, 35 mm/16 mm, 15 mts., 1966; Production: Mohan Wadhwani, Direction: P.R.S. Pillay and A.S. Thirumalai.
Southern India with its fine coastline, places of historic interest and temples is outlined in the film. Also included are the art and crafts of the region as well as the dances and the culture that still prevail.

30. **Glimpses of India-IV (Western Region):** Colour, 35 mm/16 mm, 14 mts., 1968; Production: Mohan Wadhwani, Direction: S.B. Nayampally.
The film provides glimpses of the land and people of the Western region of India—comprising of Rajas-

than, Gujarat, Goa and Maharashtra. It deals with the land, the people, their festivals and their industrial activities.

31. **Indian Muslims and their Religious Observances:** Colour, 35 mm/16 mm, 22 mts., 1971; Produced through Ashis Mukherjee, Calcutta.
The film brings out the Muslim religious life in India artistically and graphically. It dwells on the different ceremonies observed by Indian Muslims. It also shows the sacred and educational places of the Muslims in India. The undercurrent of the film is that the Muslims in India have mingled in the mainstream of the national life. The film is a beautiful, aesthetic and colourful record of Indian Muslims and their way of life.

32. **Land of Krishna:** Colour, 35 mm/16 mm, 16 mts., 1973; Produced through M/s Bhardwaj Film, Bombay. The film brings to the screen the colourful festivals in the land of Braj. It also depicts the way of life of the people and their devotion to the land of Krishna.

33. **Manipur:** Colour, 35 mm/16 mm, 16 mts., 1972; Production: Dilip Jamdar, Direction: Benoy Roy.
Manipur, the home of the famous Manipuri Dance, is often referred to as the Little paradise, 'A Kingdom of Jewels'. The film captures the beauty and enchantments of a fable land, the simple life of its people, their customs and ceremonies.

34. **The House that Ananda Built:** B/W, 35 mm/16 mm, 20 mts., 1965; Produced through Fali Bilmoria, Bombay. In this film a typical Oriya family of Ananda Karan of Nadpur Village in Mayurbhanj District has been shown. This film portrays the deep love of Ananda for his land as well as how other members of his family made progress in different vocations.

35. **Rhythm of Kerala:** Colour, 35 mm/16 mm, 16 mts., 1971; Production: Mohan Wadhwani & T.A.

Abraham, Direction: Arun Chaudhuri.
Kerala has a large number of drums which are distinctly different from drums found in other parts of India. By using the vibrant rhythm, the film unfolds the kind of life in Kerala.

36. **Weavers of Sambalpur:** Colour, 35 mm/16 mm, 10 mts., 1973; Purchased from M/s Twin Film, Bombay. The film depicts the life of the weavers of Sambalpur who are the creators of some of the finest fabrics in the country.

37. **To Catch an Elephant:** Colour, 35 mm/16 mm, 13 mts., 1972; Script & Production: N.S. Thapa, Direction: P.N. Kaul.
In Mysore the periodical capture of wild elephants is known as the *Khedda.* The film is nothing but a story of how the mightiest of mammals is caught. The film shows the difficulties encountered in trapping wild elephants in the thick forests of Mysore. The film has a special emphasis on the risky job involved requiring patience, skill and years of training.

(l) Burmah-Shell Productions

Burmah-Shell Oil Company of India planned and produced 40 half-hour documentary films with Indian production units, for distribution in various language versions within India. These films were produced between 1954-68, a partial list of which is given as below. Some of these films are available with National Film Archive, Pune, India.

1. Village in Travancore, 2. Village in West Bengal, 3. Village in East Punjab, 4. Family in Andhra, 5. Family in Bangalore, 6. Weavers of Maindargi, 7. Tanners of Jharauta, 8. The Lorry Driver, 9. Sportsman and the Carpenter, 10. Look to the Sky, 11. Martial dances of Malabar, 12. Oraons of Bihar, 13. Fisher-folk of Bombay, 14. Himalayan Tapestry, 15. Major Industirs of India—Oil, 16. Major Industries of India—Textiles, 17.

Major Industries of India—Agriculture, 18. Major Industries of India—Iron and Steel.

(m) Vide Encylopaedia Cinematographica, Institute Fur Den Wissenschftlichen Film, Gottingen, 1977; Editor G. Wolf.

1. **Bhil** (India, Jhabua district)—Gallows-swinging (Gal-Bapsi Festival) Prod: 1939, Publ: 1959. 2 min. (E. 239).
2. **Bhil** (India, Jhabua district)—From the spring festival "Holi" Prod: 1939, Publ: 1959. 2 min. (E. 240).
3. **Baiga** (India, Central Provinces)—Men's and Women's dances. Prod: 1939. Publ: 1959. $1\frac{1}{2}$ min (E. 243).
4. **Toda** (India, Nilgiri district)—Calf sacrifice. Prod: 1949. Publ: 1962. 10 min. (E 253)
5. **Kuttia Khond** (India, Orissa)—'Meriah' buffalo sacrifice. Prod: 1956; Publ: 1958. $14\frac{1}{2}$ min. (E. 179).
6. **Kuttia Khond** (India, Orissa)—Slash and burn cultivation (Harvesting and field preparation). Prod: 1955/56. Publ: 1958. Farbfilm. 15 min. (E. 194).
7. **Kuttia Khond** (India, Orissa)—Ceremonial eating of the first mango fruits and hunting oracle. Prod: 1956. Publ: 1958. Farbfilm. 3 min. (E. 195).
8. **Eastern Khond**—(India, Orissa)—Moist cultivation of rice (ploughing, harrowing, and levelling of the fields). Prod: 1956. Publ : 1958. Farbfilm. $9\frac{1}{2}$ min. (E. 193).
9. **Hindu** (India, Orissa)—Wagon Festival at Puri. Prod: 1959. Publ: 1961. $6\frac{1}{2}$ min. (E. 391).
10. **Mithila** (India, North Bihar)—Ritual preparing and taking the cannabis drink "bhang". Prod: 1973.
11. **Mithila** (India, North Bihar)—Tantra priests at the temple of Kali at Jitvarpur. Prod: 1973. Publ: 1977 Farbfilm. 4 min. (E. 2301).

12. **Mithila (India, North Bihar)**—Brahmin women at Jitvarpur painting on earth for the Satyanarayan ceremony. Prod: 1978. Publ: 1977. Farbfilm. 12 min (E. 2294).

13. **Hinduism, India**—Satyanarayan ceremony "For the welfare of the household in Jitvarpur"; Prod: 1973. Tonfilm (Komm).

14. **Mithila** (India, North Bihar)—Wall painting for religious purposes by Brahmin women in Jitvarpur; Prod: 1973. Publ: 1977. 18 min (E. 2371).

15. **Mithila** (India, North Bihar)—Kaystha women at Jitvarpur painting on earth; Prod: 1973. Publ: 1977. $14\frac{1}{2}$ min. (E. 2295).

16. **Mithila** (India, North Bihar)—Krisna figure painted on paper by Brahmin women in Jitvarpur; Prod: 1973. Publ: 1977. Farbfilm. 12 min. (E. 2368).

17. **Mithila** (India, North Bihar)—Saraswati figure painted on paper by Brahmin women in Jitvarpur; Prod: 1973. Publ:1977. Farbfilm. $10\frac{1}{2}$ min. (2369).

18. **Mithila** (India, North Bihar)—Members of the Mali caste at Jitvarpur making flower garlands; Prod: 1973. Pub: 1977. $10\frac{1}{2}$ min. (E. 2300).

19. **Mithila** (India, North Bihar)—Using pulp for the production of cultic objects; Prod: 1973. Publ: 1977. 11 min. (E.2299).

20. **Mithila** (India, North Bihar)—Kayastha women at Jitvarpur decorating their hands; Prod: 1973. Publ: 1977. $8\frac{1}{2}$ min. (E. 2297).

21. **Mithila** (India, North Bihar)—Harijan women at Jitvarpur painting on paper; Prod: 1973. Publ: 1977. Farbfilm. 13 min. (E. 2296).

22. **Mithila** (India, North Bihar)—Harijan women making mud relievos and painting on the walls of a house in Jitvarpur; Prod: 1973. Publ: 1977. Farbfilm. $17\frac{1}{2}$ min. (E. 2370).

23. **Angami and Konyak Naga** (India, Assam)—Slash and burn cultivation, Prod: 1937. Publ: 1959, $3\frac{1}{2}$ min (E. 241).

24. **Konyak Naga** (India, Assam)—Head-hunting festival; Prod: 1937. Publ: 1959. 7 min. (E. 242).

25. **Buddhism,** Tibet—Ceremonies and feasts on the occasion of the turn of 1972. I. Festive preparations and Blackhat-dance in Dehra Dun, U.P., India; Prod: 1972. Farb-Tonfilm.

26. **Buddhism,** Tibet—Ceremonies and feasts on the occasion of the turn of 1972. II Thanksgiving offering on the last day of the old year; offering for the protecting divinities. Dehra Dun, U.P., India; Prod: 1972. Farb-Tonfilm.

27. **Buddhism,** Tibet—Ceremonies and feasts on the occasion of the turn of 1972. III. Incense offering on the second day of the new year in Mussooree, U.P., India Prod: 1972 Farb-Tonfilm.

28. **Buddhism,** Tibet—Ceremonies on the occasion of the great supplication at Dharamsala, H.P. India 1972. I. Arrival of the pilgrims; audience with Dalai Lama; working on butter figures; disputations of the monks; sermon by Trijang Rinpoche; Prod: 1972. Farb-Tonfilm.

29. **Buddhism,** Tibet—Ceremonies on the occasion of the great supplication at Dharamsala. H.P.; India 1972. II. Preparing dough balls; sermon by Dalai Lama; meeting at high-noon with tea, common meal; Prod: 1972. Farb-Tonfilm.

30. **Buddhism, Tibet**—Ceremonies on the occasion of the great supplication at Dharmasala. H.P. India 1972. III. Preparing butter tea; meeting of high noon without tea. Prod : 1972. Farb-Tonfilm.

31. **Buddhism, Tibet**—Consulting the lot in the Gesar Temple at Kalimpong, West Bengal, India Prod: 1972. Farb-Tonfilm.

32. **Buddhism, Tibet**—A Tibetan astronomer speaks on the Buddhist conception of the world; Prod: 1972. Farb-Tonfilm.

33. **Tibetans**, Central Asia—Strolling minstrels at Dharamsala, H.P; India; Prod: 1972. Farb-Tonfilm.

(n) Vide Ethnographic Film, French Production, Interaudiovisuel, 1980, 25 rue Jean-Giraudoux, 75116 Paris.

1. **Happy Valleys**: Director: J. Leblond, 1973; Duration: 33 min., colour, 16 mm standard, French version; Production: Les Films de L'adagio, Distribution: Les Films de L'adagio Inter-cine-TV.
   Isolated in the heart of Himalaya, Kashmir is almost unknown to us. Nomad tribes living there have kept their ancestral habits and customs. The film is about non-Muslim Kafirs. Women in this country work in the fields. The Houzas live in a closed economy, and they may well have the secret of longvity. The Gujjars of Bakarwals are nomads in mountains as high as 15,150 ft.

2. **Mithila**: Director: L. Segarra G. Luneau, 1975; Duration: 52 min., Colour, 16 mm double band and standard, French and English versions; Production: I.N.A.; Distribution: Interama I.N.A.
   The Mithila is one of the most ancient of the Indian white kingdoms. It was founded by the Aryans in the year 1500 B.C. on the left bank of the Ganges river, and its culture is still alive today. The women keep the traditions mainly through Mithila graphic art

(drawings and paintings, and each woman knows more than 100 motifs). These allow one to communicate with the gods. In some hamlets, where traditions are maintained from morning to night and from one moon to the next, rhythm of life is governed by Vedic and Tantric prayers, rituals and magic. Krishna is the most worshipped of the gods, and when strolling players are in the village, there is mythical union between Krishna and Sita which is represented in dance and song. This osmosis between the daily material life and religious meditation gives the Mithila Kingdom a special serenity.

3. **Buddha's Smile**: Directors: J.J. Ravaux, M. Ravaux, G. Rakoff, 1974; Duration: 52 min; Colour, 16 mm double band and standard French version; Production: Les films de L'adagio; Distribution: Inter-cine TV Les films del'adagio.
   Part one of the film gives an account of the everyday life in India in a small Bonze community isolated from the rest of the world. In the monastery, days quietly pass patterned on old traditions. Part two examines the role of Buddhism and of its future in a changing world. The film ends with the Katarama Pilgrimage, which takes place in an atmosphere of collective delirium and with acts of physical mortifications.

4. **Song of the Madmen**: Director: G. Luneau, 1979; Duration: 90 min.; or 3 films of 45 min., Colour, 16 mm double band and standard original version with French subtitles; Production: Cinemarc S.E.R.D.D.A.V.; Distribution: Cinemarc.
   Bauls are wandering singers who have been travelling through Bengali villages for centuries, exalting "paths that lead to love". The word Baul literally means mentally disturbed. However, these "God's madmen" don't obey any doctrine and don't preach any religion. On the contrary they are opposed to

social or religious sectarianism. Freedom of thought is their key-note.

Their tradition is at the intersection of different trends of thought which have influenced Bengali culture; tantrism, sufism, the cult of the Kali Goddess, and the devotion to the amorous relations between Radha and Krishna.
The film shows the itinerary of different Baul singers. They meet, they gather and separate. We meet them at different stages of their zigzag itinerary through Bengal and in a festival gathering several hundreds of them.

5. **Khymba Mela, A Duo Decennial Pilgrimage to the Ganges**: Director: P. Amado 1966-67; Duration: 30 min. Colour, 16 mm Standard French version; Production: S.E.R.D.D.A.V.; Distribution: S.E.R.D.D.A.V.
Every twelve years, at the junction of the Ganges and of the Jamuna river, the largest pilgrimage in the world takes place. Ten and a half million people bathe on the same day along the sacred banks (two kilometres long).

6. **Pushkar**: Director: C. Sauvageot, 1979; Duration: 42 min., Colour, 16 mm standard, French and International versions; Production: C. Sauvageot; Distribution: Les films C. Kieffer.
Hindu society seen through the yearly Pushkar pilgrimage. Pushkar is a village situated in the Thar desert (North of India). Indian peasants come to this village because they want to be sanctified by Gurus. They also make their yearly purchases, and see the dentist. There are games and meetings at the fair. The cattle is inspected. The dromedary fair is the greatest of the country.

7. **Ma-Geig The Mother, A Than-ka Painting**: Director: C. Jest, 1967; Duration: 19 min.; Colour, 16 mm stand-

ard, French version; Production: C.N.R.S.; Distribution: S.E.R.D.D.A.V.

A detailed description of the technique of Than-ka canvas painting, representing Ma-Geig, "the mother", whose life was an example of faith, India.

8. **Amjad Ali Khan**: Directors: M. Ballero, J.C. Lubtchansky; 1971; Duration: 28 min; Colour; 16 mm double band, French version; Production: I.N.A. (Service de la Recharche), Distribution: I.N.A.
   A young musician from the north of India improvises freely on the melodic structures and rhythms of several Hindu *ragas*, accompanied by a *tabla*. At the age of five, Amjad Ali Khan was initiated in the art of the *Sarode*, a traditional stringed instrument.

9. **Rhythms from Elsewhere**: Directors: C. Dupont, P. Amado, A. Riera, 1969; Duration: 28 min., Black & White, 16 mm double band, French version; Production: I.N.A. (Service de la Recherche); Distribution: I.N.A.
   On tablas—small hand drums of India—Pandit Chatur Lal improvises on several Hindu *ragas*.
   A traditional form of music that brings us into a world of sound far different from our own. An art and a science of rhythms in search of a spiritual harmony.

10. **Vocal and Instrumental Music**: Festival de La Rochelle, 1978; Director: G. Luneau, 1978; Duration: 28 min.; Colour; 16 mm double band and standard, French version; Production: A2 (S. Genevoix); Distribution: A2.
    Classical Indian music is based on vocal music, the origins of which go back at least to the second millenium BC, the Vedic period.
    Indian tradition teaches that sound is God. This means that sound and musical experiences are in fact steps towards self-realization.

The *raga* is what colours the spirit, brings forth an emotion. It is from this point of view that all the elements of this musical art are carefully determined. The singer, Pandit Jasraj and the zitherist Kalyany Roy introduce us to the mysteries of a sonorous world.

11. **Manipuri Dances**: Festival de La Rochelle, 1978; Director: G. Luneau, 1978; Duration: 26 min., Colour, 16 mm double band and standard French version; Production: A2 (S. Genevoix); Distribution: A2. Manipur is a small State in India situated at the eastern Assam border. The valley of Manipur means "the city of the jewel". Apart from tribal dances, Manipur dances, like all classical dances, use coded gestures referring more or less directly to the "Natya Shastra". This treaty on science and dance, written two thousand years ago by the Sage Bharata precisely describes the dancer's techniques. Its aim is to provoke the *rasa* (taste) and the *bhava* (emotion). Dances generally illustrate episodes from the Gita-Govinda, a form written in the 12th century by Jayadeva. They describe the God's games (Krishna, also a flute player) with the beautiful shepherdesses of Braj in particular with Radha, his favourite one. These revels also symbolize the aspiration of individual souls (represented by the shepherdesses) with the God Krishna.

12. **The Dagar Brothers**: Director: R. Blanchard, 1965; Duration 53 min.; Black & White, 16 mm double band 35 mm standard, French version; Production: I.N.A. (Service de la recherche; Distribution: I.N.A. The brothers Moinuddin and Aminuddin Dagar sing together the long traditional Hindu song called the Dhrupad. It is an act of meditation and spiritual concentration, sustained by an obligation accompaniment of gestures as a visual translation of the melodic line. Music that can be listened to with the eyes.

13. **The Marionettes of Rajasthan**: Director: A. Klementieff, 1966: Duration 33 min.; Colour. 35 mm standard, 16 mm standard, French version; Production: I.N.A. (Service de La Recherche), Distribution: I.N.A.
    A film about a marionette theatre in Rajasthan, a State in the northwestern part of India. The puppets, in colourful costumes, are manipulated with extraordinary skill. The performance demonstrates the richness of a popular art which is over 2000 years old, but is at present in danger of extinction.

14. **Kathakali**: Director: J.C. See, 1968; Duration: 48 min., Colour, 16 mm double band and standard, French version; Production: I.N.A. (Service de La Recherche); Distribution: I.N.A.
    A performance of Kathakali by the Kerala Kalamandalam ensemble. A theatre of danced ritual, demanding much preparation, exercises of concentration and for mastery of body; work with basic figures; make-up and symbolic colours that allow the actor to recreate the heroes, demons, and gods of the great Hindu epics.

15. **The Ballad of Pabuji**: Director: G. Luneau, 1976; Duration: 52 or 70 min.; Colour, 16 mm double band and standard; French and English version; Production: I.N.A., G. Luneau; Distribution: I.N.A.
    Pabuji is a very popular legendary hero in Rajasthan (a State on the border of Pakistan in Western India). The epic tells of his birth and his adventures, presented by numerous traditional forms; ballads narration, painting, puppets, theatre, and songs make alive again the exemplary and wonderful destiny of Pabuji. The film relates one of the episodes of this legendary hero's history, by means of oral tradition and presentation of the everyday life of the inhabitants of the Thar desert. The real and the imaginary, memory and fact, reportage and direction are intermingled in the film.

Chapter IX

A Model Syllabus for Visual Anthropology

Since I had completed the Visual Anthropology Symposium, New Delhi in 1978, it generated confidence and inspiration to edit and publish the first Journal of Visual Anthropology in the country, or the Asia at least, of course in a modest beginning—the Bi-annual *Visual Anthropology Bulletin* since June, 1979. While publishing relevant news connected with ethnographic films, consequently, they also included small articles.

It was in that context that I conceived a *model syllabus* for teaching in Visual Anthropology as a part of post-graduate programme in Anthropology to suit Indian Universities. It was meant for special group of two papers carrying 200 marks. This model was published in the *Visual Anthropology Bulletin* (Volume III, No. 2, December, 1981) for circulation.

In due course, this syllabus was expanded and discussed with the members connected with a series of meetings in U.G.C.'s Curriculum Improvement Programme in the Department of Anthropology, Ranchi University (1987-89). This model syllabus is given as below for the needful:

The Subject on Visual Anthropology has four basic components viz., (A) Principles of Visual Anthropology; (B) Visual Anthropology in India; (C) Film-craft; and (D) Practical on Film-craft and the whole course is divided into 18 units as given below:

(A) Principles of Visual Anthropology

Unit-1 Visual Anthropology—Definition, scope and uses.

Unit-2 Visual Anthropology as one of the Documentation Methods in Anthropology—Photography as an Effective Medium of Communication—Its role in Visual Anthropology—Visual Communication and its Advantages over other systems—Still Photography vrs. Movie photodgraphy—Advantages and Limitations of this Method.

Unit-3 Movie Films: Feature Films, Ethnographic Films, Documentary Films, Research Films, Instructional Films—Their definitions, Scope and relevance to Visual Anthropology.

Unit-4 History and Development of Visual Anthropology—Approaches to Anthropological Films—Visual Anthropology and Analysis of Cultural Style.

Unit-5 Television and Visual Anthropology—Videotape: New Techniques of Observation and Analysis in Anthropology.

Unit-6 Film-Review, Appreciation and Criticism—Film as an Art—The Film language—Necessary conditions for Film making.

(B) Visual Anthropology in India

Unit-7 Development of Visual Anthropology in India and Ethnographic films—Present position of Ethnographic films in India.

Unit-8 Realistic and New 'Wave' Feature Films and Visual Anthropology.

Unit-9 Scope of Visual Anthropology in India—Its Uses—Urgent problems.

(C) Film-craft

Unit-10 Cine-Photography and Film—Types of cine-cameras and film gauges—Raw stock of film—Camera work—Image composition—Movement within the frame—Camera Angles—Camera

Movements—Lenses—Light Reflectors—Exposure—Meter and Measurement of light.

Unit-11 Script writing—Necessary Field conditions for shooting.

Unit-12 Sound: Use of sound in Film—Use of Music in Film—Commentary—Wild sound—Synchronisation—Making a Sound Track—Type of Tape-Recorders to be used.

Unit-13 Film Editing—Titling—Trick photography—Film preservation.

Unit-14 Film Projection and Projectors.

(D) Practical on Film-craft

Unit-15 Script writing on a given theme with all technical details and sound proposal (commentary, music, wild-sound etc. to be synchronised with the film).

Unit-16 Shooting of Film on a given theme—Duration: 3 Minutes (Minimum).

Unit-17 Review of a Film to be screened.

Unit-18 Viva on Film-craft.

Books Recommended

1. Hockings, Paul : Principles of Visual Anthropology (ed)
2. Roberge, Gaston : Chitrabani
3. Mead, Margaret : Anthropology and the Camera to Encyclopaedia of Photography, Edited by W.D. Morgan
4. Worth, Sol, John Adair : Through Navajo Eyes: An exploration in Film Communication and Anthropology
5. Collier, John, Jr. : Visual Anthropology: Photography as a Research Method

6. Heider, Karl C. : Films for Anthropological Teaching (American Anthropological Association)
7. De Brigard, Emilie : The Cinema and Social Science: A Survey of Ethnographic and Sociological Films: Reports and Papers in the Social Science 16, Paris, UNESCO
8. De Brigard, Emilie : Anthropological Cinema
9. Mead, Margaret & Macgrigor, F.C. : Growth and Cultures: A Photographic Study of Balenese Childhood
10. Sorenson, E.R. : "The Concept of the Research Film" paper presented at the Annual Meeting of the Society for Applied Anthropology, May 5, 1967, Washington, D.C.
11. Ramasaya, Terry : A Million and one *Nights*: A History of the Motion pictures
12. Pincus, E. : Guide to Film making
13. Roberege, Gaston : Film for an Ecology of Mind
14. Rangoonwala, Firoze : Seventy-five years of Indian Cinema
15. Ray, Satyajit : Our Films Their Films, New Delhi
16. Roberege, Gaston : Eisenstein's Ivans The Terrible
17. Ernest, Lindgren : The Art of the Film
18. Nilson, Vladimir : The Cinema as a Graphic Art
19. Gianfrenco, Bettetini : The Langue and Technique of the Film
20. Sahay, K.N. : "Ethnographic films in India: Prospects & Priorities and Proposals" *in* Methodology in Anthropological Film making papers of the IUAES—Intercongress, Amesterdam, 1981

21. Sahay, K.N. : "A Brief History of Ethnographic Films in India" *in Visual Anthropology Bulletin*, Vol. IV, No. 1, June, 1982

22. Sahay, K.N. : Visual Anthropology Bulletin (ed), Vol. I-IV (1979-82)

23. Sahay, K.N. : "Visual Anthropology and Indian Fiction Films", *Journal of Social Research*, Vol. 29, No. 2, September, 1986.

24. Sahay, K.N. : "Portrayal of People: Analysis of Two Indian Fiction Films and a Model Perspective in Visual Anthropology", *Journal of Social Research*, Vol. 31, No. 1-2, 1988.

25. Sahay, K.N. : "The History of Visual Anthropology in India and the Task Ahead", *Visual Anthropology*, Vol. 4, pp. 25-41, U.S.A., 1991

26. Sarkar, Kobita : Indian Cinema Today (1975)

27. Erik Barnouw & S. Krishnaswamy : Indian Film, New York

28. Aruna Vasudev & Philippe Lenglet : Indian Cinema Superbazar, New Delhi

APPENDICES

Appendix-One

Editorials of Visual Anthropology Bulletin

[The Bi-annual *Visual Anthropology Bulletin* (VAB) edited from June, 1979 to June, 1982, published four Volumes and eight issues. The Bulletin had printed 75 to 100 copies and circulated in this country and abroad for complimentary and serious subscription. By this time, I had already developed international network connected with the Commission on Visual Anthropology (IUAES). Though the Bulletin was small, containing nearly 20 pages, it was significant and a landmark in the history of Visual Anthropology in India which is still growing. The first each of the four volumes had Editorial. The Editorials may have some relevant information and perhaps, the readers may like to understand what transpired the publication of this Bulletin for four years, of course, coming out from my own pocket].

The International Symposim on Visual Anthropology held in December, 1978 during the Xth I.C.A.E.S. at New Delhi was a landmark as for the first time it enabled the few Indian scholars and agencies engaged in ethnographic film making to sit together, review the works so far done, discuss the problems of common interest with their foreign counterparts and mutually share valuable experiences of the field. Besides many fruitful sessions related to papers and films, it helped develop new contacts and inspired those of us already active in the field to do more work, and created interest among others who were new to it. There is no denying the fact that India with its multiple society and immense variety of culture promises a vast scope to Visual Anthropology and what is most urgently required is to find out proper resources and make concentrated efforts in this field by those Indian anthropologists and others who could take up this challenge. This Symposium marks the beginning of a meaningful career for Visual Anthropology in India and it will hopefully, go a long way in serving its causes in this country in particular and world in general.

It was in the wake of this development that the idea of a News Bulletin was conceived. Among other things, what struck us was, though a number of scholars and institutions were engaged in the making of ethnographic films, except those who were very active in the field, others did not know much what was happening in other parts of the world. As such, what was needed most was the publication of such a Bulletin which could acquaint the community of anthropologists and other film makers about such activities and bring them into a sort of professional fellowship. This Bulletin is expected to fulfil this objective.

VAB provides an international forum devoted to news relevant to ethnographic films including news about films, communications, reports on conferences and seminars, comments, suggestions, plannings, opportunities, short book/film reviews and discussions on specific themes circulated from time to time by VAB. Such publication materials are welcome. We have a plan to see that VAB grows into a full fledged Journal of Visual Anthropology in future depending on the availability of resources.

VAB intends to serialize names of ethnographic and other relevant films on India in some of the beginning issues. It also plans to create Associateship which can be availed by Anthropologists and others closely connected with ethnographic films from different geographical areas, the details of which will be published in due course. VAB will be published twice a year, in June and December. Items meant for publication should be *brief* as VAB has small number of pages. Materials for the first and second issues should reach the Editor preferably by April and October respectively.

VAB is a non-profit publication, its price barely covering the publication cost and postage and any financial assistance from any source will be gratefully acknowledged.

(Volume 1/No. 1/June, 1979)

VAB completes one successful year of publication; thanks to its patrons and friends who could lend their cooperation, good wishes and appreciate its humble service to the cause of Visual Anthropology.

While VAB enters the second year of publication, another significant development at Ranchi is the formation of an *Association for Visual Anthropology* (AVA) as detailed in this issue. One of the resolutions passed in the meeting of the International Commission on Visual Anthropology held at New Delhi in December 1978 aimed at forming a global network of regional and national centres in Visual Anthropology. By starting AVA with its nucleus at Ranchi the first step has been taken in this direction which will hoepfully go a long way in achieving this objective. Even though AVA makes a humble beginning, it is determined to bring like minded people interested in Ethnographic films together on a regional or countrywide level and create an awareness in them of the important role which such films can play to the scientific and human understanding of different people and their cultures and the need of preserving the fastly changing aspects of culture through the medium of film. It is sure to inspire many genuinely interested scholars and others to explore proper resources for making Ethnographic films.

In the last Delhi Symposium on Visual Anthropology held during the 1978 I.C.A.E.S., one of the films which impressed most was *Afterlife* (P—Derek Lamb; D—Ishu Patel) presented by Pierre M. Stevens of Canada. This was an *animation* and *experimental film* and depicted as to how one feels while dying. Another such Canadian film *How Death came to Earth* (D—Ishu Patel) depicts a legend from India where a story of gods and men, sun and moon and earth has been interpreted with an animation style and richness of colour and design. *Chairmen* (D—Jean-Thomas Bedard; P—Gaston Sarault) still another animation and experimental film from Canada makes an allegorical presentation of contemporary society where man has lost his freedom in the struggle to wrest recognition from the very society that is restricting his freedom. The chair is the symbol of success and without it a man is social outcast. One is also reminded of such animation and/or experimental films made elsewhere. From India, mention may be made of two experimental films produced by Film Division, Government of India viz. *Lost Child* (P—Jagat Murari; D—Mulk Raj Anand) and *Trip* (P & D—Pramod Pati). While the first is based on a famous allegorical story of Mulk Raj Anand which depicts that a child is lost from his parents in a fair—the fair being the symbol of the world and the child that of the man, the second film uses pixilation technique and depicts the transitoriness of life. Both the films reflect the basic philosophy of Hindu life. Methodologically, such films break a new ground and promise rich scope for a systematic depiction of the belief system, myths and legends, philosophy and value system of a people which otherwise remain very difficult. It is hoped that many more film makers will profitably use this type of film methodology and make further experiments on this line in near future.

It is eighteen months now that the new Chairman of the Commission on Visual Anthropology was nominated. So far more than one letter was addressed to him seeking information about the composition and activities of the present Commission, but no response was received. Subsequently, it could be known from the Secretariat of the President in March last that the Commission was still in the process of formation and the Chairman was being requested to supply relevant information. But even then nothing could be heard. It sounds unfortunate and one gets the impression that there is something seriously wrong with the Commission.

(Volume 2/No.1/June, 1980)

There has been a controversy whether or not a film made by non-anthropologist could be considered as *Ethnographic film*. There are people speaking for and against it. But the fact remains that non-anthropologists can also make Ethnographic film and some of them did contribute to the field just as several non-anthropologists had contributed to anthropological science at the beginning of its career. Admitting the fact that anthropologists have an edge over others by virtue of their training and orientation in the subject what is pertinent, at least in the *present stage of development*, is not that *who* made the film, but *how* he made the film. Visual Anthropology is probably still in its *formulatory stage* and has yet to make a systematic beginning. Hence, we may not be too obsessed by it. Films made by anthropologist may not be all 'good' films and those by others may not be necessarily devoid of anthropological insight. Systematic and depth treatment of a subject matter and realistic presentation may be some of the major criteria on the basis of which an Ethnographic film can be judged. What is required under the circumstances is, a film must be judged on its individual merit.

Some scholars think that an anthropological study is 'torn out of time and space' and what an anthropologist studies is not the *social reality itself* but a *model* based on it. Likewise, when a Visual Anthropologist goes for shooting he is also faced with a similar situation. Owing to limited footage, time and resources at his disposal, unseen factors or constraint on the choice of the varied situations which he wants to film within the period of his stay in the field, he has to make some degree of abstraction; he cannot *visually* show many things. But an Ethnographer finds himself in a better position as he can take into consideration the varied situations, all of which he may not observe himself, but knows through interview.

At every ICAES, the Commission on Visual Anthropology adopts a set of resolutions, but one wonders, what ultimately happens to it. These resolutions, no doubt, create an awareness of the existing situation and of the requirements, to the community of Visual Anthropologist, but the real good cannot be done unless we are in a position to implement them. In the absence of an effective follow-up, it remains virtually a fruitless exercise.

Some of the resolutions adopted at the meeting of the Commission on Visual Anthropology held at Delhi (1978) envisaged that 'new kind of humanistically oriented centres be created to take advantage of the multicultural potential of the visual media for furthering human understanding', 'the technologically advanced nations be encouraged to lend resources, training, and effort to developing nations', and the necessity of a 'global network of regional and national centres in Visual Anthropology be established to co-ordinate the filming, indexing, educational, archival, and research activities required.' But one does not know as to how far we have progressed in this regard. Besides, the organizers of the last Symposium on Visual Anthropology at Amsterdam who did appreciable work, in their announcement circulated earlier, included among the topics for discussion 'the drawing up and carrying out of a plan for *world-wide co-operation* in the field of Urgent Anthropological Filming', but it could not arouse adequate interest. One had a similar experience at the Delhi symposium. Is it not an indication of the kind of things going on and with what we have to content with?

If the question of securing international co-operation and devising proper means for the development of Visual Anthroplogy on global level, which an international body like the IUAES Commission or others immediately connected with it are under the obligation to look into, remain ignored, and it fails to evaluate the progress and keep a track over the matter, it may be defeating the purpose of the organization.

(Volume 3/No.1/June, 1981)

A communication received from Dr. C.S. Belshaw, the President, IUAES in April last said that the Executive at its recent meeting terminated the Commission on Visual Anthropology. "This was done essentially because no programme proposals had been received for activities between Congresses, and the general requirements for the maintenance of the Commission did not seem to be fulfilled". However, the decision of the Executive in no way affects Congress programming in this field.

It is really unfortunate that the Commission met this fate. But the manner in which the past President proposed the name of the Chairman of this Commission at the Xth ICAES in Delhi and considerations which seemingly influenced his choice, did not rule out this possibility. It was in full knowledge of the past President that a Symposium on Visual Anthropology was being organized at Delhi during the Congress on behalf of the Commission and participated by a galaxy of Visual Anthropologists from many countries. But he did not consider it proper to consult the Chairman or the Co-chairman of the Commission (who organized the Symposium) and know about them before making his choice. And of all these professionals he preferred to choose a person who did not have this much of interest to attend the Symposium even once. It is not known if it really served any useful purpose to the past President but surely it did a damage to the Commission and he shares the responsibility for its failure. Besides, it is somewhat puzzling as to why the Chairman of the Commission could remain so indifferent to the work assigned to him in spite of request from several quarters to activize the Commission.

Anyway, there lies a silver lining. The President IUAES has invited positive suggestions for the organization and programme of the Commission which must have an active series of activities apart from Congresses. Encouraging as it is, the President feels that "this is too important a topic to be shelved indefinitely". The Editor would be soon submitting a detailed proposal in this connection.

VAB has now completed three successful years and from this issue it is going to enter a significant phase; it will accommodate one or two *small articles* besides news items. To begin with, it will publish some of the papers presented at the International Symposium on Visual Anthropology organized during the Xth ICAES. The present issue includes two such papers by K.N. Sahay (India) and Sophie Ferchiou (Tunisia). Hope, it would be of interest to the readers.

(Volume 4/No.1/June, 1982)

Appendix-Two

Choreometrics and Cantometrics: A Note by Alan Lomax

[Sometime back in 1978, while being the Co-Chairman of the Commission on Visual Anthropology (IUAES 1973-78) while organizing the International Symposium on Visual Anthropology at Delhi, I had close correspondence with Dr. Alan Lomax of New York and though he could not come to the Delhi Symposium, he sent me two notes; Choreometrics and Cantrometrics—a fascinating aspect of Visual Anthropology. Later on, I had integrated the two, and published it in the *Visual Anthropology Bulletin* (Volume 2, No.1, June, 1980). It is being republished for general readership.]

Choreometrics is one of several methods developed in the course of an eighteen-year study of expressive style in relation to culture carried on in the Anthropology Department, Columbia University under the direction of Conrad Arensberg and myself and supported by the National Science Foundation, the National Institutes for Mental Health, et.al. The study applied rigorous testing methods to the description of performance behaviour on tape and film, including, singing, orchestral playing, speaking, and dancing. The systems were applied to a large sample of data drawn from a well distributed sample of cultures coming from most of the cultural regions of the world. The prime discovery is that the four systems are interrelated, producing similar distributions of culture, similar cultural geographies, and parallel correlations with elements of social structure. It appears from his study that there is a stylistic element in human behaviour that shapes human conduct and is formative in the development of all cultures and is adaptive. One of the clear findings is that style evolves as socio-economies evolve.

The first system, *Cantometrics*, comprised of 37 highly consensable parameters describing singing style, was applied to 4000 songs from 400 cultures. The data when processed by a computer programme has produced a systematic geography of song style regions and areas which corresponds to the findings of cultural anthropology. Moreover, when the relations between the measures and the system and the main traits of vocal structure were examined, correlations for more than 30 of the Cantometrics measures of social features were established, and a system emerged which makes it possible to predict social structure from the Cantometrics analysis of the song style of a culture or in reverse to predict this musical style from social structure. The prime publication is *Folk Song Style and Culture* (Transaction Press, New Brunswick, N.J.). The second publication is *Cantometrics: A Method in Musical Anthropology* (audiocassettes and handbook, University of California Extension Media Centre, Berkeley, 1977), which presents the audible scales used in the system on tape in such a fashion as to make it possible for scholars anywhere in the world to learn the system within a modest amount of time and to apply it to their own studies in order to check Cantometrics findings and to make their own analyses of other types of music that lie outside the boundaries of our investigation.

Choreometrics, a similar system, was developed in collaboration with dance experts from the Laban School. This system in toto consists of 180 measures that deal with the body parts involved in movement, the dynamics of their use, the spatial aspects of movement, the social organization of the dance or movement group, the social relations within that group, the type and level of integration that shapes the group, the manner of group coordination, the formal organization of the dance, the choreography of the dance, as well as special features of limb and middle body movement which affect the frame of dance styles.

All of these scaled and tested measures have been applied rigorously to the study of more than 500 dance films coming from several hundred cultures which represent most of the culture areas known to Anthropology. Computer evaluation of these results has resulted in a geographic taxonomy of dance styles, which closely parallels the one discovered for song style and which is closely similar to the views of cultural historians about the distribution of the main culture families of mankind.

Moreover, many connections between fundamental aspects of dance and of social structure have been established, again making it possible to predict movement from culture and culture from movement in some considerable degree. These findings have been compiled into geographic dictionaries, tables of cultural profiles, and tables of statistical correlations, and this whole body of material is in the process of being readied for publication.

The three films thus far completed (DANCE AND HUMAN HISTORY, PALM PLAY and STEP STYLE) deal with five of the most important measures in the Choreometrics system. They may be learned from the films and seem to produce high consensus among judges. They may be applied to any stretch of well authenticated and undisturbed field footage. It is hoped that in the next few years similar teaching films will be produced so as to make available a system of measures that can be used cross-culturally in the scientific investigation of human culture.

Our findings, we think will be of considerable use to both the cameraman and editors, since our movement profiles offer clues to show radical cultural differences in movement styles, which can be adjusted for in both shooting and which can add much excitement to the impact of editing. Of course, ours is only a fledgling piece of science, but enough principles of general interest have emerged to indicate that our approach may be useful to many other colleagues in ethnology. A good, first view of what we have done may be obtained by looking at the three published films. DANCE AND HUMAN HISTORY is available from the University of California Extension Media Center, Berkeley CA 94720; the two newly finished films, PALM PLAY and STEP STYLE, are available from this office (Director, Choreometrics Project, Department of Anthropology, Columbia University in the City of New York, 215 West 98th Street, Apt. 12-E, New York, N.Y. 10025, U.S.A.).

Theoretical and methodological background may be obtained by consulting the appropriate chapters on Choreometrics in *Folk Song Style and Culture.*

Appendix-Three

Association for Visual Anthropology (AVA)

[Being connected with the International Commission on Visual Anthropology, the Delhi Symposium in 1978, and the *Visual Anthropology Bulletin,* I developed a series of relevant ideas. One of them was to conceive an *Association for Visual Anthropology* published in the Bulletin (Volume 2, No.1, 1980). I did the beginning, convened two meetings, and also had formulated a Constitution. But later on, unfortunately, I had to postpone it for certain circumstances which were beyond control. However, the ideas developed in the write-up is still relevant and I may re-organize it with more fresh ideas when it is favourable.]

This is to announce the establishment of an *Association for Visual Anthropology* at Ranchi in pursuance of one of the resolutions of the meeting of the International Commission on Visual Anthropology held at Delhi in December, 1978. Brief details of the Association are given as below.

AVA would be an Association of Social Anthropologists or others who are the persons of scholarly attribute, deeply interested in, or associated with the making of 16 mm. Ethnographic films or intend to make such films, or are interested in the promotion of Ethnographic films so that it could be used for teaching and research in Anthropology or preserved as valuable records of culture, or be a medium of cultural study or cultural communication for promoting better human understanding among different groups of people, or for any other constructive purpose.

The term "Ethnographic film" will be used in a broad sense to mean not only "Ethnographic" or "Research" film as used by many Visual Anthropologists, but also such documentary or short films which make a systematic, faithful and indepth treatment of any aspect of life and culture of any community. In few cases, it may include "feature films" or so called "Art films" which make a realistic presentation of certain cross sections of the society either in contemporary time or in the past.

A person intending to be actively associated with AVA must be interested in Ethnographic films, its making and subsidiary activities, and the interest must be translated into action and productivity. Greater the interest, greater the involvement with AVA and its activities.

AVA will be a Ranchi based association and its office would be located at 48/3K, Bariatu Housing Colony, Ranchi 834009, India.

AVA will meet the following aims and objectives:

(i) AVA will strive hard to promote the cause of Visual Anthropology, particularly Ethnographic films in India which promises a vast and largely unexplored field, by encouraging specially younger generation of Anthropologists who feel the necessity of teaching Anthropology and making research through the medium of Ethnographic films, or others, who consider the necessity of making records of culture, studying, understanding or merely knowing about a culture through the medium of films.

(ii) AVA will help the dissemination of information pertaining to Ethnographic films among Indian and global community of anthropologists, others interested in or potential makers of Ethnographic films with a view to bring them into a sort of professional fellowship. The present Bulletin (VAB) will help to fulfil this objective.

(iii) AVA will explore the possibility of publishing a full-fledged Journal of Visual Anthropology in future.

(iv) AVA will organise from time to time film-shows where Ethnographic films will be screened and discussed, hold conferences, symposia and discussion-groups on Visual Anthropology and arrange lectures of such anthropologists, other scholars or experts who can talk on topics related to Ethnographic film making.

(v) AVA will explore the possibility and devise ways and means to make its own Ethnographic films usually on themes relating to Chotanagpur and Bihar in particular and India in general.

(vi) AVA will offer its general guidance in the making of Ethnographic films, specially on themes relating to Chotanagpur and Bihar, to those who need it.

(vii) AVA will make Ethnographic films in collaboration with others if its own resources permit and a suitable proposal is presented.

(viii) AVA will make research and experiments in the film as a media of preserving, studying, teaching and communicating culture.

(ix) AVA will organise from time to time brief orientation or training programme in Ethnographic film making and open a Centre dealing with such activities in future whenever its resources permit.

(x) AVA will gradully develop a library of relevant books and Ethnographic films.

AVA will enroll four types of members viz., (a) Core Member; (b) Associate; (c) Ordinary member; and (d) Honorary Member. The membership of AVA will be confined to the people in India except Honorary Membership.

(a) *Core Member*: A Core Member shall be a person nominated and specially invited by the Executive Committe for such membership for a term of five years, if he is deeply interested in Ethnographic films, has produced Ethnographic films and agrees to pay a specified sum.

(b) *Associate*: An Associate must have the experience of making 16mm. Ethnographic films. He will pay by way of annual membership fee if residing in Ranchi. In otherwise case, he will pay only. The term of membership will last for a period of three years.

(c) *Ordinary Member*: An Ordinary Member may be a Social Anthropologist or any other potential maker of Ethnographic film or a scholar who is just in agreement with the aims and objectives of AVA. He will pay by way of annual membership fee if residing in Ranchi and only in otherwise case. The term of membership will be for a period of three years.

(d) *Honorary Member*: An Honorary memberhsip shall be a conferred membership by the Executive Committee of AVA to a person who is a well known filmmaker, has made significant contributions to the field of Ethnographic films and whose association with AVA would be deemed helpful.

All categories of members shall be entitled to receive free of cost a copy of the *Visual Anthropology Bulletin,* while other publications of AVA on reduced rate. The Core members and Associates will enjoy the right of voting. Local members can participate in Film-shows and deliberations organised by AVA.

Further details can be obtained from: Dr. K.N. Sahay, Founder Secretary, Association for Visual Anthropology, 48/3K, Bariatu Housing Colony, Ranchi-834009, India.

Appendix-Four

Nippon A-V Productions of Tokyo: My Impressions

I visited Japan for a period of three weeks in June 1977 at the invitation of Dr. Masao Oka, Chairman, International Commission on Visual Anthropology and Mr. Junichi Ushiyama of the Nippon A-V Productions, Tokyo, Japan to study the position of Visual Anthropolgy there, and the various processes involved in the making of Ethnographic films. This trip was sponsored by Mr. Ushiyama and his organisation and a warm hospitality was accorded to me by the NAV during the course of my brief stay there.

For the first few days I was shown nearly fifty Ethnographic films produced by NAV on the life and culture of tribal or non-tribal communities from different parts of the world like New Guinea, African countries, South America, Indonesia, Trobriand Islands, Soloman Island, Samoa, Bangaladesh, Arctic area and even Japan itself. These films impressed me of the high technical excellence involved in their making, sense of adventure and devotion on the part of the producers, directors of films and its crew in going to some very interior and difficult areas of the world for filming the life of natives, the vivid presentation of some aspects of their life, natural shots, wonderful editing, background music befitting to the mood of the film and excellent commentaries. Some of the films could move me very deeply. I still remember the worried face of Mr. Toyotomi anxiously awaiting the air dropping of ration while on the location shooting in Africa, the scared face of Mr. Sugiyama when threatened by a 'Boss Gorilla' and looking exhausted under the scorching heat of the tropical Sun, waiting to take a few sips of water near a waterhole somewhere in Africa, the sexy and provocative dances of the Trobianders and life full of mirth and enjoyment but the very next moment the weeping and helpless faces of the women who had lost their dear ones, the 'smoked mummy' of the New Guinea tribals who finally fixed it near a tree overlooking fields which belonged to her in her life-time with the comment that she will continue to watch her field as she did in her life-time, and that way, the tribals were more human than us, the last scene of the film on the tortures of Vietnamese people said that while the Film-maker will now go back home to his peace-loving people, Commander will go on from one war front to the other torturing the innocent people, and, the dozing little child by the roadside in soiled clothes in 'Tachi's family'.

After viewing the Films, Mr. Sugiyama gave me necessary training in handling different varieties of 16 mm. and 8 mm. Movie Cameras and I took extensive notes while Mr. Sugiyama explained the things, Mr. Ikeda, the Chief Editor of NAV acquainted me with the handling of different gadgets in his laboratory and allowed me to do a little bit of editing myself. I will always remember Mr. Sugiyama and Mr. Ikeda as my first two teachers in giving first lessons in film making. Miss Ichioka one day instructed me in handling microphones, different sets of tape-recorders and took me out in a busy area of Sinjuku to try my hands on the gun-mike. She then took me to sound laboratory where I could go around and see the different studios meant for different stages of sound recording. One day earlier, Mr. Ikeda had taken me to see the developing and printing process of films in the Far Eastern Film Laboratory.

Lastly, the most awaited day came when I was taken to Katsuura on a filming trip by Mr. Kaziura, the Cameraman of NAV. The 110 kms. of train journey from Tokyo to Katsuura was of great educational value to me as I could see various big and small cities and towns, industrial centres, rural areas, and beautiful landscapes all along its route and the things which impressed me most was the fact that Japan was so neat and clean and modern amenities were available even in interior areas of Japan. I liked the Japanese Inn where I was fixed at Katsuura specially its rich menu consisting of a large variety of sea fish, shells and other sea products. Matted rooms overlooking the sea, its tiled community bath-hall though I never shared this bath with others, moving in Kimono and Slippers supplied by the Inn and its longue, were all a pleasant experience in itself. The 400 years old traditional Japanese market which I filmed, reminded me of similar open-air village market of

India. From Katsuura to Namegawa Island was a pleasant drive and the Namegawa Island itself with so many varieties of animals and birds all around, its beautiful but deserted looking Restaurants, Emporium, Acquarium, gardens, green hills and sea-view all made it look like a dreamland. I exposed 8 mm. films on the graceful movements of a group of beautiful Flamingos, Sea-lions, Elephants, Ziraff and Camels.

I understand, NAV is the leading Producer of Ethnographic Films in Japan. Its films, most of which relate to the tribal life in different parts of the world, are not only important for the Television Network in Japan but it has made significant contributions to the field of Visual Anthropology. During the course of my brief but close association with NAV, I felt as if NAV was a big family where everybody was cordial, warm and affectionate. People work very hard and with a burning zeal to contribute their best. Mr. Ushiyama, the father figure of this Institution impressed me as a large-hearted and far-sighted man. He is a lovable man, a dependable friend, a dedicated worker and possesses a keen sense of humour. He was warm, kind and generous to me and took care of my smallest needs.

Miss Ichioka was the second person in NAV who took utmost care of me. Nobody could easily believe that this young lady has lived among the tribals of the Pacific area in one of the most difficult conditions and has directed and produced some very beautiful films. She was very kind and generous to me, took due care of my comforts and training in the NAV, and made proper arrangements to show me the maximum glimpses of Tokyo.

I could also visit Sapporo for two days with the kind arrangement made by Mr. Ushiyama and I was given a warm hospitality by Dr. Okada and Dr. Kuroda of the Hokkaido University who took me around the city to the Memorial Museum, Silaoi, Shinto Shrine, Sub-way, their Institute for the study of Northern Culture, Sapporo T.V., and traditional Japanese Restaurant which played only traditional Japanese music. Sapporo impressed me as one of the most beautiful cities with rich natural sorroundings and a lovely climate. I was reminded of some of the hill stations of India. Of all the things which I saw at Hokkaido, I loved the Memorial Museum with its rich exhibits showing the gradual development of Hokkaido in a chronological sequence and its excellent 'Maruti Vision' which gives us maximum idea of the life at Hokkaido within a short span of 15 minutes. I loved to be at Shilaoi, meet the Ainu people and their chief and get myself photographed in their company with Ainu dress. The gorgeous dress of the Ainu, beautiful wood crafts and the shopping centre selling a variety of wooden works and souvenirs, also impressed me.

I was fortunate to meet nearly ten Anthropologists from different Universities of Tokyo including Dr. Chie Nakane who is very well known outside Japan. I felt highly complimented and deeply grateful to them for having assembled together to receive me in a Chinese Restaurant of Shinjuku and host a dinner to me. It was a rare occasion when so many Anthropologists could spare their busy time and collect at one place. But at the same time, it indicates the high sense of hospitality and courtesy which Japanese people show to the foreign visitors. After we finished our dinner, Professor Gamo took me to a Bar in the company of some other Anthropologists and I further enjoyed their company. Professor Gamo impressed me as warm-hearted and lovable man with jolly temperament and a rich voice for singing.

I liked the Kabuki theatre with its wonderful performance of actors. I had a sense of appreciation for the Neh show being an excellent traditional art of Japan but somehow could not sit there for a long time. I liked the musical and dance performances of the Gheisa girls in their impressive and graceful Kimonos but was amazed to see the heavy make-up of their face. I liked the Buddhist temple and shopping centre of Asakusa and Sub-way trains of Japan, specially that of Sapporo which appeared to be of the latest model and more comfortable. Shopping archades is still another lovely place where one can spend hours without being bored. I was impressed and greatly admired the angel-like 'lift-girls' in uniform in the big Departmental stores of Shinjiku who would go on speaking in a musical voice almost non-stop while operating the lift and would bow down at every five second to welcome the customers and say *Domo Arigato Gozai Mashita*. These graceful girls with Cherubic faces seemed to me the real embodiment of beauty, politeness, human warmth and feminine delicacy. It helps in understanding one of the most beautiful aspects in the Japanese culture.

I am sure, many foreigners won't take many of the traditional Japanese dishes specially the raw fish, but I loved and took with great appetite each and every kind of Japanese food and drink which I was served. I thoroughly enjoyed taking any quantity of *Sake*. I was just impressed by the richness of the Japanese food. I was amazed taking one variety of sea-product in sweet soup, some portion of that plant, I was told, was used in making explosives. I always loved taking Japanese food in Japanese Restaurants and throughout my stay in Hotel Sunlite, I regularly ordered for the Japanese breakfast. I felt sad if ever I missed it.

Today, Japan ranks among one of the most advanced nations of the world; it has made tremendous progress within the last three decades or so. One of the main reasons behind this progress is the cultural homogeneity of the Japanese people and their emotional integration. The fact that the traditional Japan used to have community baths, or it is still found in some areas of Japan, indicates the extent of psychological or emotional integration among its people which is an essential prerequisite for the progress of a nation. Secondly, religion seems to play only a secondary role in the life of many Japanese people, which also in certain respect smoothens the way to material progress. But the most interesting aspect of the Japanese culture which attracts us is that modernity and tradition survives side by side. Howsoever modern Japan may be, by and large, its people still stick to many of its beautiful cultural traditions whether it is dance or theatre, festivals, superstitions, diet-pattern, dress, sense of hospitality, flower-watching and their love for nature and the like.

The people of Japan take rich food with rich content of protein and calories, live in a neat and clean manner, labour hard and enjoy life to the maximum. It is a country of plenty and prosperity where people are disciplined and responsible. Being an oriental country, Japan seems to share certain basic characteristics with other oriental countries like India, specially as regards its love for tradition, informality, human warmth and sense of hospitality, temperament, belief-system, conservatism, emotional attachments of family life are concerned. People have adequate artistic bent of mind and sex also viewed from this angle. Howsoever, the Japanese people may modernise themselves or work under the influence of westernization, there seems to be limit to it and they will still in many respects present a contrast from the western people. Secondly, the force of tradition is so great that even for that section of Japanese who are running after Westernization a time may come when they will halt, look back and would like to return to many of their old traditions. Japan is peace-loving, but not weak, and it has vast potentialities of serving as the 'Missionary of Peace' in the whole world, like India.

I finally left Tokyo for India on the 27th June. I did it with a heavy heart as I had to part with everything, I loved and admired in Japan. When I boarded the aircraft at the Heneda, I was lost in reminiscences. Immediately after it took off, an announcement in Japanese interrupted my reverie and I became painfully aware that I was now parting company with the people speaking this language. While I was landing at Hongkong, once more, the familiar *Arigato Gozia Mashita* (expression of Thanks) on mike, addressed to the passengers dropping at Hongkong spontaneously touched my sentiment. By now Japan was left over one thousand miles behind and the voice seemed to make a note of utter melancholy on me. I heard *Arigato Gozai Mashita* for the last time while the aircraft was landing at Calcutta but by this time, this sound had ceased to have an emotional appeal in me as I had become aware that it was nothing more than a mechanical voice relayed from the cabinet of the pilot.

Appendix-Five

Jean Rouch of Paris—As I Know Him

My contact with Jean Rouch, whatsoever little, dates back to 1977 when in the capacity of Co-Chairman of the Commission on Visual Anthropology (1973-78), International Union of Anthropological and Ethnological Sciences (IUAES), I invited him to Ranchi for the first meeing of the Commission (in India) as he was one of the members of this Commission. I was supposed to share the major responsibility of organizing deliberations in Visual Anthropology during the Xth International Congress of Anthropological and Ethnological Sciences (ICAES) which was to be held at New Delhi in December 1978. He had consented to participate in the meeting, but at the eleventh hour a cable was received saying that he won't be able to come as he was suffering from some ailment and his Doctor did not advise him to travel. Instead, he would send Madam Delorme, his close associate, to represent him on his behalf. I had fruitful meeting with Delorme along with other members regarding future programmes of the Commission including those to be organized during the Congress and Jean Rouch's involvement in it.

Later, the same year I was invited by Rouch on behalf of his Organization to visit Paris for a week and discuss personally about the activities of the Commission. At Paris, among others, I visited Musee de I'Homme, the place of Jean Rouch's activities and was taken around the film laboratory and auditorium, shown a few films and was so kindly told that in case I had any film, its processing would be done free of cost for me. Rouch was a man of gentle disposition, pleasing manners, cheerful, witty and humane, looking erudite and confident. At times he talked with a marked sense of humour. Jean Rouch also came to India in 1978 and actively participated in the five day International Seminar on Visual Anthropology organized by me at New Delhi on behalf of my Commission during the Xth ICAES.

By this time I had gained impression about Jean Rouch being one of the distinguished members of the Commission and a renowned Visual Anthropologist from France who was the Chairman of the *Comite International du Film Ethnographique et Sociologique* (CIFES) formed in 1952 at the ICAES at Vienna to further preservation, production and distribution of ethnographic films. "Under Rouch's care, the genre of ethnographic films acquired scientific and political as well as artistic status in the post war decade" (Brigard, 1975, 28). In 1973 at Chicago, during the IXth ICAES it was decided to create within the existing CIFES an International Commission on Ethnographic Films (ICEF) with a view to encourage and coordinate the setting up of national or regional ethnographic film centres in the region or countries they represent and to record and preserve on sound film the whole range of human cultures now undergoing rapid change.

I could gather from Jean Rouch that between 1947 to 1975 he had produced nearly sixty eight documentary or ethnographic films and all of them were in French. Most of his films are in colour and the running time varies from 10 minutes (*Tourou et Bitti*, 1971; *Pam Kuso Kar*, 1974) to 2 hours 20 minutes (*Jaguar*, 1953; Filmography enclosed). As Rouch's Filmography is in French it is difficult for me to interpret all of them meticulously but whatever could be culled out of it, show that his films generally focus on rituals and ceremonies connected with magic and religion, initiation, circumcision, spirit possession, migrant labour, hunting, funerals, race-relations, dances, ballets, agronomy, agricultural traditions, adolescence, fetes and the like.

At the time when Bateson and Mead in early forties were engaged in studying the *Balinese character* with the aid of photography and were creating milestone in anthropological research and its methodology, Jean Rouch was then studying engineering and forming the association that "led to his becoming a leader of the ethnographic film wave in Europe and an indefatigable producer and populizer" (Brigard, 1975: 28).

Earlier, Jean Rouch came into contact with Marcel Mauss and Marcel Griaule at Musee de I'Homme and encountered Henri Langlois who later became the Director of the *Cinemathique francaise*. These contacts influenced his decision to make serious study of anthropology, during the war when he was supervising the construction of roads and bridges in French occupied West Africa. He was evidently fascinated by the Africans he came into contact during his professional assignment and as he himself confessed, "Culture conflict struck me from the start" (Deshanti and Decock, 1968: 37).

Rouch made his early films by trial and error with a 16 m/m Bell and Howell Camera acquired from flee market which he floated down the Niger with his two friends. In this process he developed his own shooting style (Rouch, 1955). While filming a hippopatamous hunt on the river, Rouch enlisted the help of Damoure Zika, a Sorko, and Dumarou Gande who later on collaborated with Rouch in research and filming. "Rouch's career has been described as one of the 'inveterate amateurism' and 'incurable dilettantism' (Marcorelles, 1963: 18). Brigard (1975: 28) rates Rouch as the 'first full-time ethnographic film professional'.

The film Rouch made on the Niger was well done. It was bought by *Actualites Francaises*, blown up to 35 m/m, narration was added to it and shown as *Au Pays des mages noirs* (Ibid). It was the year 1947. In 1955, a number of Rouch's short films in colour were blown up, combined and released as a feature, *Les fils de I'eau*.

Jean Rouch had the knack of mixing facts with elements of fiction. His *Jaguar* (1958-1967) is known as "ethnographic Science fiction". It is a film depicting northern tribesman in West Africa who migrate by the millions to the cities on the coast and then back to their villages in the dry, far north. To translate his study of migration pattern he had published earlier (1956) into audio visual, Rouch asked three of his young informant friends to react such a trip (Asch, 1955: 400).

While at Paris, Jean Rouch told the author with great gusto about another such fiction film which he was seriously contemplating showing the photograph of a Railway underbridge location where he would shoot the climax scene of the film.

Rouch was an admirer of fiction films that showed ethnographic materials and which could be anthropologically studied. In this connection he and his associate Madam Delorme were full of praise for some early films of Satyajit Ray like *Pather Panchali.* They had also stressed that it would be an excellent idea to call Satyajit Ray for the inaugural function of the International Seminar on Visual Anthropology proposed to be held at Delhi but it could not materialize due to certain reasons.

Brigard (1975: 36) states that a film of Rouch when shown to African students in Paris, caused a scandal and it marked his turning point from 'conventional documentary' to *'Cinema Veriti'*—a title earlier used by Vertov. Rouch asserted his affiliation to Dziga Vertov and Robert Flaherty and in 1963 called them as his 'masters'. While Rouch was studying Songhay religion in Accra in 1953 he was invited by the priests of Hauka sect to document sequences of a possession cult. It resulted into *Les maitres focus,* "a short film showing Hauka adepts, possessed by spirits of generals, doctors, and truck drivers from the British power structure, as they slaughter a dog, cook and eat it, march back and forth, dance violently and foam at the mouth. By including shots of the Hauka going about their menial daily work in the city, Rouch implies that the cult helps its members to cope with the strains of everyday life, particularly in the colonial situation". This film excited such a strong reaction among Europeans and Africans that they urged Rouch to destroy it. But Rouch demurred and the film went on to win a price at Venice. "However, after this experience Rouch began the 'cinema of collective improvisation' with *Jaguar,* his 'ethnographic science fiction" (Ibid, p. 36).

Whenever Jean Rouch talked about his filming plan, he stressed the necessity of doing the camera-work himself. There have been anthropologists in the past who preferred not to do the filming themselves but instead called a team of film technicians or crew for this job. Rouch expressed that personally "unless forced into a special situation", he was "violently opposed" to film crews. "With the present technique used in direct cinema (synchronic sound)" Rouch said, "the filmmaker must be the cameraman. And the ethnologist alone, in my mind, is the one who knows when, where, and how to film, i.e., to do the production" (Rouch, 1975: 91). As such, Rouch considered it indispensable to initiate anthropology students into the techniques of recording both pictures and sound. "Even if their films are technically quite inferior to the work of professionals, they will have the irreplaceable quality of real contact between the person filming those being filmed" (Rouch, 1975: 92). In the New Delhi Seminar, referred earlier, Rouch said that in France all students of anthropology are trained in making of Super 8 m/m film and there are 3 to 5 Ph.D. students in anthropological filming at a time.

Films were used to elicit responses in psychological research carried out in the beginning of the present century. It became fairly common in psychiatry during the second world war and was adapted to sociological research by Rouch and a few others in 1960's. Jean Rouch not only recorded his actor's comments and exclamations at seeing themselves on the screen as in *Jaguar*, but also used the presence of cameras and cameramen to provoke psychodramas as in *La pyramide humaine* (1959) and *La punition* (1962) (Brigard, 1975: 31).

Jean Rouch is not favourably disposed towards the use of tripod and zoom lens while shooting a film as he considered it to be a major fault. In fact, it constituted a point of criticism of some films which he viewed on the ground that it presented the shots from a 'single point of view' as if from 'an observation post'. Instead, he would say 'when I make the movie, I go into Cine-trance'. He wrote, "For me.......the only way to film is to walk about with the camera, taking it to wherever it is the most effective, and improvising a ballet in which the camera itself becomes just as much alive as the people it is filming. This would be the first synthesis between the theories of Vertov about the 'Cine-eye' and those of Flaherty about the 'participant camera......it is a question of training, of the kind of mastery of the body that proper gymnastics might allow us to acquire. Then instead of using the zoom, the cameraman-filmmaker can really get into his subject, can provide or follow a dancer, a priest, or a craftsman. He is no longer just himself but he is a 'mechanical eye' accompanied by an 'electronic ear'. It is this bizarre state of transformation in the filmmaker that I have called, by analogy with phenomena of possession, the Cine-trance (Rouch, 1975: 93-94).

Obviously, the advent of 16 m/m reduced format in postwar years was eulogized by Rouch as a great event and a technical breakthrough when instead of '35 m/m monsters', light-weight and hand-held cameras came to be more handy, useful and manupulable as discussed above. Under the circumstances it helped the revival of ethnographic films.

Rouch strongly held that the film one makes on a people must be first shown to them. At this level he considered the participation of the people to be essential. Rouch confessed that the projection of his film, *Horendi* (1972) which depicted initiation rites of possessed dancers in Niger, allowed him, by studying the film on a viewer with priests who had participated in the ritual, to gather more information in a fortnight than he could get from three months of direct observation and interviews with the same informants. This *a posteriori* information on film is creating completely new relationships between the anthropologist and the group he is studying. Some people call this feedback technique as 'shared anthropology'. Rouch called it as "audio-visual counter-gift" (Rouch, 1975: 100).

It was in this context that Rouch narrated some strange experience of persons getting possessed again when a film of spirit possession was shown to persons possessed. They say that "the spirit was calling them". In other case, Rouch added that if some people had died who appeared in film, the natives would start weeping as soon they saw their deceased friends or relatives.

References Cited

Asch, Timothy, 1975: Using film in Teaching Anthropology: One Pedagogical Approach *in* Principles of Visual Anthropology by Paul Hocking (Ed.) Mouton Publishers, Paris.

Brigard, Emilie de, 1975: The History of Ethnographic Films *in* Principles of Visual Anthropology by Paul Hockings (Ed.), Mouton Publishers, Paris.

Desanti, Dominique and Jean Decock, 1968: Cinema et ethnogrphic, *Arts d' Afrique,* 1:37-39, 76-80 as quoted in Emilie de Brigard's article referred above.

Marcorelles, Louis, 1963: *Une Esthetique du reel, le cinema direct,* Paris, UNESCO, as quoted in Emilie de Brigard's article referred above.

Rouch, Jean, 1956: Migrations au Ghana (Gold Coast) (Enquite 1953-1955), *Journal de la Societe des Africanistes* 26:33-196 as quoted in Timothy Asch's article as referred above.

Rouch, Jean, 1975: The Camera and Man *in* Principles of Visual Anthropology by Paul Hockings (Ed.) Mouton Publishers, Paris.

Rouch, Jean, 1977: *Filmographic de Jean Rouch*

A Toda beauty standing at the entrance of her dwelling.

The Onge in a canoe race.

A typical Birhor house.

Mullukurumba fishing with baskets.

A young Maria mother.

An Asur extracting iron from ore by an indigenous process in Chota Nagpur.

*Children of **Lahaul** threshing corn.*

A Shompen woman carrying a baby on her back.

Above: An Abor dance.

Left: An Andamanese couple.

Opposite above: A Riang girl carding cotton

Below: Nicobarese returning from the forest.

INDEX